Alias

BOB DYLAN

STEPHEN SCOBIE

Red Deer College Press

THE PUBLISHERS

Red Deer College Press
56 Avenue & 32 Street Box 5005
Red Deer Alberta Canada T4N 5H5

CREDITS

Cover Art & Design by Jim Brennan
Text Design by Dennis Johnson
Author photo by Jim McLaren
Printed & bound in Canada by Gagné Printing Ltée

ACKNOWLEDGMENTS

The Publishers gratefully acknowledge the financial contribution of the Alberta Foundation for the Literary Arts, Alberta Culture & Multiculturalism, the Canada Council, Red Deer College & Radio 7 CKRD.

Special thanks to Colleen Donnelly, Mary Scobie, Carolyn Dearden and Clark Daniels for their assistance in preparation of this book.

CANADIAN CATALOGUING IN PUBLICATION DATA

Scobie, Stephen, 1943–
Alias Bob Dylan
ISBN 0-88995-069-5
1. Dylan, Bob, 1941– —Criticism and interpretation.
I. Title. ML420.D98S36 1991   782.42'162'0092   C91-091109-6

DEDICATION

This book owes much to the many people who have,
over the years, shared, encouraged, or tolerated my passion
for Bob Dylan. First, then, it is for Maureen, whom I
abandoned on a Saturday afternoon in 1966 to go
to Bellingham in search of *Blonde on Blonde*.
Then it is for Brishkai, who gave me the opportunity
to teach a course on Dylan at the University of Victoria,
and thus got the whole thing rolling.
It is for all the students in that course and in the
Dylan discussion group which grew out of it: especially
for Eric and Jane, who keep us keeping on.
This book is for Martin, who taught that course
with me, and for Trevor with his marvellous gifts. It is for
Simon in memory of those seminars whose traces can
still be read in Chapters 3 and 8. It is for Robin,
who always covers his tracks.
This book is also for Jean-Louis and Françoise in the
gardens at Versailles; and for Roger, Ken, and the Cat, 'masters
of the bluff and masters of the proposition.'
And it is for Jim, who drove with me to Hibbing and
Duluth, down Highway 61.

A NOTE ON QUOTATIONS

Most of the quotations from Bob Dylan lyrics in this book are taken from Bob Dylan, *Lyrics, 1962–1985* (New York: Alfred A. Knopf, 1985). All such quotations are noted parenthetically in the text, using the abbreviation L; for example, 'Blowin' in the Wind' is noted as (L 53). For a fuller discussion of the status of this volume as a source text, see Chapter 2.

Any quotations from Bob Dylan lyrics given in the text without parenthetical page citation have been transcribed directly from the recordings. This occurs either when I am quoting from a song not included in *Lyrics, 1962 – 1985* or when I am quoting from a recording in which the words of the actual performance differ significantly from the text printed in *Lyrics, 1962–1985*.

Quotations from albums issued since 1985 are transcribed directly from the recordings. Those from *Oh Mercy* are noted parenthetically as OM; see Chapter 9, note 1, for quotations from 'Brownsville Girl.' In the Postscript, quotations from *Under the Red Sky* are taken from lyrics published on the sleeve.

All quotations from Bob Dylan, *Tarantula* (New York: Macmillan, 1971) are noted parenthetically in the text, using the abbreviation T.

Unless otherwise noted, all quotations from the Bible are from the King James Authorized Version.

All other quotations are noted parenthetically, with the sources listed in 'Works Cited.'

COPYRIGHT CITATIONS

CONTENTS

to my students:
i take it for granted that youve all read
& understood freud–dostoevsky–st.
michael–confucius–coco joe–einstein–
melville–porgy snaker–john zulu–kafka–
sartre–smallfry–& tolstoy–all right then–
what my work is–is merely picking up where
they left off–nothing more–there you have
it in a nutshell–now i'm giving you my
book–i expct you all to jump right in–
the exam will be in two weeks–everybody
has to bring their own eraser.
                your professor
                herold the professor

Bob Dylan, Tarantula

FRANK IS THE KEY

The Chippewa called it The Hill of Three Waters. Long before precise topographical surveys, the Chippewa understood that there was something significant about this spot that we would now, in our language, designate as a site two or three miles to the north of the town of Hibbing, Minnesota. It is a triple continental divide. A raindrop falling at this precise spot (or a teardrop falling) would divide into three equal parts, with three equal chances of flowing north (into the Hudson Bay), south (into the Mississippi River system and thus to the Gulf of Mexico), or east (by way of the Great Lakes to the St Lawrence River and the Atlantic Ocean). Topographically, Hibbing could be considered the center of North America.

The exact spot at which this triple divide occurs is no longer accessible to the public. It falls within the boundaries of the Hull Rust Mine, the largest opencast iron mine in North America. 'Since ore shipping began in 1895, more than 1.4 billion tons of earth have been removed ... [leaving a] vast pit yawning more than three miles long, up to 2 miles wide, and 535 feet deep.'[1] The pit of the Hull Rust Mine (filled now with water, like a man-made lake) extends as far as the eye can see, its levels of red earth and ore exposed like a stratified geological map. At the Observation Complex, a mounted sign records that the Chippewa name for this site meant The Hill of Three Waters; it does not record what the Chippewa word was.

Mining began in this area in the early 1890s. Legend attributes the origin to the moment when the German prospector Franz Dietrich von Ahlen 'stuck his head out of a tent on a 40 degree below zero January morning in 1893 and said, "I believe there is iron under me. My bones feel rusty and chilly"' (Hull Rust pamphlet). Within a couple of years, the mine and the town were started, and von

Ahlen, like so many immigrants before and since, had changed his name. Franz had become Frank; von Ahlen had become his mother's maiden name: Hibbing.

By 1912 Hibbing was a prosperous, thriving community laid out on a grid system over many blocks. It boasted an Opera House and a grandiose Library donated by Andrew Carnegie (Carnegie's U.S. Steel Corporation was the holding company for several Hibbing mines). Unfortunately, by 1912 it was also clear that the richest deposits of iron ore lay directly under the town site. Action was delayed by the First World War (to the winning of which iron ore mined in Hibbing made no small contribution), but from the early 1920s on, the town of Hibbing was, simply, moved.

Most wooden buildings—houses, hospitals, schools—were hoisted from their foundations, mounted on steel wheels, and moved two miles south—to the suburb of Alice, which now became, in effect, Hibbing. Some more ornate stone buildings, like the Lincoln School and the Carnegie Library, could not be moved; some other buildings, like the Sellers Hotel, didn't make it, but collapsed spectacularly on the way. The move went on for thirty years; it was still happening in the late 1940s and early 1950s when Bobby Zimmerman was growing up in the new town.

Today what is left of old north Hibbing is minimal and eerie. The stone steps leading up to the Lincoln School, between 2nd and 3rd Streets, are still there; standing on them you can see the remaining street signs and the cracked pavement outlines of the streets as they once were, lined by neat rows of trees. The corner of 2nd and Lincoln is clearly marked, but there is nothing there. A couple of blocks to the north, the last signs of old Hibbing disappear into the vast open pit of the Hull Rust Mine.

Forty years ago much more was still visible:

old north Hibbing...
deserted
already dead
with its old stone courthouse
decayin' in the wind...
the old school
where my mother went to
rottin' shiverin' but still livin'

standin' cold and lonesome

arms cut off

with even the moon bypassin' its jagged body

pretendin' not t' see.... (L 107)

Imagine the young Robert Zimmerman, alias Bob Dylan, walking through the ruins of old Hibbing. The Minnesota wind blows cold as death across the Mesabi Iron Range. The open pit of the mine lays the countryside bare, like the scar of open-heart surgery. The foundations of the old buildings disappear into another year's grass. Two miles to the south is the solid middle-class town of Hibbing: where his father, Abraham, works in Micka Electric, a furniture and appliance store (now called Brownie's) on 5th Avenue; where his mother, Beatty Stone Zimmerman, works in the Feldman's store on Howard Street; where the family lives at 2425 East 7th Avenue, a tiny, boxlike house on a corner lot close to Hibbing High School. This is where the legend and the name begin.

Hibbing is a displaced center.

Hibbing is a ghost.

Hibbing is a double of itself.

Hibbing is an alias, a pseudonym, written in the name of the mother.

In 1957 a band featuring Bobby Zimmerman played at Hibbing High's Jacket Jamboree Talent Festival.[2] The band replaced Bob's first group, the Golden Chords, which had fallen apart the year before. This group, which was nameless, 'featured Chuck Nara on drums, Bill Marinec on bass, and Larry Fabbro on electric guitar, with Bob on piano, guitar, and lead vocals' (Shelton 42). According to Bill Marinec, Bobby Zimmerman was a perfectionist, drilling and rehearsing the band for weeks before. He knew exactly what he wanted.

For many readers of the standard biographers, 'the auditorium of Hibbing High School' must evoke something modest: a school gymnasium, perhaps, with folding chairs set out over the lines of the basketball court. Nothing could be farther from the truth.

Hibbing High School was built in 1926, financed by money from the mining companies as they moved the town southward. In 1920s' money it cost 3.9 million dollars; a picture of it was featured in the 1935 *National Geographic* (LXVII 316). The auditorium, modeled on a Broadway theater, the Capitol, seats 1825 spectators. The ceilings are in molded plaster, and the ornate walls feature paintings of decorous Classical nudes. Two large, formal boxes flank the stage. The chandeliers were made of glass imported from Belgium and Czechoslovakia. The stage has a loft 90 feet high with room for over 60 drops. The roof is covered in gold leaf to improve the acoustics, which are superb: even under the back balcony, every word from the stage is crystal clear. Every stage that Bob Dylan has played on for the past thirty years has been, after the Hibbing High School Auditorium, an anticlimax.

Bob had his band well prepared. They were to hit their first notes at full volume the moment the curtains began to open. The front rows would be filled with jocks, the privileged elite of the school: the H-Club, the lettermen. They could be relied on not to understand. Few people had heard rock 'n' roll in Hibbing in 1957; none had ever been played in a setting as distinguished as the Hibbing High School Auditorium. Legends abound as to this performance. Some say that the audience laughed, some say that it booed. Some claim that the teachers tried to cut off the power—a claim identical to the one made about the Newport Folk Festival eight years later. Some who were there, like Larry Furlong and Jackie O'Reilly, admit that they don't remember what the audience reaction was. They all remember Bobby pounding at the piano, like a demented imitation of Little Richard, singing 'Rock 'n' Roll Is Here To Stay.'

Part of the legend is that Bobby Zimmerman broke the foot-pedal on the school's Steinway piano. The Steinway is still there, backstage, at the Hibbing High School. The pedal has been repaired.

No one in Hibbing says 'Bob Zimmerman'; they all say 'Bobby.' ('My uncle beat up Bobby Zimmerman once and threw him in a trash-can for being such a wimp.') For weeks after the concert, Bill Marinec recalls, people looked at Bobby strangely and didn't say a word.

First and foremost, before even being a songwriter, Bob Dylan is a performer. He exists on stage. He has never given any audience anything close to what they expected.

This book is about performance.

This book is about displaced centers, ghosts, doubles, aliases, and pseudonyms.

Franz Dietrich von Ahlen became Frank Hibbing; Robert Zimmerman became Bob Dylan. Hibbing was von Ahlen's mother's maiden name; Bobby's mother was Beatty Stone. Like a rolling stone. The pseudonym suppresses the name of the father; eventually, in the figure of Isis, Bob Dylan returns to the name of the mother.

In the liner notes to *John Wesley Harding* there are three kings, who believe that 'the key is Frank!' (L 265). 'Frank,' says the first king, 'Mr. Dylan has come out with a new record. This record, of course, features none but his own songs and we understand that you're the key.' 'That's right,' Frank replies, 'I am.'

I do not believe that there is any one 'key' to the work of Bob Dylan in the sense that any one fact or approach can unlock and explain all the mysteries of his career. But I do want to suggest, in another sense of the word, that this book is written 'in the key of' Frank—Frank Hibbing.

Frank Hibbing's statue stands in a quiet park in Hibbing, Minnesota. Wearing his pack and hiking boots, he faces west and north toward the mine, toward the Hill of Three Waters. There is as yet no statue of Bobby Zimmerman in Hibbing, Minnesota. Nor one of Bob Dylan, either.

I AND I: BOB DYLAN AS TEXT

'Who are you?' Bob Dylan was asked in 1972. 'That's a good question,' he replied.

Actually, the exchange takes place as part of the dialogue for Sam Peckinpah's film *Pat Garrett and Billy the Kid*. The question is asked by James Coburn, who is playing Garrett, and answered by Dylan, who is playing—

Well, what is the name of Dylan's character? The question is repeated later in the film by Billy and his gang, and produces the following exchange:

–What's your name, boy?

–Alias.

–Alias what?

–Alias anything you please.

–What do we call you?

–Alias.

–Hell, just call him Alias.

–That's what I'd do.

–Alias it is.

Usually, an alias substitutes one name for another: 'Bob Dylan' for 'Robert Allen Zimmerman.' But in Dylan's case the alias is doubled, because 'alias' refers to itself as the process of renaming, the gesture of displaced and disguised identity. Bob Dylan *is* Alias: always someone else, always a deferral, always a ghost. 'Alias' is the signature he writes into his text.

This book, although it makes some limited use of biographical information, is not really concerned with Bob Dylan as biography. Rather, it deals with the alias Bob Dylan: 'Bob Dylan' as text. This text, however, like an alias, is multiple and shifting, for there are many different 'texts' of Bob Dylan. There are his songs, which exist in various modes: as recordings, as live performances, as lyrics printed on the page. There are his writings in poetry or allusive poetic prose. There is the film that he wrote and directed, *Renaldo and Clara*. All are, in one sense or another, conventional aesthetic 'texts.' But other aspects of Dylan's career also may be read as texts or as essential component parts of the text that is 'Bob Dylan.' There are the texts of his life, his public career, and his name.

In the Preface I have already indicated how this textual reading might work. Starting from the historical and geographical facts about Hibbing, I presented them as a symbolic construct that would provide a 'key' for the understanding of Robert Zimmerman/Bob Dylan. This chapter will set out in more detail the theoretical and methodological considerations involved in talking about Bob Dylan as text. In doing so I would like to begin with certain details about my personal experience of Dylan's work.

It is said that all members of a certain generation can remember what they were doing when they heard of John F. Kennedy's assassination. I was in the Library of the University of St Andrews in Scotland when a fellow student brought in the news, which quickly spread in whispers around the reading room. I packed up my books and went back to my lodgings—and played over and over a recording I had recently bought of Peter Paul and Mary singing 'Blowin' in the Wind.'

> Yes, 'n' how many deaths will it take till he knows
> That too many people have died? (L 53).

Twenty-seven years later it is still Kennedy that I think of when I hear these lines.

Of course, November of 1963 was a little late to be catching up with Bob Dylan. For the previous year or so, I had been in thrall to Joan Baez and was regularly attending the St Andrews Folk Club, listening to the great Scottish singer Archie Fisher. Around the end of 1963, I had begun to notice that several very striking songs—'Blowin' in the Wind' itself, a recent Baez recording of 'Don't Think Twice, It's All Right', and an incredible piece called 'It's a Hard Rain's A-Gonna Fall' on a Pete Seeger album—were all credited to a B. Dylan. The first recording of Dylan himself that I ever heard was a single track, of 'Blowin' in the Wind,' on a CBS sampler album. Most of my friends at St Andrews disliked it intensely. 'It's his song,' said one, 'so I suppose he can ruin it if he wants to.' But Dylan's voice, startling in its contrast to the Baez purity of tone, did not put me off at all. I was hooked, landed, gone—a lifetime convert.

Through 1964 I managed to catch up on the first two Dylan albums and keep pace with the new ones. Since I was also listening to The Rolling Stones, I had no trouble in accepting, indeed welcoming, Bob Dylan's move to rock 'n' roll. In 1965 I wrote a letter to the editor of *The Glasgow Herald*, defending *Bringing It All Back Home* against a hostile review. Later that year I moved to Canada, and in March, 1966, I finally saw Dylan: in Vancouver in concert with the Hawks, loud, badly amplified, and totally exhilarating.

So far this is a fan's story, and I have always remained a fan of Bob Dylan. I collect his recordings, both official and unofficial; I know many songs by heart; I have read all the biographies; I keep up to date with the rumors of what he is doing—will he tour this year, when is his next album coming out? My interest in Dylan's work is inextricably bound up with the memories and emotions of my private life. In ways more far-reaching than I will ever be able to understand, Dylan's words and music have defined the conditions of those memories and emotions.

But there is another aspect of my autobiography that is equally relevant to this study. In the Library of the University of St Andrews in November, 1963, what I was doing was studying for an Honors degree in English literature, and for the last twenty years, I have made my living as a teacher and a critic within the mainstream of the University academy. As such I was trained in and still write in a discipline that in several crucial ways is opposed to the 'fan's story' that I have just told.

The orthodox discourse of the discipline has little place for fans. Of course it is presumed that you *like*, say, William Shakespeare; if you are a biographical scholar you are even entitled to an obsessive interest in the trivia of his life and times. But even so, the rhetoric of the discipline is one of calm objectivity, measured judgment, and careful discrimination. You're not supposed to go to a concert and scream like a teenager. And you're not supposed to begin a 'serious literary study' with trivial personal reminiscences.

Within the traditional pose of objectivity, a good deal of positive evaluation does, of course, go on, but much of it is done silently and implicitly. The very act of writing on a canonical author includes the presumed judgment that the author is worth writing about, that he (or more rarely she) is 'a great writer': that's why he's in the canon in the first place.

Recently, however, the discipline has been faced with a drastic reexamination of the problems of canonicity: which works appropriately make up the curriculum of literary studies. There is still a traditional view that is strongly resistant, to the study of contemporary authors, especially those who work in mixed media and above all those who work in a popular, commercial milieu. That traditional view is under fire and in retreat, but no new consensus of canonicity is emerging. The whole point is that the very idea of 'canon' itself is now in question.

There is, of course, a kind of 'reverse' canon outside the University, an anti-academic one. Dylan has always been claimed by various schools of purists, from folk music devotees to born-again Christians, who demand that his works be interpreted exclusively in their terms. Those who see Dylan as an essentially 'popular' artist often react with hostility to any treatment of his work that uses the vocabulary of academic literary criticism.[1] A study like this one is thus liable to attack from both sides, for being both too academic and not academic enough.

While the opening up of the concept of 'the canon' might seem to facilitate a study of Dylan, other recent critical theory developments have moved in different directions against my 'fan's story.' In the various forms of New Criticism, structuralism, and poststructuralism, recent literary study has focused on the text to the exclusion of the author: an exclusion that reaches its rhetorical climax in Roland Barthes' essay 'The Death of the Author.' If I follow this methodology, how can I then pursue an obsessive interest in everything connected with the figure of the biographical author Bob Dylan? How can I justify traveling to Hibbing, Minnesota to gawk at his childhood bedroom?

The theory of the death of the Author is, however, much more sophisticated than any simplistic dismissal of biographical information. At its most radical it calls into question the way we view not only authors but all so-called 'individuals.' It depends upon a fundamental questioning of the notion of personality, of the self. In what sense can an author (or indeed anybody) be said to be an autonomous, coherent individual? Or to what extent are our selves and our images of ourselves the product of networks of intertextual traces (of language, of history, of society, of the unconscious)? Such skepticism about individuality—the notion that we are not singular entities but variable and multiple personalities—is also a major concern of Bob Dylan's work. In this sense, far from being opposed to critical theory, Dylan's work thematizes one of its central questions.

What dies in 'the death of the Author' is not the literal author but his authority: that is, the position of the author as the final criterion by which every reading of a work is to be measured and judged. Traditional criticism saw its purpose as the recovery and restatement, 'in other words,' of the original intention of the author. If a reading could be proved to be consonant with what could be known (or more often surmised) of the author's original state of mind, then it was a good or valid reading; if a reading seemed to exceed or run contrary to authorial intention, then it was a bad or invalid one.

Such a position is, of course, very limiting. It has great difficulty in accounting for any difference between the cultural contexts of the original author and the present reader. For instance, no twentieth century reader of Sophocles' *Oedipus Rex* can avoid seeing Freudian psychology as at least part of the meaning of the text—but it is a part that clearly cannot be attributed to the intention of the author.[2] Again, what is being disputed is not what can be known of the author's biography and intentions but the authority accorded to such knowledge. 'The author' is not so much the source or origin of his texts but rather *another* text, to be read with as much care, intelligence, and attention as one would devote to the reading of a poem. What one can know about an author's life is thus a text, made up of all the formal biographies or newspaper stories or just plain gossip that has entered public circulation. Similarly, what one can know about his intentions is another text, derived from diaries, letters, interviews, discarded drafts, etc. None of these texts can be taken simply; none (least of all works of fiction or poetry) can be accepted as reliable or unmediated statements of autobiography. All such texts take their place within the larger 'text' to which we may attach, for the sake of convenience, an author's name—such as 'Bob Dylan.'

Let us look briefly at an example of how this approach might operate in a particular interpretation. It has been suggested[3] that John Wesley Harding, the name of the outlaw, the song, and the album, is a reference to God, whose Jewish name Jehovah, or Jaweh, could be transliterated from Hebrew (which lacks separate letters for vowels) as the initials JWH. (One could then further suggest that the G, which Dylan adds to the historically correct spelling Hardin, supplies the English 'God.')

A strictly biographical approach would have to seek evidence that Dylan knew that JWH could stand for Jaweh (a reasonable surmise, since he was brought up as a Jew), that he remembered this when he chose the name, and that he intended his listeners to make this connection. (A more subtle version would hold that both the memory and intention were unconscious.) Evidence could be sought in interviews and other reported statements by Dylan about 'John Wesley Harding.' Failing that, a scholar might always hope that after Dylan's death some letter or diary entry might be found in his papers to corroborate the point. In any event, these strategies would refer the interpretation back to the author: would, as Barthes says, seek an 'explanation' in 'the author, his person, his life, his tastes, his passions' (*Image-Music-Text* 143).

A post-Barthesian reading would not discount what could be known about Dylan's biography. *It is* relevant that he had a Jewish upbringing and that *John Wesley Harding* is a deeply religious album, which in many ways prefigures the Christian albums of ten years later. But such concerns would no longer dominate or determine the reading, nor would the reading be proved 'wrong' if Dylan himself were to scoff at it and say, 'I never intended any such thing.' The author's intention, writes Jacques Derrida, 'is not annulled ... but rather *inscribed* within a system which it no longer dominates' (OG 243). As soon as such a reading has been suggested, it enters the textual system of *John Wesley Harding*, and it must be evaluated in terms of what it can offer to a reading of that system, not in terms of what it has to offer for anyone's understanding of the biographical person Bob Dylan.

The necessity of making this kind of distinction will become more acute when we deal with songs that are more ostensibly autobiographical, especially those that refer to Dylan's love life. Such songs should be approached as dramatic images, not as clues in some biographical crossword puzzle. Dylan claimed that his song 'Sara' should be read in reference not to his wife but to the Biblical wife of Abraham. In a later chapter I will examine some ramifications of that intertextual chain; but the point to be made here is that, however one reads it, the interest of 'Sara' is as a textual construct that includes both the biographical and the Biblical references. What the song does not do (and should not be asked to do) is offer any simple, transparent report on the state of the Dylans' marriage.

This is not to say that the biography or the public career is irrelevant to the songs. Dylan insists on their relevance, especially in the setting that has repeatedly proven the most vital and productive milieu for his art: live performance. Dylan's concerts over the years have played an endless series of variations on his public image, on what an audience expects of him. This was perhaps most clearly demonstrated in the self-consciously mythopoeic Rolling Thunder Revue, but it is no less evident in other tours. Any given concert, in its selection and arrangement of old songs, provides another 'text' of Bob Dylan, another complete but momentary alias.

If we read 'Bob Dylan' not as a person but as a textual system, it is a great advantage that Bob Dylan (or should we here say, Robert Zimmerman) has exhibited an exceptionally high degree of self-consciousness in his collaboration in that creation. Any author who adopts a pseudonym is, by that very gesture, foregrounding the writing of his life as a text. The assumed name is a kind of mask: 'It's Halloween,' Dylan announced to a New York audience on October 31, 1964. 'I have my Bob Dylan mask on.'

The image of the mask has been central throughout Bob Dylan's career. In his 1989 album, *Oh Mercy*, the sinister 'Man in the Long Black Coat' is described as having 'a face like a mask' (OM). And right at the beginning, the mask makes a curiously 'accidental' appearance. In the famous review that Robert Shelton wrote for *The New York Times*, September 28, 1961, is the phrase 'his musicmaking has the mark of originality and inspiration' (McGregor 18). When this review was reprinted on the back cover of the first album, 'mark' was misprinted as 'mask.' Bob Dylan has been wearing the mask of originality ever since.

Classical theater used the mask both to conceal identity and to express character. The mask hid the face of the actor, whose individuality was not important: he existed only to serve the role. At the same time the stylized designs of the face gave expression to the dramatic reality of the fictional character.[4] Actor and character coexisted as each other's doubles; the voice was the ghost within the mask.

Ezra Pound used the Classical mask, the persona, as an image for what the poet does in the act of writing:

> In the 'search for oneself,' in the search for 'sincere self-expression,' one gropes, one finds some seeming verity. One says 'I am' this, that, or the other, and with the words scarcely uttered one ceases to be that thing.
>
> I began this search for the real in a book called *Personae*, casting off, as it were, complete masks of the self in each

poem. I continued in a long series of translations, which
were but more elaborate masks. ('Vorticism' 1914.)

One could see this as an uncannily accurate description of the early Dylan
'casting off' (the term means both creating and discarding) the masks of himself as
protest singer, rock star, country boy, before embarking on the 'translations' of
other people's songs which he released in 1970 under the paradoxical title *Self-
Portrait*.

Pound's use of quotation marks indicates a degree of skepticism about such
phrases as 'search for oneself' and 'sincere self-expression.' The mask always casts
identity into doubt: to say 'I am' something is already to cease to be that something. Bob Dylan has made frequent comments on the instability and indeterminacy of his projected identity. His 1983 song 'I and I' explicitly thematizes the
mask of divided identity and relates it to the indivisibility of God (Jaweh, I AM
THAT I AM). In a 1985 interview he commented in relation to this song:

> Sometimes the 'you' in my songs is me talking to me. Other
> times I can be talking to somebody else.... It's up to you to
> figure out who's who. A lot of times it's 'you' talking to 'you.'
> The 'I,' like in 'I and I,' also changes. It could be I, or it could
> be the 'I' who created me. And also, it could be another per-
> son who's saying 'I.' When I say 'I' right now, I don't know
> who I'm talking about (Cohen, 'Don't Ask Me' 39).

The result is that the personal pronouns in Bob Dylan's songs tend to be highly
mobile and indeterminate in reference. Anthony Scaduto quotes Dylan as saying,
'when I used words like "he" and "it" and "they" and talking about other people, I
was really talking about nobody but me' (249).

In late 1985 Dylan also said, on the liner notes to *Biograph*, 'I don't think of
myself as Bob Dylan. It's like Rimbaud said, "I is another." '[5] Rimbaud's line has
been widely quoted in support of the postmodern sense of the self not as a meta-
physical entity but as the result of multiple and interlocking systems of discourse.
It can serve as a motto not only for Dylan but for a whole theory of the divided
self, or rather of the impossibility of an *un*divided self. Its use of the third person
'is' instead of the first person 'am' serves to dislodge 'I' from its privileged position
as syntactic and ideological subject.

The idea that each of us is an absolutely unique, coherent, self-contained, autonomous individual has increasingly been attacked as a myth of relatively recent origin. The psychoanalytical dimension of the unconscious deprives the rational mind of its total sovereignty over knowledge and intention. Social and economic analyses of power and discourse show that the rhetoric of individualism serves particular political ends by creating privileged subject-positions. The philosophical and linguistic investigations of poststructuralism argue that language itself necessarily implies that our consciousness of the world or of ourselves operates by deferral and division. Underlying such views is the metaphor of the world as a text: that is, not as something natural but as something culturally produced; not as something self-evident and self-explanatory but as something subject to all the complex processes of writing, reading, and interpretation; not as something separate from us but as something that simultaneously forms us and is formed by us. The world as text has many authors/many others. Rimbaud's 'Je est un autre' can equally well be read 'Je est un auteur.'

The traditional authority of the I (and especially of the *male* I) has taken many forms and operated through many metaphors. One such metaphor, to which the critical discourse of feminism has paid particular attention, is the *gaze* of the controlling eye, which surveys and dominates its chosen field. In film theory, the spectator (predominantly male) occupies the subject-position. He chooses what to look at, and the freedom of his gaze reflects the freedom of his volition and movement through the plot. The object of the gaze (here theorized as female) exists only to be seen. Whether as Hollywood pinup or hard-core model, she is fixed in time and space under the eye/I of the gaze.

Bob Dylan has long been fascinated by the cinema and by the authoritative structure of the gaze. In his film *Renaldo and Clara*, the camera is clearly an instrument of power enforcing reluctant acquiescence from the men, and especially women, whom he 'directs' to 'perform' themselves. Many of Dylan's narrative songs have constructed elliptical, subtly disjointed scenarios, which invite consideration in cinematic terms. At the same time he himself has always been uneasy under the camera's eye. His appearances in rock videos have been awkward and unconvincing. In 'Jokerman' he squints back at the camera, returning its gaze in a guarded and secretive fashion as if it were an enemy to be very wary of. His most characteristic role, here as elsewhere, has been that of Alias, the man who is always someone else (un autre).

The power of the gaze is that it comes from a fully realized and privileged subject-position: the one who looks is always an I. This gives rise to the central I/eye pun of identity. Vision, the enabling medium of the eye, acts as a metaphor for the enabling power of the subject, so a reference to 'eye' carries implicitly the notion of an 'I,' the linguistic assertion of personality. Much contemporary psychological, sociological, and linguistic theory challenges the primacy of this 'I.' The 'I' is seen as the product of various discourses of power, and as always uncertain and divided within itself. The very word 'I' is divided between the I who writes and the I who is written, so there is no refuge, even in the first-person pronoun (or in the proper name), for the traditional sense of unique and coherent personality.

Bob Dylan's work participates in this interrogation of the I, and he too uses the I/eye equivocation. 'I cannot say the word eye any more,' he wrote in 1965 on the liner notes for *Highway 61 Revisited*: '... when I speak this word eye, it is as if I am speaking of somebody's eye that I faintly remember.... there is no eye—there is only a series of mouths—long live the mouths' (L 210). There is no eye, and there is no I (and I). This eye/I pun recurs frequently—in, for instance, 'Abandoned Love' (1974): 'Everybody's wearing a disguise / To hide what they've got left behind their eyes' (L 393). In the course of this book, I will repeatedly return to the possibility of reading 'eye' as 'I,' always with the further implication that the I is unstable, unknowable, unspeakable. 'I cannot say the word eye any more' (1965); 'When I say "I" right now, I don't know who I'm talking about' (1985).

A mask usually has two openings: for the eye and for the mouth. Commenting on the passage from the *Highway 61* notes, Neil Corcoran writes,

> Any Dylan song is what Bob Dylan chooses to do next with
> his breath and his mouth; and in decentring and destabilis-
> ing the authority of the 'eye' or 'I,' Dylan refuses the bur-
> den of his past, and allows himself the possibility of actually
> 'keeping on,' neither a slave to, nor a denier of, his own
> extraordinary history and his own extraordinary fame (97).

The medium that Dylan has chiefly worked in is not a visual one, controlled by the eye/I, but an aural one, conveyed through 'a series of mouths,' a succession of voices. 'Voice' can, of course, serve just as strongly as vision as a metaphor for a secure and recognizable personal identity. We speak of artists who have 'found

24

their voice' as a mark of unique style. But what is Bob Dylan's voice? During his career, he has adopted a remarkable range of voices, from folkie twang to mellow country, from the hoarse blues shout to 'that thin, that wild mercury sound' of rock 'n' roll. It is in his voice, in the 'series of mouths,' that Dylan has sought both to create and to escape his assumed identity.

Nowhere is this variety more apparent than in the strange, casual collection of ventriloquistic performances of other people's songs that Dylan entitled *Self-Portrait*. Produced early in 1970, the record was a dramatic disavowal of the newly ended decade and of its various images of Bob Dylan as protest singer, as rock 'n' roll Messiah, as original songwriter. The 'self' was here 'portrayed' as alias, as the amalgam of its influences: old songs from the folk, blues, pop, and country and western idioms; contemporary songs by other writers; carelessly understated performances of his own 'greatest hits.' On the opening song of the album, Dylan himself does not sing: even his voice has been replaced by 'un autre.' In this presentation of the self not as a unified author but as the sum of its intertextual traces, *Self-Portrait* is a remarkably poststructuralist album, a thorough deconstruction of Bob Dylan's power, authority, and identity.

Self-Portrait was Dylan's most systematic statement of his view of the self as other. Critics who have developed the implications of Rimbaud's aphorism have stressed the degree to which the self, the 'I,' has to be regarded as a construct of language and discourse. This construct is always implicitly a narrative one. Richard Kearney speaks of 'the narrative self' and says that 'To reply to the question "who?" is to tell one's story to the other' (395). The chapters of this book describe Bob Dylan's attempts to tell himself to various respective 'others': to other singers, to past and present lovers, to the ultimate audience of God.

For the identity of the 'other' in Rimbaud's phrase is no less problematic than the identity of the self. There are many ways one can define 'the other':

1. The other is an image of absolute alterity, everything that is set off from me, which I do not know or comprehend. The other is the sign of the *difference* that everywhere confronts me. In this sense 'I is an other' is the expression of the paradox that I am defined by what I do not understand or control; 'I' can only be thought in relation to everything that is not I.

2. The other is the one whom we face in all ethical or political situ-

25

ations: 'we live in a political world' (OM). It is the face of a starving child, a refugee, a victim of torture. It is this other to whom we acknowledge responsibility in all our civic actions. It is this other who was addressed, for instance, in the 1985 Live Aid concert, at which Bob Dylan, with more honesty than tact, pointed out that the other is close to home as well as overseas. It is this other to whom he sings, '[If] I just turn my back when you silently die / What good am I?' (OM).

3. The other is the one whom we meet in our personal relationships, the immediate 'you' with whom we share our daily lives. In popular songs this 'you' is overwhelmingly the lover: desired or possessed, celebrated or lost. In love songs 'I' is the story told to this 'you.' It is the oldest story in the world, and every time it is told anew.

4. For an artist, especially a performer, the other is the audience. In many Dylan songs the 'you' is implicitly the listener, and the listener is frequently envisaged with such immediacy that it is as if he or she is actually present. For instance, in 'What Was It You Wanted?', Dylan addresses his interlocutor, promising to be 'back in a minute.' There follows a brief harmonica break, in which the singer is, as it were, 'away'; then he returns to say, 'What was it you wanted? / You can tell me, I'm back / We can start it all over / Get it back on the track' (OM). The self-reflexive gesture is emphasized by the double meaning of 'track': the voice returns from the absence of the instrumental break, but both voice and harmonica are equally present/absent on the recorded 'track.'

As in many songs, the 'you' of 'What Was It You Wanted?' could be interpreted in terms of all the above categories. It could be a love song to an excessively demanding woman, or it could be a prayer to a no less demanding God. It could be an internal dialogue in which Dylan attempts to understand what the 'you' who is also 'I' demands of him. But it also could be addressed to Dylan's audience, with whom he has a continuing and ambivalent relationship.

In the early stages of his career, there was an evident craving for attention and fame, but simultaneously (as in his performance in the Hibbing High School Auditorium), there was an uncompromising refusal to do anything that an audience might expect. This refusal might, of course, be seen as an inverted ploy for both attention and fame: Dylan's attraction would be that he could always be expected to do the unexpected. The 1964 Halloween concert is in some respects a love-in between Dylan and his audience; yet even there he is leading them away from the familiar. The order of songs carefully alternates between the well-established protest songs like 'The Times They Are A-Changin'' or 'Who Killed Davey Moore?' and the radically new idiom of 'Mr Tambourine Man' or 'Gates of Eden.'

Several songs from that period—the whimsical 'Hero Blues' or the manifesto 'My Back Pages'—were directly produced by Dylan's resistance to the audience demands of people like Irwin Silber, whose November, 1964 'Open Letter to Bob Dylan' attempted to direct him back to the paths of folk-protest virtue. The confrontation became open and violent in the electric concerts of 1965 and 1966, from the largely apocryphal booing at Newport to the anguished cry of 'Judas!' from an outraged fan in Manchester. But Dylan's resistance to his audience was also a form of response to it, and his art was being shaped by the various strategies and forms which that resistance took.

The same process can be traced at every stage of his career. *Self-Portrait* takes disavowal to be the formative force of identity, a gesture repeated in 1988 by the even more eclectic *Down in the Groove*. In his almost continuous concert tours since 1974, Dylan has alternately courted and rebuffed his audiences. In 1978 he offered them familiar songs in outrageously unfamiliar arrangements. In the early gospel tours, he frustrated their desire to hear the old songs, but by 1981 he was reintroducing them like rewards. In 1988-89 he steadfastly refused to speak to audiences at all, moving from song to song without a word of introduction or thanks. In these concerts the audience might just as well not have been present— except that Dylan and his band were offering them magnificent music. Above all else (even, I would argue, his songwriting), Bob Dylan is a creation of live performances. It is on the stage that he creates his Alias. 'Bob Dylan' exists only in relation to the audience, and this is never more true than on the occasions where he is ostentatiously ignoring or resisting it.

The audience, then—the listeners, critics, fans; the Stephen Scobie who writes this book and the Stephen Scobie who listened to 'Blowin' in the Wind' on November 22, 1963; I and I—are all part of the intertextual system that we must read as 'Bob Dylan.' We wear a mask too, the mask of the Other, of Rimbaud's 'autre.' The singer on the stage is himself involved in our presence: 'A million faces at my feet,' Dylan sings, 'but all I see are dark eyes' (L 500). Dark I's.

THE TEXT OF BOB DYLAN

In April, 1987, Bob Dylan joined the Irish group U2 on stage in one of their concerts and sang 'Knockin' on Heaven's Door' with them. In the middle of the song, U2's lead singer, Bono, starts improvising a new verse: 'Well, the time has come / For this wounded world to start changing….' Then he comments: 'You know, I used to make up my own words to Bob Dylan songs. He says he doesn't mind.' And Dylan responds: 'Well, I do it too.'

The extent to which Bob Dylan has been willing to make up new words and new music to Bob Dylan songs poses another set of problems for the critic. If in the last chapter I was discussing the whole image and career of 'Bob Dylan' as a kind of text, I must turn in this chapter to the text of Bob Dylan: the words, the music, the performances, and the various forms in which these elements are available to us.

Traditional literary scholarship is always anxious to establish a definitive text, which will then be a stable and unchanging object of study. Researchers attempt to reconstitute from the flawed and incomplete printed versions of Shakespeare's plays what he 'actually' wrote. These arguments are usually phrased in terms of authorial intention: what did Shakespeare mean to write in this line? But since authors of this stature are assumed to be geniuses, there is always the temptation to argue that the 'best' line (or what the editor thinks is the best line) must surely be what the author intended. Thus accidental improvements in the text, caused by misprints or obscure handwriting, may be incorporated on the grounds that the more ordinary reading was 'unworthy' of this author. Editorial scholars also have to decide between early and late versions: is the first inspiration preferable to the later revision? Despite these problems, the aim remains unquestioned: the definitive text, the stable object of study.

For Dylan there is no definitive text. There is only a shifting body of work, in which the songs change with each performance and in which the printed text has a limited authority. Every time a critic quotes from a Dylan song, the quotation is in some way provisional, hedged around with qualifications. The purpose of this chapter is to set out some of these qualifications, so that they can then be understood to hover over every other set of quotation marks in this book.

It is often difficult for listeners to determine exactly what the lyrics of a Bob Dylan song are—he has never been noted for clear enunciation. I remember my amazement when I first saw a printed text of 'Subterranean Homesick Blues' and compared it with my notes of what I thought he'd been singing! *All Across the Telegraph* includes an amusing section of 'reported mishearings' (268-9), which range from the comic—Rosemary 'took a cabbage into town' (for 'carriage')—to the plausibly poetic—'She's delicate and seems like veneer' (for 'the mirror'). One reason for these difficulties was that Dylan, like The Rolling Stones, never printed the song lyrics on the album jacket or sleeve, as if he were insisting that the words should be heard, even misheard, rather than read. It was not until *Empire Burlesque* in 1985 that printed words appeared as part of an album package.[1]

Of course, the words were published in other places—as sheet music, for instance—and many early songs appeared in magazines like *Sing Out*. But no major collection of Dylan lyrics was in print until Knopf brought out *Writings and Drawings* in 1973. This edition was then updated and reissued as *Lyrics, 1962-1985*, and it is this volume that has the best claim to be the definitive printed text of Dylan's songs.

But it's a very shaky claim. There are several ways in which *Lyrics* fails to be a definitive collection. In the first place it is drastically incomplete: Clinton Heylin lists the titles of 48 songs officially copyrighted by Dylan that are not included in *Lyrics*.[2] Although most of these songs were unreleased at that time, several are of major importance: 'Angelina,' 'Blind Willie McTell,' 'Foot of Pride,' 'Yonder Comes Sin'....

Secondly, *Lyrics* prints only one version of each song. Given Dylan's habit of extensive rewriting, this cannot help but produce an incomplete picture. A good example is 'Tangled Up In Blue,' released on *Blood on the Tracks* in 1975. This song has gone through many variations in its lyrics. During the 1978 tour Dylan changed the reference to 'an Italian poet,' substituting a series of chapter-and-

verse Biblical citations, which seemed to be random and changed with every performance. For the 1984 tour he revised the lyrics much more thoroughly, and this
new version was released on *Real Live*. In the sleeve notes to *Biograph*, Dylan commented, 'On *Real Live* it's more like it should have been.... The imagery is better
and more the way I would have liked it than on the original recording.' Why then
is it the 1975 version that is reissued on *Biograph* and the 1975 text that is printed
in *Lyrics?* In cases like this, *Lyrics* could make a stronger claim to be a definitive
text if it printed at least the 1984 version alongside the original text. (A scholarly
edition of the variorum Bob Dylan text will eventually have to include all the 1978
Biblical citations as well.)

It is not that *Lyrics* sticks slavishly to the text of the original recordings. Far
from it. *Lyrics* is full of revisions, from the occasionally altered word to the completely rewritten song. Whether these changes are always for the better is open to
debate. On 'Precious Angel,' for instance, Dylan sings the marvelously sensuous
and erotic lines 'You're the queen of my flesh, girl, you're my woman, you're my
delight, / You're the lamp of my soul, girl, and you torch up the night.' *Lyrics*
prints 'you *touch* up the night' (L 426). In other cases the rewriting is wholesale:
'Goin' to Acapulco' bears little resemblance to the text sung on *The Basement
Tapes*, and the jokes in 'I Shall Be Free' have been extensively reworked despite the
fact that Dylan has not sung the song in public since 1963.

And there are other annoyances. The order of songs is sometimes different
from the order in which they appear on the albums; the *Basement Tapes* lyrics
appear, illogically, neither at the date on which they were recorded nor at the date
on which they were released. And so on. *Lyrics*, in other words, bears many signs
of carelessness and incompletion, as if Dylan lacked interest in publishing a complete, properly edited, and definitive text. Yet at the same time it shows such
extensive revisions that one can only conclude that it was put together with a good
deal of attention and care.[3]

This divided response, that the book is both carefully considered and slop-
pily casual, is characteristic of the problems of Dylan's text. A similar division is
apparent in many recordings, where some songs are tight, word-perfect performances and others are slipshod and hurried, with the mistakes and stumbles left in
the released track rather than corrected in another take. (On *Self-Portrait*, for
example, Dylan completely messes up one verse of 'Days of '49' and comments

'Oh, my goodness' audibly between verses.) In contrast to singers who spend weeks in the studio honing and perfecting their material, Dylan likes to move in and out of the studio as quickly as possible. The whole of *Another Side of Bob Dylan* was recorded in a single day: June 9, 1964. Occasionally, he has gone back and rerecorded songs, as he did for *Blood on the Tracks*, and recently he has allowed more elaborate studio productions, like *Infidels* and *Oh Mercy*. But to a great extent, he seems to have ignored the technical possibilities of modern recording studios and attempted to preserve the spontaneity and rough edges of live performance.[4]

At the same time it must be remembered that Dylan in the mid-1960s was at the technological front line. He was one of the first performers to use the full power of electronic amplification. What many people who heard Bob Dylan and the Hawks in 1965-66 reacted to most strongly, whether positively or negatively, was the sheer volume. Dylan has never rejected the technological capacities of his music, but he has never allowed himself to be dominated by them either. He has never become a fetishist for the perfect sound system or the flawless recording. In the same way, he has always shown disdain for the commercial and marketing aspects of his profession. He doesn't release the kind of albums his fans expect. In concert tours he ignores his most recent releases and doesn't even say 'Hullo, it's nice to be here.' Dylan has moved into the world of the mass media and its technological capitalism, but he continues to treat it as if it were a coffeehouse in Greenwich Village.

All this returns us to *Lyrics*. The book is presented as if it were what the fans and scholars might expect: the definitive collection, carefully edited, which would then be the reference point for all Bob Dylan studies. But this expectation is then subverted. Bob Dylan isn't interested in a definitive text any more than he is in becoming a model commercial rock star. Paul Williams describes the effect as 'Dylan thumbing his nose at or trying to erase ... his art even as he anthologizes it, still eating the document' (229). But for all its imperfections *Lyrics* is still the best we've got. Most quotations in this book continue to use it as their source.

One other major way in which *Lyrics* is not definitive is simply that it is only the lyrics. The words presented in isolation from music and performance are as incomplete as a musical score or the script of a play. It is this incompletion which underscores the often-made distinction that Bob Dylan is not, strictly speaking, a poet: he is a songwriter.

Alone on the page, Dylan's words may seem flat or clumsy—but often enough it is precisely those 'clumsy' lines that work best in performance. In the printed lyrics the line 'And you wouldn't know it would happen like this' (L 239) seems prosaic and drab amidst the imagistic pyrotechnics of 'Sad-Eyed Lady of the Lowlands.' Yet in performance it soars. 'What Dylan "means" in a song,' writes John Herdman,

> is not always what the words say: the sense may be con-
> veyed through the *tensions* between words, expression and
> musical mood. Dylan's voice does not just interpret his
> lyrics, it gives them life. His marvellous timing and
> breath-control, his capacity for drawing out lines almost
> to breaking-point, his emotional subtlety and inspired
> phrasing, make it one of his greatest artistic assets (6).

Dylan's voice has, of course, been the subject of more abuse than praise. In a witty article for *The Telegraph*, Bert Cartwright assembled from twenty years of reviews and journalism the many and desperate metaphors with which critics have sought to describe it. It has been characterized as a whine, whether nasal or ade-noidal, and as a growl, a howl, a croak, and a wail. It has been compared to a wide range of animals caught in barbed wire, to police sirens and acupuncture, and to 'the death scream of a circular saw.' *Time* claimed that 'At its very best, his voice sounds as if it were drifting over the walls of a tuberculosis sanitarium—but that's part of the charm.'5

Rather than attempt to compete with such inspired imagery, I note that Dylan's voice, as part of Dylan's text, contributes to the general indeterminacy that I am describing. 'Voice' is often seen as a guarantee of individuality and authenticity: we say that an artist has 'found his voice.' But Dylan's voice changes, from record to record and from concert to concert. It offers no privileged access to a stable 'I' behind the songs; it too refuses the stamp of the definitive. Whether it is a growl or a whine, the smooth country inflections of *Nashville Skyline* or the hard, angry rasp of *Highway 61 Revisited*, it adjusts itself to the emotional needs of the song and the performance. Conventional musical notions of beauty or tuneful-ness are simply irrelevant: Dylan's voice is the most varied and expressive of the instruments he plays.

A simple proof of this may be found by listening to other singers performing Bob Dylan's songs. The songs themselves are so strong that these singers will often produce enjoyable versions,[6] but very few if any are better than Dylan's own recordings. Perhaps only Jimi Hendrix, with 'All Along the Watchtower,' has succeeded in redefining a Dylan song.

Consideration of Dylan's vocal phrasing brings up one further and final problem in the printed *Lyrics:* that of lineation. How does the text indicate the pauses for line-breaks and rhymes? Dylan frequently weaves convoluted patterns of internal rhymes, or rhymes that distort the semantic pattern of the line-break. In 'When the Night Comes Falling from the Sky,' the *Lyrics* text reads, 'You will seek me and you'll find me / In the wasteland of your mind' (L 496), whereas the spacing on the recording is clearly 'You will seek me and you'll find / Me in the wasteland of your mind'—which may look awkward on the page but works well in performance because of the stressed alliteration of 'me' and 'mind.'

Sometimes Dylan's phrasing cuts across the regular printed lines to such an extent that he produces an aural equivalent of free verse. For instance, these lines from 'I Dreamed I Saw St. Augustine' are printed as

> With a blanket underneath his arm
> And a coat of solid gold,
> Searching for the very souls
> Whom already have been sold.
> ....
> No martyr is among ye now
> Whom you can call your own,
> So go on your way accordingly
> But know you're not alone (L 256).

The recording on *John Wesley Harding* follows this line pattern faithfully enough. However, a transcription of the performance Dylan gave in London on October 17, 1987, might well be set out like this:

> With a blanket under-
> neath his arm
> and a coat of
> solid gold,
> searching for the

very souls
whom already have been
sold.

....

No martyr is
among you now
that you can
call your own,
so go on your way a-
ccording-
ly
but know
you're not a-
lone.

Here the rhythmic pattern is closer to open-form verse, the kind of stress on unexpected line-breaks we might find in a poet like Robert Creeley or Denise Levertov. In this performance the voice is played as an instrument more interested in the rhythmic pattern than in the strict meaning of the words. It makes no sense to insert two major pauses in the middle of 'accordingly,' even if it does produce a nice pun on 'chording.' What it does do is illustrate what Dylan meant, as long ago as the sleeve notes to *Highway 61 Revisited*, when he wrote, 'the songs on this specific record are not so much songs but rather exercises in tonal breath control' (L 210).

Dylan has often been criticized for indulging in such 'exercises,' as if he should pay as much attention to the meaning of his words as his critics feel compelled to do. It seems somehow decadent to indulge in rhythmic frills when the song is about Important Topics like racial prejudice or nuclear war. But I think this criticism is misguided: its approach is a narrowly thematic one that sees form as mere decoration rather than a formal one that sees the musical effects as intrinsic to the content. Again, it reads Dylan's works as poems rather than songs.

The importance of the music in the Dylan text cannot be overstressed, but it is also very difficult to discuss. Some critics, such as Betsy Bowden and Wilfrid Mellers, have used technical musical vocabulary to describe shifts of key and modulations of rhythm, but in my view this approach has met with limited success.

The effect of the music, though pervasive, can only partly be articulated; the music acts as 'the unconscious of the text.' This phrase comes from the French critic Catherine Clément. Although she is writing about the relation of words and music in opera, I believe that her account is also highly suggestive for song:

> A double, inseparable scene: the words give rise to the
> music and the music develops the language, gives it
> dialect, envelops it, thwarts or reinforces it. Conscious and
> unconscious: the words are aligned with the legible, ratio-
> nal side of a conscious discourse, and the music is the
> unconscious of the text, that which gives it depth of field
> and relief, that which attributes a past to the text, a mem-
> ory, one perceptible not to the listener's consciousness but
> to his enchanted unconsciousnesses (21).

The music is the context within which the text lives: it allows the text to be, it justifies the text's existence. The music provides a rhythm, a beat, an emotional ambience. It does not have to 'say' anything itself; it just has to be there, in the background, on the threshold of the unconscious, like a ghost.

Clément says that the music may either 'thwart' or 'reinforce' the words. The music does not have to repeat or support the meaning of the words; it is equally capable of undermining the words or acting in ironic counterpart to them. In either event the meaning of the music will always modify what the words ostensibly say. In any art form the very act of creation is such a positive gesture that it tends to counteract even the most pessimistic and tragic world view. There is a kind of joy, even in *King Lear* or *Guernica*, at the affirmation of something being made. In music, with its strongly rhythmical effects, and with its sense of an implied community of listeners, this joy is always there. Leonard Cohen phrased it memorably in his novel *The Favourite Game* in a scene in which his hero listens to Pat Boone singing[7]:

> *I can tell you, people,*
> *The news was not so good.*
>
> The news is great. The news is sad but it's in a song so it's
> not so bad (97).

In song the news can never be completely bad. For Dylan the sheer joy of music-making has always been a major part of whatever meaning his songs may convey.

So the music can change the total effect of a song in different performances even if the words remain identical. No performance of a song ever stands alone— it is necessarily accompanied by the intertext of previous performances and the audience's awareness of the previous performances. For example, the rhythmic variation of the 1987 'St. Augustine' plays with and against the audience's memory of the *John Wesley Harding* recording. It is only because of that memory that it can be understood as a variation in the first place.

Dylan has frequently explored the possibilities of varying the musical setting of his lyrics. In 1971[8] the single 'George Jackson' offered the same words in different settings on its A and B sides. The A side is sung solo with acoustic guitar and harmonica while the B side adds steel guitar, drums, and two backup singers. The A side is intense and angry, a protest against the defeat of George Jackson's death; the B side is solemn, hymnic, and unexpectedly tender, a celebration of the victory of George Jackson's life. The words do not change: but the music changes the meaning of the song. Further, the performance depends upon the audience's knowledge of Dylan's past. In 1971 the return to acoustic guitar and harmonica was a deliberate evocation (what semiotic critics would call a 'coding') of Dylan's early 1960s style of protest music. Increasingly, Dylan would work with the accumulation of his own history, weaving that context into the meaning of each performance.

Nowhere has this variability been more evident than in Dylan's evolving treatment of what is perhaps his most famous single song: 'Like a Rolling Stone' (L 191-2). The lyrics present a complex portrait of a character who has recently experienced a drastic reversal of fortune. I will call her 'Miss Lonely' (the only name the song attributes to her), but it should be borne in mind that the 'you' of a Dylan song is always a multiple other and that in some ways the addressee is also Bob Dylan himself, the audience, or even God. The words allow for a wide range of emotional response. They express anger and a certain amount of gloating at the woman's plight; the song has often been seen as primarily an act of revenge. But there is also a sense that Miss Lonely has liberated herself and that living 'out on the street' is greatly to be preferred to 'the finest school.' Paul Nelson saw the ending as 'clearly optimistic and triumphant, a soaring of the spirit into a new and more productive present' (McGregor 107). While there are negative connotations to being 'on your own ... without a home ... with no direction home,' there is also a sense of freedom, honesty, and self-reliance. Dylan's whole musical career up to 1965, especially his inheritance of the Woody Guthrie tradition, would suggest that to be 'like a rolling stone' is a far from undesirable destiny. Each verse builds up to the climactic moment of release on 'How does it feel?'—it is the pattern of male sexual orgasm or, more learnedly, of Aristotelian catharsis. But the question has no simple answer, as I hope to show with a survey of six selected performances (selected out of the dozens if not hundreds of times Dylan has performed the song over twenty-five years).

The original recording, June 15, 1965, already reflects the range of possibilities. At the time it seemed like a vitriolic performance, but in retrospect Dylan's voice sounds almost mellow. He is fully involved here with the characterization: this version is about Miss Lonely in ways that few of the later versions would be. (Or indeed could be: inevitably, every subsequent performance is about 'Like a Rolling Stone'; that is, about itself and the song's history.) The band drives hard and direct toward the climax of 'How does it feel?', but Al Kooper's organ track (added, so legend has it, almost by accident) hints at more hymnic and celebratory moods. It remains a great rock 'n' roll recording and as close to a definitive performance as one can ever get with Dylan; it also remains the touchstone from which all subsequent variations will derive their meaning.

Perhaps the most famous bootleg recording of Dylan features 'Like a Rolling Stone.' It dates from Manchester Free Trade Hall, May 17, 1966. The audiences on this tour were openly hostile to Dylan's electric music, which they chose to see as a betrayal of folk music purity. Someone in the crowd yells out 'Judas!', and there is a smattering of applause and embarrassed laughter. 'I don't believe you,' Dylan says, ironically quoting the title of one of his acoustic songs recently translated into an electric arrangement. 'You're a liar!' Then he steps back from the microphone and shouts (barely audible on the tape) 'You're a fucking liar!'—whereupon The Hawks slam in with the opening chords of 'Like a Rolling Stone.' There is no doubt about the mood of this version: it's pure venom. The anger, however, is directed not at the character, Miss Lonely, but at the audience—and by extension at all the audiences who for the past year had been reacting with such incomprehension to the changes in Dylan's art. The vocal is pitched much higher than on the original recording, and it seems right on the edge of control. The band is dominated by pounding and obtrusive drums, but Robbie

Robertson's guitar matches the agony of Dylan's voice.

Three years later, the performance at the Isle of Wight, August 31, 1969, took place in a completely different context. It was Dylan's first major concert appearance since his withdrawal into seclusion in 1966, and it was to be his last until he resumed touring in 1974. As might be expected, he and The Band were under-rehearsed, and the version of 'Like a Rolling Stone' is, to put it mildly, a mess. A genial mess, though. Dylan sings in long tumbling runs that slide down the scale like waterfalls. In the second verse he forgets the words and sings the same line three times, his mumble retreating into deeper obscurity than ever. No attempt is made to build up to 'How does it feel?' Two points need to be made about this performance. First, it in no way displaces or annuls the original. Indeed, it works only with reference to the original; Dylan is relying on his audience's familiarity with the song. Hey, he's saying, it's no big deal; it's just a song, not a way of life. We can have fun with it too. And secondly, Dylan chose to release this version officially as part of *Self-Portrait*. In that context it participates in the remarkable deconstruction of his image that is that album's ironic project. No other song could have made the point quite as forcefully.

When Dylan resumed touring in 1974, his relationship with his audience was very different from what it had been eight years previously. Now the concerts were a celebration of the times he and they had been through together. The political context of Watergate gave new emphasis to lines like 'even the President of the United States / Sometimes must have / To stand naked' (L 177). As is evident in the version released on *Before the Flood*, 'Like a Rolling Stone' became the climax of this celebration. The voice now stressed the liberation rather than the put-down, and the dominant instrument was Garth Hudson's organ, whose rolling five-note phrase after each line of the chorus transformed the song into an anthem. The answer to 'How does it feel?' was unequivocal: it feels great. Welcome back, Bob. It feels wonderful.

By 1980-81 the context had changed again. In his first concerts after his conversion to fundamentalist Christianity, Dylan had resolutely played only the new religious songs. When he began to reintroduce older songs into the act, one of the first was 'Like a Rolling Stone.' In the new context, Miss Lonely became a lost soul who had missed her true 'direction home' to Christ.[9] All anger had been replaced by Christian compassion and forgiveness. Dylan's voice was mournful and sympathetic, and the music had become, quite literally, more tuneful. Whereas the lines of the verse in previous versions had been sung as long runs on a single note with only a few embellishments, this version has a complex and lovely melody carefully worked out and sustained through all four verses.

In 1988, working with the trio led by G. E. Smith on guitar, Dylan attempted 'Like a Rolling Stone' without keyboards for the first time. The arrangement is thoroughly reworked: there is an instrumental bridge passage before the last verse, and Smith takes long guitar solos. In many ways this rendition has returned more closely to the 1965 original than any of the intermediaries: the 1988 'Like a Rolling Stone' is a straight-ahead rock song, which once again balances between the anger of the personal attack, the liberation of the chorus, and the joy of its own music.

So what is the text of 'Like a Rolling Stone'? It is surely the accumulation of all performances, the song's total history. The text is not a fixed set of words or music but a fluid space, a performance area, which sets out a musical and thematic field within which any one version can only be provisional. Dylan minimizes the importance of a stable text as *product* and maximizes the importance of the *process* of singing or listening.

Of course, Dylan is also willing to change the words of a song as well as the music. As an example let me look at three different versions of 'Going, Going, Gone.' This song first appeared on *Planet Waves* (1974), an album largely devoted to songs celebrating married love. It depicts a singer who has reached some extreme point, 'the top of the end' (L 342), which may be religious, political, psychological, or emotional. The context of the album suggests that this too is a love song, an interpretation which is reinforced by the bridge passage:

> Grandma said, 'Boy, go and follow your heart
> And you'll be fine at the end of the line.
> All that's gold doesn't shine.
> Don't you and your one true love ever part.'

'Grandma' implies a traditional source of proverbial wisdom, so the possible naiveté of the advice is distanced through the imputed speaker. Moreover, the proverb—'All that glisters isn't gold'—is reversed, a technique that was characteristic of Dylan's writing in this period.

Two years later Dylan returned to the song during the Rolling Thunder

Revue tour. By this time the love relationships being depicted in Dylan's songs were strained and on the point of collapse. This version opens with the same verse as the original but follows it with a completely new one:

> I'm in love with you, baby,
>
> But you got to understand
>
> That you want to be free,
>
> So let go of my hand.

The separation is here attributed to the woman's desire 'to be free,' a desire that she herself still has to 'understand.' The onus is on her to leave him. Another new verse follows:

> I was living on the road
>
> With my head in the dust,
>
> So I've just got to go
>
> Before it's all diamonds and rust.

Now it is the man who feels that it's up to him to leave. If the song is to be interpreted biographically, in relation to the breakup of Dylan's marriage to Sara, the level of personal reference is complicated here by the phrase 'diamonds and rust' —which was the title of a song that Joan Baez wrote about *her* relationship to Bob Dylan. At the time of this performance, both Sara Dylan and Joan Baez were on the Rolling Thunder tour and engaged in the filming of *Renaldo and Clara*.

In this version the bridge passage runs:

> Papa says, 'Son, go and follow your heart
>
> And you'll be fine at the end of the line.
>
> All that's gold isn't meant to shine.
>
> Don't you and your life-long dream ever part.'

'Grandma' has been replaced as the source of conventional wisdom by 'Papa,' a switch that is in keeping with Dylan's obsession at this time with the figure of the dying father. Now the gold not only 'doesn't shine,' it isn't even 'meant to shine' (this is the version of the line printed in *Lyrics*), and the 'one true love' becomes the more desperate but less specific 'life-long dream.'

A third version appears on the 1978 album *Bob Dylan at Budokan*, and it gives us a completely new set of words:

> Well, I just reached a place
>
> Where I can't stay awake.

I've got to leave you, baby,
Before my heart will break
....

Now from Boston to Birmingham
Is a two-day ride,
But I got to be goin' now
'cos I'm so dissatisfied.

This version, with its long, drawn-out repetition of the final chorus, is fully committed to separation, and the wish to go is now unequivocally on the man's side. Biographical speculation would point out that this version comes after the divorce from Sara; there is also the curious point that the Baez reference has been replaced by an oblique one to Emmylou Harris, backup singer on *Desire*, and author of the song 'From Boulder to Birmingham.' The bridge passage finds a woman back in the advice-giving role:

Now my Mama always said, 'Go and follow your heart
And you'll be fine to the end of the line.
All that's gold wasn't meant to shine

—'wasn't' now, the relationship firmly relegated to the past tense—

Just don't put your horse in front of your cart.'

This brilliant last line does at least three things. It reverses a cliché, which now advises against conventional arrangements such as marriage. It comments by omission on the naive expectations of the previous versions that the singer and his one true love/life-long dream would never part. And it is a joke shared with the audience by playing its outrageousness against their memories of previous versions.

Not all of Dylan's revisions have been as drastic as those to 'Going, Going, Gone.' Often he will change only a single line or image. Sometimes the changes may be no more than passing jokes in performance. For instance, in 'Knockin' on Heaven's Door,' the lines 'Mama, put my guns in the ground / I can't shoot them anymore' (L 337) appeared on one occasion as 'Mama, put my guns right into the ground / I can't screw them down the floor' (Milan, June 19, 1989).

At other times the rewriting is the result of a protracted effort to get the song right, as Dylan shows in his comments about 'Caribbean Wind' on the *Biograph* sleeve notes:

Sometimes you'll write something to be very inspired, and

you won't quite finish it for one reason or another. Then
you'll go back and try and pick it up, and the inspiration is
just gone. Either you get it all, and you can leave a few little pieces to fill in, or you're always trying to finish it off.
Then it's a struggle. The inspiration's gone and you can't
remember why you started it in the first place. Frustration
sets in. I think there's four different sets of lyrics to this,
maybe I got it right, I don't know. I had to leave it. I just
dropped it.

While this comment simply describes the process of revision that any artist goes
through, in Bob Dylan's case the process takes place at least partly in public. One
of the 'four different sets of lyrics' to 'Caribbean Wind' was performed in concert
(San Francisco, November 11, 1980) and is available on tape. Again the critic faces
the problem of the indeterminacy of the Dylan text. 'Caribbean Wind' has no
definitive set of words. The listener has the opportunity of judging between two
versions (and I personally cannot say which I prefer).

It seems safe to say that Dylan never regards a song as unalterably finished.
At any time he is prepared to come back and rework the lyrics or the music—and
equally, he may abandon these revisions and return to the 'original' text. But his
continuing commitment to the performance and reinterpretation of his old songs
means that the text is never definitively closed.

Paul Williams, the most perceptive critic of Dylan as a performer, sums up
much of the argument I have been making when he writes:

Listening to these unreleased alternate takes is a reminder
that when Dylan is fully involved in the music he's making, every performance of every song is new and different
and exciting. The music is so fluid, so expressive of what
Dylan is feeling moment to moment, that it would be mis-
leading to suggest that one melodic or rhythmic or lyrical
variant is more true to the song's intention than another.
That assumes a specific intent that precedes the writing
and performing of a song, whereas all the evidence is that
Dylan's songs ... express a constantly shifting intent which
is feeling-based and unconscious at least as much as it is

43

deliberate, conscious, premeditated (138).

This discussion brings us to the question of bootlegs. Many of the perfor-mances I have cited—the Manchester version of 'Like a Rolling Stone,' the Rolling Thunder version of 'Going, Going, Gone,' the San Francisco recording of 'Caribbean Wind'—are not officially released. Rather, they circulate as unofficial, bootleg tapes.

The first widely circulated Bob Dylan bootleg was the so-called *Great White Wonder*, which came out in 1969. It was a haphazard double-album collection of recordings from the early years of Dylan's career, often of other people's songs, and from the 'Basement Tapes' recorded with The Band in Woodstock. Sound quality was generally poor, and the album took its name from the complete lack of sleeve notes, illustrations, or even track listings.

In the twenty years since, bootlegging has become a more sophisticated enterprise. Sound quality has greatly improved, and the sheer amount of under-ground Dylan material in circulation is staggering. Bootleg Dylan falls into two major categories: studio outtakes and concert recordings. Studio outtakes consist of songs recorded in studios, usually during the sessions that produce official albums. They thus may include alternate versions of songs that do appear on the albums, with different words and/or music, and also songs that for one reason or another were not released. Concert recordings are tapes made of live perfor-mances, usually by audience members carrying concealed microphones, though occasionally by direct tap out of the soundboard. Clinton Heylin reports that out of 485 live Dylan shows between 1974 and 1987 there are only 27 for which no known tape exists (407). The tours of 1988-90 have been even more thoroughly documented.

Why is Dylan bootlegged on a scale vastly greater than that of any other pop performer? The answer has to include the semimythical status that Dylan attained in the early 1960s and that he has never lost over the years. Consciously or unconsciously, he has cultivated an air of mystery. His most trivial statements take on an oracular status. *Great White Wonder* appeared when Dylan was in seclu-sion; his very secretiveness fed the desire for hidden Dylan songs. Even in recent years, when he has been touring almost constantly, the fear that he might again lapse into silence has given his performances a scarcity value.

This is paradoxical, for Dylan bootlegs are anything but scarce. Indeed, the main reason for their persistence is simply that so much interesting material is available. Again the variability of the Dylan text comes into play. There would be little point in taping 485 live shows from most pop singers, because they vary their songs so little in performance: one concert is pretty much a carbon copy of any other. But no two Dylan shows, even on consecutive nights, are ever quite the same. Even a survey as cursory as my six selected performances of 'Like a Rolling Stone' shows the range and richness of the concert material.

With the studio outtakes there is the even more interesting problem that Dylan has chosen not to release much of his best work. Many unreleased songs circulated widely in bootleg before they were finally officially released. *Biograph* (1985) made available such major titles as 'Lay Down Your Weary Tune' and 'Caribbean Wind.' The 1991 release of *The Bootleg Series Volumes 1-3* has at last added 'Farewell Angelina,' 'Blind Willie McTell,' and many more. (The release of this collection will—not before time—render half the bootleg industry obsolete.) The words for some of these songs appear in *Lyrics*, but as noted, several of them are not acknowledged even there.

What is the critic to do with this material? To begin with, certain legal questions arise. These are, after all, illegal recordings. Some bootleggers undoubtedly make money, though my experience has been that the people I am in touch with do not sell tapes but exchange them freely, and are collectors who will buy everything that Dylan officially releases. Bob Dylan has suffered no financial loss from any of the people I am in touch with. Many such collectors object strongly to the term 'bootleg,' which implies sale for profit. They take their motto from Dylan himself: 'To live outside the law, you must be honest' (L 233). Before publishing this book I obtained permission from Dylan's agent for all quotations used.

There is an ethical problem too. One may argue that the work has a right to be heard that supersedes the author's right to control his creations—but who is to make this decision? As a critic using rejected material, I am setting myself up to second-guess and judge Bob Dylan's editorial choices. While critics regularly do this when sifting through the manuscripts of a dead author, it is rarely that we have the chance to do so while the author is still alive. Sometimes, of course, I agree with Dylan's decisions: I would not want to see the embarrassing 'Julius and Ethel' included on *Infidels*, and the 1970 recordings of 'Yesterday' and 'Da Doo Ron Ron' are strictly for fanatics only.

In other cases, however, I have to assert my critical judgment that Dylan has been drastically wrong in the choices he made. *Shot of Love* (1981) is often seen as one of his weakest albums: but if you add in its outtakes—'Angelina,' 'Caribbean Wind,' and 'The Groom's Still Waiting at the Altar'—the assessment is dramatically changed. As I will argue in Chapter Seven, these three songs present a fascinating mixture of surrealist and Christian imagery, and they show Dylan's verbal art reemerging from the straightjacket of fundamentalist rhetoric. Dylan may have felt that they were unresolved or imperfect: yet their very incompletion makes them more interesting artistic objects than the smooth banalities of 'Watered-Down Love' or 'In the Summertime,' which did make it to the album.

The more one explores the bootleg material, the more such questions arise. By what right of authorship could one justify withholding release of 'Lay Down Your Weary Tune' for twenty years? Why were we never meant to hear 'She's Your Lover Now'? Whatever possessed him to suppress 'Blind Willie McTell' for so long?

Such questions challenge the privileged position of the author as the ultimate source and arbiter of his work. They point to another way in which the text has escaped the author's jurisdiction and control. This excess of the text over the author, evident in its most concrete form in the bootlegs, is also what I have been arguing all the way through this chapter: that the Dylan text is indeterminate, nondefinitive, divided against itself and away from its author. In this sense 'the text of Bob Dylan' rejoins 'Bob Dylan as text': the songs in all their manifestations are only part of the total text, which also includes the biography, the interviews, and all the phenomena of Bob Dylan's public career (phenomena that include the assiduous wielders of concealed microphones at every concert). This is a text that remains open: a disseminated text that gives no guarantee of any unitary self originating it. In all their indeterminacy, Bob Dylan's songs only show in another aspect the split between I and I. The text too proclaims, in every moment of its performance, 'Je est un autre.'

CHAPTER THREE

CALL ME ANY NAME YOU LIKE

Bob Dylan became 'Bob Dylan,' so he says, by accident. In October, 1959, he walked into a Minneapolis coffeehouse, The Ten O'Clock Scholar, and asked for a job as a folk singer. The owner asked his name, and he answered, off the top of his head, 'Bob Dylan.'

So the story goes. We have, of course, no way of confirming it and no way of knowing to what extent this gesture of self-naming was premeditated. The name 'Dylan' may have occurred to him at random. At one stage he claimed that he had taken it from an uncle called Dillon, but genealogical research shows no trace of any such person. He always denied that he chose the name because of any conscious association with Dylan Thomas; this may be so, though it would not rule out unconscious association. Apart from a fondness for elaborate imagery, there is no evidence in Bob Dylan's work of any direct influence from Dylan Thomas.

For Bobby Zimmerman in 1959, fresh out of Hibbing, the particular name he chose was less important than the simple gesture of assuming a new name. It was part of an extended program of self-recreation, along with the way he dressed, the way he talked, and the stories he told about his past. 'Bob Dylan' became the seal and signature of his new persona: it sealed him off definitively from Hibbing, from Robert Zimmerman, and from Abraham Zimmerman. It was the signature that guaranteed the authenticity of what he had become. The name Bob Dylan is Bob Dylan's first and most enduring work of art.

Recent critical theory has paid a good deal of attention to the concept of 'signature.' The author's name presented on a title page or copyright notice occupies a marginal site, not part of the text but not separate from it either. It reaches out from the text to that historical world where the 'author' leads his biographical existence, yet it also brings the author's name into the text as part of its verbal structure and play. As Peggy Kamuf puts it, 'At the edge of the work, the dividing trait of the signature pulls in both directions at once: appropriating the text under the sign of the name, expropriating the name into the play of the text' (13).

As a gesture of appropriation, the signature claims both the text and the name as property. It claims ownership of the text in the name of the author, a name to which certain legal and economic rights can be attached. The most obvious of these is copyright, an individual's claim to the ownership of a text. Only you can sign your signature; it seals the assertion our society makes of unique, inimitable individuality. The proper name is your property; it guarantees the authenticity of your claim to be, for example, 'Bob Dylan.'

Yet at the same time, as Jacques Derrida has shown,[1] the signature depends for this very effect on its iterability: the fact that it is not a unique and singular event but must be able to be reproduced on various separate occasions. One signature can only be authenticated by reference to a different instance of the same signature. This iterability means that the signature can always be reproduced, forged, quoted, inserted into all the possible contexts of language. This is the gesture that Kamuf calls 'expropriation': the signature enters the text and thus moves outside the sole control and intentionality of the author. The proper name is not just your property; it can no longer guarantee the authenticity of your claim to be, for example, 'Bob Dylan.'

The proper name lives on as that which exceeds individual identity. A public name like 'Bob Dylan' is no longer within the control of the man who happens to bear it; it has gone beyond him. In a 1977 interview with Allen Ginsberg, Dylan himself said, 'Nobody's Bob Dylan. Bobby Dylan's long gone…. Let's say that in real life Bob Dylan fixes his name on the public. He can retrieve that name at will. Anything else the public makes of it is its business' (28). The view of the proper name that I am advancing here would be in general agreement with this statement —except that it may be severely doubted whether any author can 'retrieve that name at will.' Once the name is signed, it is on its own.

The proper name 'lives on' in both senses of that phrase. The name is a kind of parasite, which lives on the author and at his expense; it also lives on in the sense that it survives. Its effects continue even after the author's death, and while the author is still alive, the proper name accompanies him as a sort of ghost.

'Lenny Bruce is dead,' sings Bob Dylan, 'but his ghost lives on and on' (L 455). In the same way Frank Hibbing lives on and on in the ghost town that bears his pseudonym.

'To be dead,' writes Derrida, 'means that no profit or deficit, no good or evil ... can *ever return again* to the bearer of the name. Only the name can inherit, and this is why the name, to be distinguished from the bearer, is always and *a priori* a dead man's name, a name of death' (EO 7). For Derrida this link between death and the signature is so strong that he can state, 'When I sign, I am already dead' (G 19bi). As we shall see, this is a connection that Bob Dylan also makes in relation to his proper (assumed) name.

This problem of the signature in Dylan's work can be seen in a curious song from *Self-Portrait*, the album whose very title invites the kind of puzzling self-reference involved in the deployment of the proper name. The copyright notice on the record label confidently attributes the song 'Belle Isle' to the authorship of 'B. Dylan.' In his book *Song and Dance Man*, Michael Gray accepted this attribution and wrote a wonderful commentary on the wittiness of what he took to be Dylan's parody of traditional folk song modes. Unfortunately for Michael Gray, 'Belle Isle' *is* a traditional folk song that shows up in many different versions all over the world, especially in Newfoundland. The text that Dylan sings is almost identical with that contained in the magazine *Sing Out* or in Edith Fowkes' *Penguin Book of Canadian Folk Songs*. So Gray issued a massive mea culpa, a long article in which he traced the history and provenance of the song 'Belle Isle,' which was now regarded as definitively not by 'B. Dylan.'[2]

Still, it could well be argued that Gray's original reading is the better one. The signature 'B. Dylan' on the record label is an illegitimate act of appropriation, a claim to legal ownership of a text to which he is not entitled. But equally, the text of 'Belle Isle' now includes that false signature. Dylan has failed to appropriate the song, but his claim to 'authorship' has been expropriated into the play of its text. 'Belle Isle,' after all, is *about* mistaken and disguised identity. It tells of a young man who returns to the sweetheart he has left years before; not revealing his identity, he attempts to seduce her, but she remains true to her memory of her absent love. He then reveals himself:

'Young maiden, I wish not to banter,
'Tis true I came here in disguise.

I came here to fulfill our last promise,

And hoped to give you a surprise.'

She (improbably, I have always thought) forgives his deception, and they live happily ever after. In the song the false identity (the assumed name) becomes the means of establishing the authenticity of the girl's love, and that love in turn guarantees the truth behind the false name. 'B. Dylan' (alias Robert Zimmerman) then claims this song on an album whose 'self-portrait' is largely made up of songs by other people. The overstated, sentimental verses are sung by Dylan with an air of seeming sincerity, which, Gray argues, turns the whole performance into parody. But the levels of parody and irony are much more complex than Gray allows for. The song resonates with Dylan's sense of the sheer instability of identity, the impossibility of self-portrait, the paradoxes of the signature.

So it is not surprising that many early 'Bob Dylan' songs are filled with paradoxical references to names and naming. On the one hand, there are assertions of the name (the signature) in its traditional role as guarantor of authenticity. 'Train A-Travelin'' addresses a series of rhetorically loaded questions to its audience: 'Do the kill-crazy bandits and the haters get you down? / Does the preachin' and the politics spin your head around?' If the listener gives the affirmative responses which the form of these questions already presupposes, then, the last line of every verse repeats, 'you heard my voice a-singin' and you know my name' (L 30). But the name which the 1960s listener would know, and which would guarantee the authority of that singing voice, would, of course, be 'Bob Dylan,' the assumed name that Robert Zimmerman is writing into the text of his own life.

On the other hand, there are songs and poems that put into question this unproblematical trust in the efficacy of naming. Of particular interest here is 'Advice to Geraldine on Her Miscellaneous Birthday,' a poem written in 1964. The poem takes the form of an extended series of admonitions to an unspecified listener. In a typical paradox, Dylan's advice to her is not to take advice: 'do Not create anything,' he warns, 'it will be / misinterpreted' (L 125). The danger of creating anything, a text, is not just the risk of misinterpretation, it is that the text persists. It lives on and, like a parasite, it lives on you: 'it will not change. / it will follow you the / rest of your life.' Thus the author's attempt to appropriate the text, to regard it as property over which he can exercise some control (the right, for instance, to specify what is or is not a misinterpretation) is bound to fail. The

50

appropriative gesture of the signature is itself expropriated by the text's capacity to survive beyond the control of the author's name. The echo of the two names suggests that even the name itself is split: 'Dylan,' male author, is shadowed by 'Ger*aldine*,' female audience. What remains is a strategy of resistance not only to the demands of audiences and hangers-on but also to the traditional modes of self-recognition and identification: 'when told t' look at / yourself,' Dylan's advice to Geraldine ends, 'never look. when asked / t' give your real name ... never give it.'

Naming gives authority. By 1964 a Bob Dylan song had come to mean a style of writing that was recognizable, like a signature, and the name Bob Dylan lent authority to what its bearer had to say on social and political questions. 'Blowin' in the Wind' (even if it is strikingly vague about specific courses of political action) had become his 'signature tune.' Dylan was to become increasingly uncomfortable with the role in which 'Bob Dylan' had been cast, and he attempted a whole series of disclaimers of his imposed status as a prophet, a folk Messiah, a spokesman for his generation. The problem was that it appeared as if such disclaimers also would have to be disclaimers of the name Bob Dylan, which he had so urgently and carefully nourished as the basis of his career. Eventually, he was successful in resolving this problem by making 'Bob Dylan' stand not for any imposed role but for the very act of resistance to imposed roles. But the traces of this struggle can still be read in the various references to names and naming in his early poems and songs.

Take, for instance, the opening lines of 'With God On Our Side.' Dylan's song is based on the Irish ballad 'The Patriot Game,' which begins by establishing the identity and thus the authority of its narrator: 'Oh my name is O'Hanlon / I'm just gone sixteen.' But Dylan deliberately refuses these specifics of naming. Instead his opening—'Oh my name it is nothin' / My age it means less' (L 93)— attempts to base the rhetorical authority of his song on the singer's anonymity, his representativeness, rather than on the personal charisma of 'Bob Dylan.' In terms of his advice to Geraldine, he is refusing to give his real name.

Again the paradox arises: what was Bob Dylan's 'real' name? The evasion of 'My name it is nothin'' did not return the original listener to anyone called Robert Zimmerman. At the time this song was written (April, 1963), that name was still unknown, and the singer's voice signs this song too with the authority of 'Bob Dylan.' The very gesture of refusing the name works inversely to increase the authority of the suppressed signature.

Similarly, in 'Long Time Gone' (also written in 1963), Dylan attempts to disclaim prophetic status, but again in a way that necessarily involves him in the issues of name and signature.

> If I can't help somebody
> With a word or song,
> If I can't show somebody
> They are travelin' wrong.
> But I know I ain't no prophet
> An' I ain't no prophet's son.
> I'm just a long time a-comin'
> An' I'll be a long time gone (L 27).

The form of the disclaimer is curiously ambiguous. The argument seems to be that the singer is placed in the position of a prophet 'helping' and 'showing' the way, 'but' he wants to disavow that burden and authority. However, the syntax of the sentence is incomplete: 'if' opens a condition, but no conclusion follows. We are not sure whether the singer *is* in a position to help and show. This uncertainty is accentuated by the negative form of the verb: 'can't' displaces the positive 'can,' which the sequence of the argument seems to require. The negative form suggests that the fear is not so much that he is a prophet as that he might not be one after all.

Moreover, the disavowal of prophetic status extends beyond the singer to his father, his past, his name. 'I ain't no prophet's son,' sings Robert Zimmerman, son of Abraham Zimmerman. In the Old Testament, Abraham is the prophet who is prepared to sacrifice Isaac, his son. Two years after 'Long Time Gone,' in 'Highway 61 Revisited,' Bob Dylan would perform a ferociously ironic replay of this primal scene: 'God said to Abraham, "Kill me a son"' (L 202). The surname also enters this anti-prophetic play: the German word 'Zimmerman' means 'carpenter.' In view of Dylan's later fascination with Jesus, it is interesting that in the name he suppressed he was both a carpenter and a carpenter's son.

The adoption of a pseudonym is a denial of the past, of history, of the patronymic, and it always carries strong connotations of an Oedipal struggle against the father. The forging (in both possible senses of the word) of the name 'Bob Dylan' involved a wholesale recasting of the singer's past, and one of the most interesting texts in this process is 'My Life in a Stolen Moment' (L 70-72). Dylan wrote this poem in 1963 in response to increasing demands for autobiographical statements from him. In a typically evasive gesture, it weaves together elements of fact and fiction that later biographers have worked to unravel. It begins accurately enough in 'the Iron Range Country up north,' in Hibbing, where to this day, 'You can stand at one end of ... the main drag an' see clear past the city limits at the other end.' But soon it takes off into fantasy, claiming that he had run away from home at the ages of 10, 12, 13, 15, 15 1/2, 17, and 18. A more or less truthful account of Zimmerman's brief attendance at the University of Minnesota is succeeded by an imagined odyssey through Texas, California, Oregon, New Mexico, and Louisiana, and by hitchhiking on Highways 61, 51, 75, 169, 37, 66, and 22. The list of numbers, like the earlier list of ages, attempts to give an appearance of exact detail to vouch for the fabrications, but the over-explicitness of detail becomes comic, so the effect is parodic. The claim to truthfulness is simultaneously being made and being mocked.

Then come these curious lines:

> Got jailed for suspicion of armed robbery
> Got held four hours on a murder rap
> Got busted for looking like I do
> An' I never done none a them things

The denial in this last line seems to refer only to the false accusations of robbery and murder: but strictly speaking it should refer to all the immediately previous lines—in which case one of the things 'I never done' was 'looking like I do.' This is an intriguing reading, for it introduces the idea of a fundamental split in the 'I,' who, in his assumed identity, can no longer resemble himself. However, this denial infects not just the three preceding lines but the entire previous poem: if the protagonist never committed 'armed robbery,' neither presumably did he hitchhike on Highways 61, 51, 75, 169, 37, 66, or 22. By this time the admission has undermined not only the poem's inventions but also its truths: Hibbing and 'the Iron Range Country up north' have also disappeared into the gap opened up by 'I never done none a them things.'

My argument here is not that these effects were in any way *intended* by the author of 'My Life in a Stolen Moment.' Rather, the text always escapes the author's control—or is 'stolen' from it. These songs and poems return obsessively to the issues of naming because the signature 'Bob Dylan' is expropriating the texts Robert Zimmerman is attempting to write in its name. The gaps and contradictions, the points of slippage in the discourse around the concept of naming, are the inevitable results of this expropriation. Dylan himself, Robert Shelton records, saw 'My Life in a Stolen Moment' as a text of uncertain authorship: 'he often denied it, saying others had "made" him write it' (24). In an interview with Shelton in 1966, Dylan says: 'I don't disavow it. It is just not me. Somebody else wrote that.' But the 'other,' the 'somebody else,' is also Dylan himself: 'It was bled from my hand and from my arm ... by my brain' (Shelton 360-61).

So another of the effects of signature is this sense of internal self-displacement, of the 'other' who is always at play within the site of the self. Long before he had read Rimbaud's 'Je est un autre,' Bob Dylan was working with this idea. One possible biographical reference for the 'Girl of the North Country' is a woman called Echo: and all the 'others' in Dylan's early songs can be seen as echoes, as aspects of himself that come back to him. Even in a seemingly nonpersonal protest song like the anti-nuclear 'Let Me Die In My Footsteps' (L 21), there is a subtle ambiguity in the title phrase. To be in someone's footsteps is most often, idiomatically, to *follow* him (like the page of Good King Wenceslas), to put your foot in the trace of the other. So the expressed desire of this song is for the singer to live (and to die) in his own footsteps, in the trace of himself that he has already left behind. The footstep, like the signature, is a sign of presence which can only be read in the signer's absence. These images of footsteps, echoes, and naming come together in 'Tomorrow Is a Long Time,' where Dylan portrays a state of separation from the loved one as also an alienation from these images of the self: 'I can't hear the echo of my footsteps,' he sings, 'can't remember the sound of my own name' (L 42).

Most of this early equivocation around names and naming was, of course, an internal drama intended, as it were, for Dylan's ears only. For the audience who heard 'Tomorrow Is a Long Time' in 1962, 'the sound of my own name' was still unproblematically 'Bob Dylan'; and Robert Zimmerman, singing the song, must have been aware of the irony of what was being concealed. But from November, 1963 on, the facts of Dylan's background as Zimmerman were widely known,[3] and the curious paradox is that they made it *easier* for Dylan to develop his assumed identity, his alias. The game was now being played with the audience's full knowledge; the mask could be worn in public and could be publicly displayed *as a mask*.

This is the point of the famous comment to the audience at New York Philharmonic Hall on October 31, 1964. 'Don't let that scare you,' he says, referring probably to the song he had just finished, the scary 'Gates of Eden'. 'It's just Halloween' (pause); 'I have my Bob Dylan mask on' (laughter, loud applause); 'I'm mask-erading.' And then he begins 'If You Gotta Go, Go Now,' with its wonderfully comic version of his disavowal of prophetic status:

> It ain't that I'm questionin' you
>
> To take part in any quiz
>
> It's just that I ain't got no watch
>
> An' you keep askin' me what time it is (L 158).

Now the audience can laugh with him at the idea of a Bob Dylan mask: Bob Dylan has become the name of this kind of disavowal.[4] Over the next year he was to break decisively with the folk music establishment and its demands for what 'Bob Dylan' should be. In doing so, he was to create another mask of Bob Dylan, rock star, from which another escape would become necessary, so this movement from one mask to another, rather than any achieved position within the movement, became what the name Bob Dylan signed and stood for.

In the 1965 song 'Farewell Angelina,' Dylan wrote: 'Call me any name you like / I will never deny it' (L 184). But in a typical gesture of evasion and deferral, he did not sing it himself. 'Farewell Angelina' was given to Joan Baez to sing; until 1991 there was no known recording—official or unofficial, studio, concert, or bootleg—of Bob Dylan singing those lines.

As Dylan moved into the kaleidoscopic imagery of 1965 and 1966, the concern with his own name was caught up in the great flood of other names—historical, fictional, legendary—of the hordes of characters who inhabit Highway 61 and Desolation Row.[5] Naming in these songs is so dispersed that there is no possibility of identification: 'All these people that you mention,' Dylan comments, 'I had to rearrange their faces / And give them all another name' (L 206). With so many names to choose from, no single name can exert the authority of the signature. The singer's signature appears only in the acrostic of the title *Blonde on Blonde*: BoB.

In *Tarantula*, written in 1965-66, naming and the changing of names are everywhere: 'invent me a signature,' says one of the book's many characters (T

130), and Dylan certainly obliges.

> dear tom
> have i ever told you that i
> think your name ought to be
> bill. it doesnt really matter
> of course, but you know, i like
> to be comfortable around people.
> how is margy? or martha? or
> whatever the hell her name is?
> listen: when you arrive & you
> hear somebody yelling 'willy' it'll
> be me that's who... (T 37-8)

But who is 'me'? Each section of the book ends with a verse letter, signed in a bewildering variety of names, the very first of which is 'your double / Silly Eyes' (T 11). In the same way as 'Geraldine' echoed 'Dylan,' the reader here is seen as the double of the author. The signature itself is doubled in its turn: the eye/I pun of divided identity is presented in the plural, Silly *Eyes*. In the next few pages, the narrator is warned that a woman will 'split your eyes' (T 15), and he admits that 'my eyes are two used car lots' (T 14). The I continues to be doubled, and it comes like a used car, secondhand, from the other.

The most remarkable passage on naming in *Tarantula* is the self-composed epitaph:

> here lies bob dylan
> murdered
> from behind
> by trembling flesh
> who after being refused by Lazarus...
> was amazed to discover
> that he was already
> a streetcar &
> that was exactly the end
> of bob dylan
> ....
> here lies bob dylan

demolished by Vienna politeness—

which will now claim to have invented him...

boy dylan—killed by a discarded Oedipus

who turned

around

to investigate a ghost

& discovered that

the ghost too

was more than one person (T 118-20)

'When I sign,' wrote Derrida, 'I am already dead.' When the name 'Bob Dylan' appears in Bob Dylan's text, it is as an epitaph, a sign of death.[6]

The naming here is explicitly linked to the Oedipal scenario of the father's murder, in which 'Bob' is reduced to the childish 'boy.' Naming is appropriated by the 'Vienna politeness' of Sigmund Freud, which 'will now claim to have invented' ('invent me a signature') the name Bob Dylan. As a rejection of the father's name, the adoption of a pseudonym always carries this Oedipal charge. Freud's account of the Oedipus complex attempts to describe the way in which desire is transferred from one object to another; in this passage the 'trembling flesh' transfers from the dead Lazarus to the 'murdered' Bob Dylan only to find that he too has been transformed into a streetcar (named Desire?).

Simultaneously, Dylan also casts himself in the role of the father killed *by* Oedipus. In Sophocles' play, Oedipus set out 'to investigate a ghost' and discovered that the truth of the ghost lay in his own proper name: Oedipus, swollen foot, who bears as a scar the murderous signature of his father. Again we see the proper name as ghost, as that which lives on (Zimmerman, the carpenter). The ghost is 'more than one person': involved here are the ghosts not only of Oedipus and of Sigmund Freud but those of Frank Hibbing, Abraham Zimmerman, and Bob Dylan.

Yet all these references also converge upon one person, just as Oedipus discovered that the alien murderer he was seeking was himself. The gesture of Oedipus, upon discovering the truth, was to blind himself, the splitting of his eyes confirming the awful singularity of his I. The author of a self-composed epitaph views himself from the outside, as Rimbaud's 'other,' but he also must recognize that these doublings occur within himself, within the first person. As Dylan writes later in the book, 'it is not that there is no Receptive for anything written or acted in the first person—it is just that there is no Second person' (T 134).

Another point of identification with Oedipus for Dylan is that Oedipus became, to some degree innocently, an outlaw. In the 1969 song 'Wanted Man,' Dylan again plays with the paradoxes of naming. The song is full of proper names—'Wanted man in Tallahassee, wanted man in Baton Rouge ... Wanted man by Lucy Watson, wanted man by Jeannie Brown'—but it gives no name for the central character—'If you ever see me comin' and if you know who I am, / Don't you breathe it to nobody 'cause you know I'm on the lam' (L 279). As a 'wanted man,' he is, like Oedipus, the focus of desire: always on the move, never to be pinned down. The very lack of a name, in the midst of so many other names, allows for this elusiveness. But in a sense, the repetition of 'wanted man' turns that phrase itself into a kind of name: the name of desire, the name of namelessness.

The 'wanted man' literally provides Bob Dylan's alias in Sam Peckinpah's 1973 film, *Pat Garrett and Billy the Kid*, in which he plays a character whose name is simply Alias.[7] In this process of substitution, one name slides into another, refusing to fix on any single name as authoritative or originary. What the name 'Alias' denotes is the refusal of naming. More extreme than a simple pseudonym, it not only rejects the name of the father, it also rejects the possibility of founding a new patronymic.

Peckinpah's film presents a series of doubled images, and it adumbrates the obsession with the image of the failed or dying father that was to dominate Dylan's work in the 1970s in such albums as *Desire*. By the end of the decade, 'the Name of the Father' had shifted in his work to its orthodox religious sense as the unnamed name of God. In Dylan's Christian songs the theme of naming again comes to the forefront, most obviously in 'Gotta Serve Somebody':

> You may call me Terry, you may call me Timmy,
> You may call me Bobby, you may call me Zimmy,
> You may call me R. J., you may call me Ray,
> You may call me anything but no matter what you say
> You're gonna have to serve somebody... (L 424).

In one sense this is a restatement of 'Farewell Angelina': 'Call me any name you like./ I will never deny it.' The specific name, these lines insist, is unimportant; in the eyes of the Lord all names are equal. Names are arbitrary signs with no inherent connection to the essential reality of the persons they signify. No matter what you call me, the ultimate truth of my existence remains unchanged. This argument is supported by the apparently random choice of most names on this list: there has never been any biographical motivation for associating Bob Dylan with Terry, Timmy, R.J., or Ray.[8]

But one name on the list—Zimmy—is more ambiguous in its effect. As the only appearance of the name Zimmerman in the entire Dylan canon, it both dismisses and appeals to the essential reality of the name behind the mask. This name too is unimportant, the song says, but in saying it, in quoting *this* name, the song reasserts that naming is not simply arbitrary. The proper name is not detachable from the character of its bearer but is written into the text of what and who the bearer has become. 'Zimmy,' after all, is not just the singer's name: it is also his father's name. In *Tarantula* 'boy dylan' had been killed by a 'discarded Oedipus,' the man who in turn had killed his father; here Bob Dylan reasserts the name of *his* father, in a boyish, contracted form, as ironically that which is immaterial to the Name of the Father.

A similar ambiguity plays through another song on the same album, 'Man Gave Names to All the Animals.' Genesis presents the naming of the animals as the first and quintessential human task given to Adam by God. Yet this task already prefigures the Fall, by limiting the infinite wonders of the natural world inside the restrictions of human speech. The names are arbitrary, the product of human language (and *languages*—'pig' is also cochon, Schwein, etc.). Dylan's song presents Adam going through a process in which the names appear to be suggested by the natural characteristics of the animals themselves—

> He saw an animal leavin' a muddy trail,
>
> Real dirty face and a curly tail.
>
> He wasn't too small and he wasn't too big

—but in which the name is made inevitable by the arbitrary characteristics of English-language rhyme—

> 'Ah, think I'll call it a pig' (L 434).

For most of the song, the effect is comic, and one can easily imagine it as a children's song in which the audience is encouraged to participate in Adam's task by supplying the expected rhyme. But as John Hinchey suggests, in the later verses this becomes too easy, too predictable, as Adam, 'in love with the sound of his own voice' (22), approaches the moment of the Fall. At the end of the song, the rhyming effect is brilliantly turned against itself by the abrupt ending, in which the singer *refuses to name* the animal that rhymes with 'lake.' The missing name is, in Derrida's phrase, 'un nom de mort'—a dead man's name, the name of death. It is as if Dylan, by declining to repeat Adam's recognition of the serpent, is attempting to replay the Genesis story without the Fall and thereby to return to the Edenic state in which naming was natural and innocent.

But as all the songs of this period insist, we are not in an Edenic state but in a fallen world. Adam does in fact name the snake, and thus he enters the realm of the Symbolic (which the French psychoanalyst Jacques Lacan calls 'the Name of the Father'). As Hinchey says, 'Adam's consciousness will never return to the state of unselfconscious rapport with the animate world he loses by naming things' (22). Naming, then, has lost its innocence, whether you call me by a fictional name ('Timmy') or by my 'real' name ('Zimmy'). Yet the 'real' name is still there, calling attention to itself by its open appeal to the audience's knowledge of Bob Dylan's biography and by the distance it still maintains from the 'B. Dylan' to whom this song, like 'Belle Isle,' is copyrighted.

The name 'Bob Dylan' lives on, and for the songs of the religious period it is still a problem. These songs are full of the singer's troubling sense of his unworthiness, his division both from God and from himself. As in the earlier songs, this division often focuses on the singer's name. 'Every Grain of Sand' associates it with temptation and sin: 'I gaze into the doorway of temptation's angry flame / And every time I pass that way I always hear my name' (L 462). One version of 'Caribbean Wind' attempts to kill it off altogether:

Stars on my balcony, buzz in my head, slayin' Bob Dylan in my bed,
Street band playin' 'Nearer My God To Thee.'

Just as 'Zimmy' is the only occurrence of that name in a Dylan song, so this is the only time that the actual name 'Bob Dylan' appears in the text of a song. (The name appears in several titles, such as 'Bob Dylan's 115th Dream,' but not in the words.) As in *Tarantula*, the appearance of the signature is a signal of death: moving nearer to God, Bob Dylan has to slay 'Bob Dylan.' Here he lies, murdered by trembling flesh. (The ultimate naming in these songs, both of God and of himself, takes the doubled form of 'I and I'—but a detailed discussion of this act of naming must wait until Chapter Seven.)

Later in the 1980s 'Bob Dylan' was slain in a more lighthearted way as Dylan assumed yet more pseudonyms. As one of the Traveling Wilburys, he was again able to play Alias—and again the point of the play was that the audience was in on the joke. Although the names Harrison, Orbison, Petty, Lynn, and Dylan never appear on the album, everyone knew who they were. The Wilbury masks are an ironic acknowledgment of the impossibility of anonymity. Dylan's chosen first name here is 'Lucky,' and this name also resonates through his lyrics.

It is, for instance, the name of the 'Minstrel Boy,' who appears on *Self-Portrait* as an image of the artist attempting to cope with the demands of a commercial audience: 'Who's gonna throw that minstrel boy a coin? / Who's gonna let it down easy to save his soul?' (L 280). At other times 'lucky' appears not as a name but as an adjective. In retrospect, however, these references too speak to the later alias. 'Lucky' is often an ironic adjective for Dylan, who is wary of all simple twists of fate. In 'Pledging My Time' luck is lethal:

Well, they sent for an ambulance

And one was sent.

Somebody got lucky

But it was an accident (L 222).

And in 'Idiot Wind' Dylan prefaces a song of intense personal anguish with a brief flight of fictional fancy: 'They say I shot a man named Gray and took his wife to Italy, / She inherited a million bucks and when she died it came to me. / I can't help it if I'm lucky' (L 367).

When the second Wilbury album was released in 1990, everything had shifted again. (For one thing the second album was entitled *Volume 3*!) All the Wilbury aliases had changed, as if the names themselves lacked inherent stability or permanence. Dylan now appeared as 'Boo' Wilbury. The name evokes the Deep South, but it also responds ironically to Dylan's audience. Twenty-five years after Newport, Dylan adopts the audience's booing as his name and signature—or, perhaps more precisely, *counter*-signature.

The *Oxford English Dictionary* defines 'to countersign' as 'To sign (a document) opposite to, or alongside, or in addition to, another signature; to add one's signature to a document already signed (by another) for authentication or confirmation; to confirm, sanction, ratify.' Peggy Kamuf suggests that an author can and inevitably must countersign his work[9]: must add and keep on adding new instances of signature to confirm, sanction, and ratify what has already been claimed in its name. Because the play and structure of the text always expropriate the signature, no instance of signature can ever stand outside the text definitively enough to guarantee its authenticity. All signatures must be repeated, cited and re-cited, countersigned.

'Countersignature' is one way of describing what Bob Dylan has been doing obsessively since 1974: that is, *performing his signature* in concert. There is a curious ambiguity in the values that our culture attaches to performance. On the one hand, we value 'live' performance as a guarantee of the author's *presence*. At poetry readings we want to hear authors read their own works in their own voices, and at concerts we want to see our favorite stars 'live,' even if 'live' means a tiny figure on a stadium stage, enlarged perhaps on a television screen. The outrage that greeted the revelation that the 'singers' of Milli Vanilli had been lip-synced by other performers testifies to the importance attributed to the presence of the live performer. Performance is the seal of authenticity, of sincere self-expression, of assured personal communication.[10]

Yet 'performance' is viewed with great suspicion. 'It's a clever performance,' we say, implying that somehow it's not real. To perform is to pretend that you are something you are not, and this notion of falsity is as much at the heart of our idea of performance as is its previous sense. The activity of performance is always a doubled one, a re-citation, a repetition of a text that exists prior to the moment of performance. The singer is always divided into I and I: the person who performs this song for you now and the person who previously wrote it. (Improvisation compresses but does not eliminate this split.) Any given performance of 'Like a Rolling Stone' is haunted by the echoes of past performances and by the ghost of the man who wrote it and who is *no longer there*, even if, in another incarnation, he is now on stage singing it. Absence always shadows the value of presence: a 'live' performance is also a performance of death.

'A singer must die,' Leonard Cohen wrote—and sang—'for the lie in his voice.' I don't think that this line means that only those singers who lie must die, as opposed to those singers who don't lie and thus can live; I think it means that all singers lie, that performance is a lie, and that all such lying performances have death built into them as part of their structure.

This ambivalence in the notion of 'performance' repeats the ambiguity, the double-edged nature of the signature, with which I began this chapter. A signature must be, like a live performance, unique, the guarantee of presence and personality; yet a signature must always be capable of being repeated, forged, reinscribed—in a word, countersigned. When I say that Dylan in concert is 'performing his signature,' I am saying that he is being simultaneously genuine and false, that he is simultaneously delivering us his presence and standing back from it, denying any possibility that he is *really* there. What we see and hear on the stage in front of us is not the singer but his alias, not the person but his *name*.

'It's just Halloween,' said Bob Dylan in 1964, 'I have my Bob Dylan mask on.' In the Rolling Thunder Revue concerts of 1975-76, the singer on stage wore a transparent mask and sang to his audience, 'You can almost think that you're seein' double' (L 300). In the film *Renaldo and Clara*, improvised during this tour, Bob Dylan appears as a character called Renaldo while the part of 'Bob Dylan' is played by Ronnie Hawkins. (You may call me Renaldo, you may call me Ronnie.) The 1978 tour offered outrageous musical reworkings of the standard repertoire, ranging from the whimsical (the reggae version of 'Don't Look Twice') to the profound (the wonderful, slowed-down, saxophone version of 'Tangled Up In Blue'). The 'religious' performances of 1979-80 countersigned the past by ostentatiously excluding it, by not including any of the old songs. The tours of 1988-89 were marked by the number of songs Dylan brought back into his repertoire after absences of ten or twenty years: 'Subterranean Homesick Blues,' 'Tears of Rage,' or traditional folk material like 'Banks of the Pontchartrain' (a variation on the 'Belle Isle' story line) and 'Wagoner's Lad' (which contains the lines: 'If I'm writ on your books, love, / Just you cross out my name').

Each tour, practically each concert, has presented a new version of 'Bob Dylan.' Like a signature, each version is unique yet simultaneously recognizable, because it must refer to previous versions of the 'same' signature. And by virtue of that very combination of sameness and difference, no version can be final. Each signature calls out for another, counter-, signature. That is why the project that Dylan embarked on in 1988 has become known quite seriously as 'the tour that never ends.' There can be no ending to it: the more concerts Dylan plays, the more necessary it becomes that he continues playing. As he sings in 'Tangled Up In Blue,' 'The only thing I knew how to do / Was to keep on keepin' on' (L 358).

This project of countersignature might be seen as a limited, sterile, inward-turning one, especially in comparison to the flamboyant extroversion of Dylan's lyrics in the mid-60s. But what I have attempted to argue here is that signature, the staging and performance of the name Bob Dylan, has always been at the center of Dylan's career. Indeed it *is* his career. The simple strategy of disguise by which the young Robert Zimmerman attempted to make a name for himself (literally) has turned into the lifelong core of his invention of himself. The problem of Bob Dylan's signature is at the center of the fascination he continues to exert over all those who think that they know his name.

C H A P T E R   F O U R
I FEEL I COULD ALMOST SING

At the beginning of 'You Angel You,' from the album *Planet Waves*, the singer, attempting to express the happiness he feels with his 'angel,' declares, 'I feel I could almost sing' (L 348). But he *is* singing—so the line turns on itself in a self-reflexive twist by which the ostensible content of the statement (I am not yet singing, though I feel I could) is modified to the point of reversal by the form (I am singing).

In this chapter I want to examine statements Bob Dylan has made about his position as a singer: about his art, its sources and inspirations, and about other artists. The statements I will be discussing are not those made by Dylan during the many interviews (seriously handled or otherwise) he has given throughout his career but those made *in the songs themselves*. The Other that he addresses in these songs is *himself as artist:* even, or especially, when that address is diverted through an other 'other,' as happens in the songs dedicated to other singers or artists.

These songs are all subject to that self-reflexive twist. Saying 'I feel I could almost sing' in an interview is very different from singing the same words in a song. The song has already, by its very existence, transcended the creative impasse that the words describe: this is the familiar paradox of the artist's anti-art pose. If someone tells you that he can no longer write a good poem but does so in a good poem, how is he to be believed?[1]

At the same time, the song loops round on itself. It returns the singer imaginatively to the moment of the impasse. The song reenacts the difficulty of its own creation and renews the always unfulfilled desire for its own origin. So another recurring motif is that of the 'Eternal Circle' (L 117). As Aidan Day says, discussing the song of that name:

> The closing of the circle of this song, its completion, does

not close the larger cycle—the eternal, temporally unclos-
able circle of creativity—within which the work has its
beginning and its end. As an object of desire, beckoning
towards creation, the creative spirit is realized in this song
and simultaneously ... she always lies beyond it, like echo
to a sound or shadow to the figure which casts it (31).

This motif of the echo or the shadow recurs in several of Dylan's songs about his creativity. It is further extended in such images as trace, brother, and ghost, all of which repeat the structural relationship that the alias has to the proper name. The source of inspiration is presented as *one step removed*, deferred beyond the point where it can be immediately grasped, and always elusive and indefinable.

The circular motif is implicit in the very nature of song, in the repetition of the same tune in verse after verse, and in the return of a chorus after these verses.[2] 'Lay Down Your Weary Tune' is one song that strongly thematizes this formal characteristic. The circle is a traditional emblem of unity, and the vision in this song is of a mystical or pantheistic unity between all the elements of man and nature. The verses present this unity in a series of images that unite natural phenomena (breeze, dawn) with cultural artifacts (bugle, drums)—

The morning breeze like a bugle blew

Against the drums of dawn

—while the chorus draws a conclusion and advises the singer to

Lay down your weary tune, lay down,

Lay down the song you strum,

And rest yourself 'neath the strength of strings

No voice can hope to hum (L 120).

The recurrence of the chorus is emphasized because it has the same tune as the verse. As Michael Gray comments, this device 'doubles the sense of unity which covers the whole song' (193). The song moves in a circle from chorus to verse to chorus, but each element is itself a circle, the repetition of the tune.

The sense of unity is also expressed in the synaesthetic nature of the images: one sense-impression is consistently conveyed in terms of another. Thus the blowing of the breeze (touch) is registered in terms of the blowing of a bugle (sound); the two different but allied senses of 'blew' mediate the comparison. The 'river's mirror' is 'watched' (sight) as something which can be heard: a guitar's 'strum.' Hearing is the master-term in all these analogies, and what is heard is always music.

Dylan's presentation of these movements between senses is rapid and compressed. Take the line 'The cryin' rain like a trumpet sang.' We begin with a familiar comparison, the visual correspondence between rain and teardrops. But the dominant aural metaphor of the song transforms 'crying' into its alternate sense, so that the cry becomes a sound. The sound of the rain is then compared to the sound of a trumpet, furthering the analogical correspondence of natural phenomena and cultural artifacts. But even the sound of the trumpet is immediately modified, by another comparison, into a human voice singing. The human voice thus stands at the midpoint between rain and trumpet: natural because it is human and cultural because it is singing.

The circle is also timeless. Although the lyrics do refer to temporal progression (dawn, autumn), they present images of cyclical recurrence (hours of the day, seasons of the year). The song's dominant feeling is of a moment suspended in time, the moment of the mystic caught up in the rapture of his vision. In the face of this vastness, the individual singer seems reduced to insignificance. He is advised to lay down his weary tune and take refuge in that 'strength of strings' so much greater than his own strength.

But this ostensible meaning of the chorus is put into question by its form. In the first place, who is the 'you' addressed? If the 'you' needs this advice, needs to be told the limitations of his song, then the 'I' must be someone of superior insight, someone who has already realized and transcended those limitations. But this dialogue is surely an internal one: most likely the 'you' is Dylan himself, who thus appears in the song as both first and second person, the 'I' of the verses and the 'you' of the chorus.

Secondly, the self-reflexive twist enters this song too, for 'Lay Down Your Weary Tune' does not obey its own advice. The singer advised to stop singing does not stop singing: indeed, we only know about the advice because it is contained in the song we are hearing. To the extent that this song successfully creates the image of unity, it embodies the 'strength of strings'; its voice (Dylan's voice) does in fact hum what 'No voice can hope to hum.' So the very existence of the song transcends the limitations set out in the lyrics of the song.

'Lay Down Your Weary Tune' presents a grand vision of transcendence in both man and nature, and it uses music as the mediating term of this comparison. The human creation of music, both by voice and by instruments, becomes the image for the beauty and infinity of the natural world. This metaphor also occurs in other Dylan songs. 'Chimes of Freedom,' for instance, replays the sense of mystic unity found in 'Lay Down Your Weary Tune' but adds the experience of the social world. The chimes are heard not just by a solitary watcher on the shoreline but by a group of friends in the city, and they toll for the refugees, the rebel, the outcast: 'every hung-up person in the whole wide universe' (L 133). The metaphor of this song presents a thunderstorm as 'majestic bells' playing in a 'wild cathedral evening.' Synaesthesia is used again, since it is the flashes of lightning (visual) rather than the crashes of the thunder (aural) that are presented as 'chimes.'

In these songs the site and source of inspiration are located outside the singer: in the shoreline of 'Lay Down Your Weary Tune' or in the thunder and lightning of 'Chimes of Freedom.' Yet that 'outside' is always potentially interiorized, since the natural metaphor is a metaphor *for* the creative power of the singer himself. This paradox of inspiration, as something simultaneously coming to the artist from somewhere else and arising from within his imagination, has traditionally been presented through the figure of the Muse. As a goddess, a figure separate from the artist, the Muse is the external source of inspiration, something that the artist cannot fully control. Yet she is also the projection of the artist's inner creativity; when he addresses her, he is also addressing himself.

I say 'she,' for the Muse is traditionally female. Most Dylan songs that can be interpreted as addresses to his Muse recognize this tradition. But in one striking case, the Muse is male: *Mister* Tambourine Man.[3] Perhaps because he is male, and because he plays a musical instrument, he is more clearly and closely related to the singer than the female figures tend to be. Moreover, the tambourine is an instrument that cannot carry a tune by itself: it needs the cooperation of the singer if music is to be created.

'Mr Tambourine Man' is in many ways an extension of the imagery of 'Lay Down Your Weary Tune.' Again the setting is a shoreline, the meeting of earth, sea, and sky; again the singer is alone. The song begins in the evening but looks forward to the renewal of the cycle in the 'jingle jangle morning' (L 172). In that image the sound of the tambourine is synaesthetically transferred to the natural scene. While the earlier song had at least ostensibly seen the singer's 'weary tune' as futile and inadequate, 'Mr Tambourine Man' welcomes his participation in the music and the dance. The singer asks the Muse to 'play a song for me,' and responds that he will 'come followin' you' and 'dance beneath the diamond sky.' Most obviously, Dylan will respond with lovely harmonica solos which have been a feature of the song from its original recording on *Bringing It All Back Home* to the 1989 concerts.

This brings us again to the self-reflexive twist of songs about making songs. Aidan Day, in his perceptive account of this song, points out that the repeated 'play a song for me' can be read as desperate, 'as much a plea as an injunction.... "Mr Tambourine Man" comprises an account of what it is to be inspired from the immediate vantage point of not being so' (20). Yet Day also acknowledges that 'the work itself evidences an attainment of the creative moment which its speaker spends so much time anticipating' (24). Such an attainment is always temporary: desire renews itself in the moment of its own accomplishment, and the cycle of creation begins again.

For most of the song, the relationship between the singer and his Muse is based on a clearly defined distance. The singer must appeal to the Muse for inspiration; must prepare himself by stripping his senses and ridding himself of obligations ('there is no place I'm going to'); and then must follow, be 'ready to go anywhere.' But in the third stanza, the interaction becomes more complex[4]:

> And if you hear vague traces of skippin' reels of rhyme
> To your tambourine in time, it's just a ragged clown behind,
> I wouldn't pay it any mind, it's just a shadow you're
> Seein' that he's chasin'.

A third figure—the 'ragged clown'—enters, and then even a fourth—the 'shadow' seen by the Tambourine Man and chased by the clown. Now it is the singer's turn to give advice and even comfort to his Muse: 'I wouldn't pay it any mind.' The Tambourine Man can see only shadows and hear only 'traces' of the 'reels of rhyme,' rhyme being the verbal art possessed by a singer but not a tambourine player. At the same time, the clown needs the Tambourine Man to see the shadow that he's chasing. Poetic inspiration is deferred, passed from one figure to another along a chain of substitutions, from the Tambourine Man to the singer to the clown to the shadow. And what is the shadow a shadow *of?* Aidan Day comments,

'Poetic language and poetic power chase each other in a circle of mutual implication, an incessant shadow-play' (26).

The 'mutual implication' of singer and Muse is also evident in 'Eternal Circle.' Here the Muse is a woman who stands in the audience while the singer plays a song but who disappears by the end of it. The link between them is established by the familiar I/eye pun: 'She called with her eyes / To the tune I's a-playin'' (L 117). Eye and I continue to interact throughout the song: her face reflects his words; his 'eyes danced a circle / Across her clear outline'; looking at the audience he pretends that 'of all the eyes out there / I could see none.'

But when he looks for her at the end of the song, he finds that 'her shadow was missin'.' While the Tambourine Man had only *seen* a shadow, here the woman *is* a shadow—and an absent one at that. The shadow, like the 'vague traces … of rhyme,' stands in for the full, unmediated experience that can only be posited, never realized. The work of art is always a trace.[5] All the artist can do in his desire for the missing, deferred origin is to enter the eternal circle of creation again: 'So I picked up my guitar / And began the next song.'

Both 'Eternal Circle' and 'Mr Tambourine Man' present the cooperative relationship, even mutual identification, of singer and Muse. In other songs Dylan has stressed the distance and the demands of the Muse, the degree to which he is at times at her mercy:

> You will start out standing
> Proud to steal her anything she sees.
> But you will win up peeking through her keyhole
> Down upon your knees (L 163).

Although 'She Belongs To Me' has been widely read as a love song, I agree with Bill Allison[6] that it also can be interpreted as another account of the singer and the Muse. Here the Muse is dominant: she has everything she needs, she's an artist, she's beyond the reach of the Law, she should be worshiped on ritual occasions. By contrast, the singer is simply a 'walking antique' in her collection. His position on his knees is not so much one of prayer as one of humiliation. The only vision she vouchsafes him is a voyeur's peek.

Yet again the ostensible meaning of the lyrics is modified by the performance—the last verse is a genuinely joyful celebration—and, interestingly, by the title. Allison points out that 'Me' appears only in the title, not in the verses, and suggests that this 'Me' is to be identified with the 'You' of the lyrics. So the Muse, who makes these extreme demands of the singer, nevertheless belongs to him. She is the shadow that he is chasing, but she is also *his* shadow.

This Muse 'wears an Egyptian ring,' sometimes in performance an 'Egyptian red ring.' The ring, a symbol of eternity, is associated with the ancient female goddesses of wisdom and fertility such as Isis, who was worshiped by the Egyptians as 'thou lady of the red apparel' (Walker 454). In the 1970s Dylan was interested in the figure of the Great Goddess. In a later chapter I will be discussing his song 'Isis'; other associated songs such as 'Oh, Sister' and 'Golden Loom' evoke the spiritual and creative powers of the 'Sweet Goddess / Born of a blinding light and a changing wind' (L 343). After Dylan's conversion to Christianity, the Muse figure was transformed into 'Precious Angel' and 'Covenant Woman.' In 'Caribbean Wind' she appears to him while he is 'playing a show in Miami in the theater of divine comedy' (L 466). In all these cases the Muse is an external force, a divine or semidivine creature to be worshiped, Beatrice to the Dante of *The Divine Comedy*. Yet in each case she is also internalized, the partner in the dialogue of I and I. 'Isis' is a song about a marriage, and it ends with an ecstatic 'Yes!' She belongs to me.

There is, however, a darker, negative characteristic of the Muse: or perhaps we should say, there is also a false Muse. This anti-Muse is addressed in 'Dirge.' 'I hate myself for lovin' you' (L 347), the song opens, and immediately we plunge into the internal debate. This 'you' is no less a part of Dylan than the you addressed self-reflexively in 'Lay Down Your Weary Tune' and 'She Belongs To Me.' In the song she is never identified, not even as 'she.' Only the conventions of address by a male singer might lead one to suppose that the 'you' is a woman. She stands in stark contrast to the 'you' addressed in the other songs on *Planet Waves*, yet she is as much a part of the singer as the woman to whom he sings, 'You're the other half of what I am' (L 350). 'We stared into each other's eyes,' Dylan sings in 'Dirge,' because they *are* each other's I's. Their relationship has been one of weakness and need, of simultaneous hate and love. This 'you' has, like Bob Dylan, sung 'songs of freedom' but also has shown him mercy beyond what he could have guessed. At the same time, she is 'a painted face on a trip down Suicide Road.' This is the false Muse of fame, commercial success, 'a moment's glory.'

'Dirge' is a bitter and impassioned rejection of the anti-Muse, but the song recognizes that the need and the love were real. The ending is ambiguous: 'I hate myself for lovin' you, but I should get over that.' Is it the love or the hate that he has to get over? Can they be distinguished from each other? This too is a Muse who belongs to me.

So far I have dealt with Dylan's attitudes toward his music and its sources of inspiration entirely from the perspective of Dylan as a solitary, unique figure. But the Muse, in whatever aspect, belongs to many other people as well. The singer of 'Dirge' may have 'paid the price of solitude,' but no singer is ever truly alone or 'out of debt.' The way any given work is necessarily situated within the context of other works is part of what is referred to as 'intertextuality.' Any text is always part of the accumulating intertext, building and rebuilding on what is already waiting there. I take this phrasing from Dylan himself, in '11 Outlined Epitaphs':

> Yes, I am a thief of thoughts
> not, I pray, a stealer of souls
> I have built an' rebuilt
> upon what is waitin'
> ....
>
> on what has been opened
> before my time
> a word, a tune, a story, a line
> keys in the wind t' unlock my mind (L 112).

It is not just that 'influence' is inescapable; it is that 'influence' is too puny and limited a word. Dylan acknowledged this in 'My Life in a Stolen Moment.' 'I can't tell you the influences,' he writes, ''cause there's too many to mention an' I might leave one out.' He lists singers like Woody Guthrie and Big Joe Williams, 'records you hear but one time,' the call of the coyote, the meow of the tomcat, and the 'train whistle moan.' 'Open up yer eyes an' ears an' yer influenced,' the passage concludes, 'there's nothing you can do about it' (L 72). This is not simply a denial of the responsibility of acknowledging sources; it is a recognition that the sources are everywhere, so widespread that they will never all be tracked down.[7]

Dylan has been wary of acknowledging the literary intertext. While statements like 'My Life in a Stolen Moment' pay tribute to the heritage of song, his references to poets and novelists have been more ambivalent or dismissive. Although he quotes with approval Rimbaud's 'Je est un autre,' Rimbaud's one direct appearance in the text of a song is a lighthearted disavowal of any comparison:

> Situations have ended sad,
>
> Relationships have all been bad.
>
> Mine've been like Verlaine's and Rimbaud.
>
> But there's no way I can compare
>
> All those scenes to this affair,
>
> You're gonna make me lonesome when you go (L 355).

American literary modernism fares no better. The reading of 'all of / F. Scott Fitzgerald's books' is a dubious accomplishment of the unfortunate Mister Jones, while Ezra Pound and T.S. Eliot appear only as irrelevant figures 'Fighting in the captain's tower' of the *Titanic* as it sinks (L 198, 206). And in the liner notes to *Bringing It All Back Home*, Dylan attempts to dissociate himself completely from tradition:

> i would not want t' be bach. mozart. tolstoy. joe hill.
>
> gertrude stein or james dean/they are all dead. the Great
>
> books've been written. the Great sayings have all been said
>
> (L 182).

This attempt remains unsuccessful, however, as 'My Life in a Stolen Moment' could have predicted. Bob Dylan formed the mask of 'Bob Dylan' from many intertextual elements (not the least of which was James Dean). The debt is paid most interestingly in those songs and poems that pay tribute to other artists. The rest of this chapter will look at three of these evocations: Woody Guthrie, Lenny Bruce, and Blind Willie McTell. In each case the sincerity of Dylan's tribute is not in question, but that sincerity in no way interferes with the songs' self-reflexiveness. Guthrie, Bruce, and McTell are indeed praised for their accomplishments, but they are also projections of Dylan's view of himself as an artist. As Allen Ginsberg said in reference to 'Lenny Bruce,' 'He's really talking about himself also, and all us artists' (*All Across the Telegraph* 173).[8]

'Song to Woody' was Bob Dylan's first major composition, and all the biographical accounts testify to the importance he attached to his meetings with Woody Guthrie and the song he had written for his idol. Robert Shelton quotes Dylan as having told Izzy Young, 'When I wrote "Song to Woody" in February, I gave Woody the paper I wrote the song on. Woody liked my song' (Shelton 102).

(Of course he also told Young that he had first met Woody Guthrie when he was thirteen!)

The song works hard to establish the connection between its author and its subject. The first line of the second verse—'Hey, hey, Woody Guthrie, I wrote you a song' (L 6)—is almost childish in its delight: a delight that seems to arise as much from the fact that *I* wrote it as from the fact that it's *for* 'you.' The lyrics underline that connection between 'I' and 'you' in the singer's claim that *'I'm* seein' *your* world' and in the even more convoluted reciprocity of 'I know that you know / All the things that I'm a-sayin'.' The fourth verse evokes 'Cisco an' Sonny an' Leadbelly too' and enlists Bob Dylan by unspoken implication as the latest in that line.

The intimacy between author and subject is also established by the song's appropriation of Guthrie's own music. The tune was one that Guthrie had used, and the words contain more than just echoes. Terry Alexander Gans comments:

> Incorporated freely into the song are Guthrie lines such
> as: 'come with the dust and are gone with the wind,' from
> 'Pastures of Plenty'; and 'hittin' some hard travelin',' from
> 'Lincoln Highway.' Thus Dylan pays tribute to Guthrie by
> letting the man write some of the song for him (67-68).

By quoting Woody Guthrie as part of his own song, Dylan is projecting Guthrie as a part of himself: not just 'you and I' but already 'I and I' in embryonic form.

The paradoxes and contradictions of this project of self-creation are evident in the last two lines: 'The very last thing that I'd want to do / Is to say I've been hittin' some hard travelin' too.' The young Dylan had, of course, been saying just that, spinning tall tales about the extent of his travels in an attempt to make himself seem more like, say, Woody Guthrie. However, the strict grammatical and idiomatic sense of the words he writes contradicts what he apparently wants to say. The 'very last thing that [anyone] would want to do' is normally something that he truly does *not* wish to do; but the sense of Dylan's lines, conveyed despite the words, is that he *does* want to do some hard traveling—or at least to be able to *say* that he's done some. When he does say it, he uses, as Gans noted, a quotation from Woody Guthrie. In the ambiguities of these lines, the strain of Dylan's appropriation of Guthrie threatens to overcome the song; in performance, of course, Dylan blithely sings the lines as if there were no ambiguity there.[9]

A later poem, 'Last Thoughts on Woody Guthrie,' is a conscious attempt to move beyond the image of Bob Dylan as Woody Guthrie's disciple; the most important word in the title is 'Last.' The poem is a long, rambling piece of free association verse. In the one recorded performance, Dylan wisely rattles through it at top speed so that its sheer energy and abundance make up for the weak lines and lame rhymes. It has strikingly little to say about Woody Guthrie or even about music, but its extended sentence[10] eventually works round to the familiar imagistic association of religion, music, and natural grandeur:

> You'll find God in the church of your choice
> You'll find Woody Guthrie in Brooklyn State Hospital
>
> And though it's only my opinion
> I may be right or wrong
> You'll find them both
> In the Grand Canyon
> At sundown (L 36).

This ending, however, feels forced and unconvincing, a rhetorical gesture rather than an achieved resolution.

There is a more telling 'last thought' on Woody Guthrie in '11 Outlined Epitaphs,' where Dylan writes that Guthrie was his 'last idol' precisely because he 'shatter[ed] even himself / as an idol' (L 111). By the time Dylan wrote this, he too was idolized and feeling the restrictions imposed by such a role. So his iconoclasm of Guthrie is intended to shatter his own image too, as the end of the poem makes clear:

> you ask 'how does it feel t' be an idol?'
> it'd be silly of me t' answer, wouldn't it...?

Dylan's final and finest tribute to Woody Guthrie is his magnificent performance of 'Pretty Boy Floyd' on the Smithsonian album *A Vision Shared*.

Like Woody Guthrie, Lenny Bruce was an outsider, an iconoclastic rebel. 'He was an outlaw,' Dylan sings, 'that's for sure' (L 455). Allen Ginsberg has commented on Dylan's 'unexpected sympathy for Lenny Bruce at a time when he [Dylan] was supposed to be a Born Again moralist Christian, and he was coming out for the injured and the insulted and the wounded and the supposedly damned' (*All Across the Telegraph* 173). One point of sympathy between the two artists may be that 'Lenny Bruce,' like 'Bob Dylan,' is an assumed name: the comedian was born Leonard Alfred Schneider.

As early as *Tarantula* Dylan had written of a character called 'lenny' (whom I take to be Lenny Bruce): 'you know he's some kind of robber yet you trust him & you cannot ignore him' (T 54). In Lenny Bruce, Dylan assimilates the figure of the artist to the figure of the outlaw. In a later chapter I will be discussing in more detail the outlaw in Dylan's work, but here it is worth noting that 'the thief' is a recurring image for Dylan himself and for the artist.[11]

What Dylan values in Lenny Bruce is his clear insight, uncompromising honesty, and the way he compelled his audiences to look at themselves with similar insight and honesty. In *Tarantula*

> lenny can take the bad out of you & leave you all good &
>
> he can take the good out of you & leave you all bad / if
>
> you think youre smart & know things, lenny plays with
>
> your head & he contradicts everything youve been taught
>
> about people ... lenny i'm sure is already in a resentful
>
> heaven (T 54-57).

The first sentence is reminiscent of the Muse in 'She Belongs To Me': 'She can take the dark out of the nighttime / And paint the daytime black' (L 163). In the song the portrayal is less paradoxical. Lenny Bruce 'sure was funny and he sure told the truth.... He just took the folks in high places and he shined a light in their beds.'

As a result, Dylan claims, the people whom he attacked 'said that he was sick.... They stamped him and they labeled him like they do with pants and shirts.' Here we begin to see the implicit identification of author and subject. Dylan too has resisted being stamped and labeled. In the song that immediately precedes 'Lenny Bruce' on *Shot of Love*, he presents a picture of himself as similarly rejected by those who cannot bear the truth of the message he brings:

> He's the property of Jesus
>
> Resent him to the bone
>
> You got something better
>
> You've got a heart of stone (L 456).

But Dylan's relationship with Bruce in the song is more complex than a simple identification of two persecuted truth-tellers. The line 'He was an outlaw, that's for sure' is followed by 'More of an outlaw than you ever were.' The 'you' involves us in the familiar complexity and fluidity of Dylan's pronouns. Again the most obvious interpretation is to see it as self-addressed: the line is an acknowledgment that Lenny Bruce's alienation was more radical and fatal than anything Bob Dylan had achieved. But the implicit identification of the two nevertheless claims for the singer the outlaw status that this line qualifies.

Later in the song Dylan appears in an almost ostentatious *first* person, offering an odd biographical anecdote: 'I rode with him in a taxi once, only for a mile and a half, / Seemed like it took a couple of months.' The meeting with Bruce is presented as a timeless moment like the moment of the mystic's contemplation in 'Lay Down Your Weary Tune' or 'Mr Tambourine Man,' but here the object of contemplation is not a natural scene but a mundane taxi ride. The Muse has become another artist, a defeated comedian laying down his weary tune. This use of the first person brings Dylan closer to Bruce by claiming firsthand knowledge and simultaneously distances him further by showing how tenuous and fleeting their contact was. It also sets up a triangular relationship between 'he' (Lenny Bruce), 'I' (Bob Dylan), and the 'you' of 'More of an outlaw than you ever were.'

This 'you' reappears only in the last line of the song: 'Lenny Bruce was bad, he was the brother that you never had.' 'Bad' balances between its literal meaning (what the 'Born Again moralist Christian' would see in Bruce's drug abuse) and its idiomatic use as black slang for 'good.' (It also recalls the line in *Tarantula* in which bad and good change places.) Bad Lenny Bruce is now 'the brother that you never had.'[12] Dylan's 'you,' who is also 'I,' is the brother of the 'he.' Dylan's appropriation of Lenny Bruce is thus much more complex than his appropriation of Woody Guthrie. Instead of a simple identification, we get a relationship deflected through a double screen of pronouns, both the 'I' who 'rode with him' and the 'you' who was less an outlaw than he was and who never had a brother to ride with.

The brother here is similar to the shadow and trace of 'Mr Tambourine Man.' A relationship at one remove is implied, a deferred identification. Lenny Bruce is also a 'ghost,' who 'lives on and on.' Like the shadow and the trace, the ghost is marginal and parasitical, absent and yet present. Lenny Bruce stands in these relationships (ghost, shadow, brother) to both 'you' and 'I.' He *is* 'your' brother and he *is not*, since 'you never had' a brother. He is both close to Bob

Dylan (both are scorned for the truth they tell) and distant (a casual acquaintance who once shared a brief taxi ride). Reciprocally, 'you' and 'I' are both the brothers whom Lenny Bruce never had—the brothers who might have saved his life, who might have helped him to make it to Synanon. If 'his ghost lives on and on,' it lives on as a shadow, as a brother, as the trace of the art he once created. It lives on also in the song that Bob Dylan sings about him.

The explicit drama played out in the shifting pronouns of 'Lenny Bruce' is implicit in 'Blind Willie McTell.' Unlike the tributes to Guthrie and Bruce, this song makes no claim for a personal relationship between the author and subject: indeed, the whole point is McTell's *absence*. The singer remains unobtrusive, an observer only. What he sees is a 'vision of desolation and expected destruction' (Bauldie, *All Across the Telegraph* 199): a world in which 'power and greed and corruptible seed / Seem to be all that there is.' This world is evoked through a series of concise imagistic tableaux, mainly relics of the Old South, the birthplace of the blues: 'big plantations burning,' 'the ghost of slavery ships,' 'a chain gang on the highway.' The scene is universalized in one sweeping phrase, 'All the way from New Orleans to Jerusalem,' which unites the old world and the new while implying also the 'New' Jerusalem of the Apocalypse.

In a perceptive commentary on the song, John Bauldie argues that its central point is not simply that the world is in this desperate state but also that no singer (no prophet) can adequately lament it:

> The problem which brought this song into being is the singer's feeling of being unable to shoulder the responsibility that he's always liked to think he inherited from those ghosts who haunt the darker side of his street—Robert Johnson, Leadbelly, Blind Lemon Jefferson, Blind Willie McTell. How can Bob Dylan offer appropriate homage, how can he address and relieve the oppression? He cannot.... It's that knowledge that is being bewailed—not just the fact that no-one can sing the blues like Blind Willie McTell but that Bob Dylan knows that no-one can (200).

But here, of course, we encounter the self-reflexive twist again. To the extent that Dylan has succeeded in presenting the desperation of vision, he *has*

'shouldered the responsibility' of the blues. Bauldie concludes his article by writing,

> The irony is that in attempting to express that inadequacy,
> in lamenting the oppression of his knowledge, Bob Dylan
> sings the blues indeed: and such a soul-rending blues as
> any of the old bluesmen—Blind Willie McTell, Robert
> Johnson—might have sold their souls to be able to sing
> (202).

My argument has been that this 'irony' is structurally built into this kind of song.
Just like 'Lay Down Your Weary Tune' and 'Mr Tambourine Man,' the existence
of 'Blind Willie McTell' as a song must necessarily modify to the point of reversal
the ostensible meaning of the lyrics.

In this sense Bob Dylan 'becomes' Blind Willie McTell: the song is even
more closely about himself than 'Song to Woody' or 'Lenny Bruce.' By singing
the blues *like* Blind Willie McTell, Dylan identifies the old bluesman as the
'brother [he] never had.' Although the word 'you' is never used in this song, the
relationship is as much implicit as it was with Woody Guthrie. Hey, hey, Blind
Willie, I wrote you a song.

There are, however, further ironies at work here. Each verse of the song
leads up to the refrain, 'I know no one can sing the blues / Like Blind Willie
McTell,' so each verse has to provide a rhyme for 'McTell.' It's not a difficult word
to rhyme, and Dylan runs through the obvious choices: fell, well, bell, yell. The
one that he does *not* use is the most obvious of all: tell. (The closest he gets to it is
as part of 'St. James hotel.') What Blind Willie did in his blues was to *tell* the
truth; this prophetic task is inscribed in his name; it is his signature. But the song
refuses to 'tell.' The absence of the word is like the absence of Blind Willie: an
absence at the center of the song so glaring that it draws attention to itself. At the
same time, just as 'blind' Willie 'sees,' this song tells its own refusal to tell. By
singing that no can sing the blues, Dylan proves that he can.

The history of the song pushes these ironies even further, for 'Blind Willie
McTell' was, of course, a bootleg.[13] Recorded as an outtake for *Infidels*, the song
was not released until *The Bootleg Series* in 1991; unlike many other unreleased
songs, its text is not even included in *Lyrics*. It is a story that Dylan refused to tell.
Asked about it by *Rolling Stone* in 1984, he said simply, 'I didn't think I recorded it

right.' So why not go back and record it again? It is as if Dylan's suppression of this song was an attempt to act out the absence that the song inscribes. No one will sing the blues like Blind Willie McTell, and no one will hear or sing 'Blind Willie McTell.'

Among those who had heard the song, Bob Dylan appeared to be a minority of one in his opinion of it. Critic after critic acclaimed it as one of his masterpieces. So here it was the bootleg network that made the self-reflexive twist possible and enabled us to tell what 'Blind Willie McTell' refuses to tell. Bob Dylan may say, 'I feel I could *almost* sing,' but in this case he *is* singing. Gloriously.

BIG GIRLS AND
SAD-EYED LADIES

Love songs of one kind or another—contented love or rejected love, care-
less love or abandoned love—make up the great majority of popular songs. Bob
Dylan's songs are no exception. From the lovely 'Girl of the North Country' to
the haunting 'Most of the Time,' Dylan has produced a memorable array of
images of love.

In trying to write about these songs, the critic's first temptation is to take a
biographical approach: to identify the women about whom the songs were written
and relate them to what is generally known of Dylan's private life. But this
approach poses major problems, which fall into three main areas.

First, the biographical material is incomplete and inadequate. There are too
many details that, despite the prying of biographers, we simply do not know. The
major figures in this story—Dylan and his wife, Sara—have maintained a tight
hold on their privacy. Other people who have spoken about their relationships
with Bob Dylan have often done so from clearly self-interested and biased positions, either for or against him. Much of what can be said about Dylan's marriage
must remain pure (or impure) speculation. Further, the very notion of biographical 'fact' is problematic. 'Fact' is always the product of discourse and can seldom
be appealed to in any direct or unmediated way. So how can any of this material
be used as a basis for judging whether the songs give an accurate portrayal of what
happened, or whether they are to be read as fictional variations?

Secondly, even in cases where enough biographical material is available to
identify discrepancies or inventions in the songs, we have no way of knowing how
or why those discrepancies arose. The writer may have forgotten details and be
making an honest mistake, he may be deliberately distorting the record in an

effort at self-justification, or he may simply be using the facts as the foundation for a fictional construct. Nothing says that poetry has to be factually accurate. The very nature of linguistic utterance always involves a split between the I who writes and the I who is written: a certain degree of fictionalization is inevitable in any statement. The more complex the statement becomes (by being shaped into a song, for instance), the less 'reliable' it is as a record of fact.

And thirdly, even if these problems could somehow be resolved with absolute or even relative certainty, the question remains: So what? What purpose has been served by a biographical reference? Does it really contribute anything worthwhile to our critical understanding and appreciation of the songs themselves? In cases where the biographical record may clarify an ambiguity in the text, does that clarification improve the text by making it more understandable, or does it diminish the text by reducing the possibilities of interpretation? If, for instance, we conclude that 'She's Your Lover Now' is 'really' about Edie Sedgwick and Bob Neuwirth,[1] does that knowledge increase or diminish our enjoyment of the song's wit and intricacy? The purpose of criticism is not to pander to the curiosity of gossip but to respond to the complexity of the texts themselves.

Fair enough: but 'the texts themselves' are not always as pure and self-enclosed as that phrase often suggests. The texts are caught up in the intertext of, for instance, proper names. When Bob Dylan sings about a woman called Sara, he is right to insist that the song need not and should not be taken as referring exclusively to his wife. Indeed, it may be at some level 'about' the Biblical Sara. But he would be naive to claim also that Sara Dylan can be entirely excluded from the intertext of this song; his use of the name ensures her presence there.

In fact, for all his reticence about his private life, Dylan has frequently 'staged' it in his art. What I mean by 'staging' is the process by which an actual person, identifiable to the audience either by name or some publicly accessible biographical detail, is projected into the text as a quasi-fictional character. The effect is most obvious in a song like 'Sara' or in *Renaldo and Clara*. In that movie two factors are of equal importance: that it is about two fictional characters called Renaldo and Clara, and that they are played by actors identified as Bob and Sara Dylan. An audience must balance these two elements. The film cannot be read as a transparent account of what went on between Bob and Sara—it must be approached as a work of fiction. Simultaneously, that fiction takes its particular shape, resonance, and authority from the identities of the actors. This kind of staging of autobiography takes place not only in *Renaldo and Clara* but also in many songs.

So, while admitting the force of the three problems, and while remaining unable to answer adequately any of the objections they raise, I still have to respond to the love songs at least partly in biographical terms, if only because those are the terms the songs themselves invite. The other to whom Bob Dylan tells the story of himself is sometimes clearly a very specific 'you.' At the same time, of course, the other is as always 'I.'

The relationship between 'I' and 'you' in Dylan's love songs is seldom clear-cut. Characteristically, the songs display an ambivalent attitude of the singer, who is divided between loving and hating, praising and blaming. This ambivalence often extends into a kind of reciprocity between the two lovers, a feeling that their positions are, for better or worse, interchangeable.

The ambivalence is given early and definitive expression in 'Don't Think Twice, It's All Right.' This is a song of parting that evenly balances tenderness and bitterness. The moments of regret—'Still I wish there was somethin' you would do or say'—are matched by flashes of vindictive reproach—'You just kinda wasted my precious time' (L 61). The singer hints that there *is* still something that the woman could 'do or say' but simultaneously insists that 'It ain't no use,' no matter what she does. His gift of his heart is countered by her demand for his soul, but equally he admits that she is in the light while he is 'on the dark side of the road.' Even the title is ambivalent: despite its ostensible reassurance, he clearly wishes that she would think twice, and it is obviously *not* 'all right.'[2]

Such divisions cannot be contained within one side of a relationship: they infect both parties and inevitably produce a kind of reciprocity. 'One Too Many Mornings' refuses to lay blame, insisting that 'You're right from your side, / I'm right from mine' (L 94). The two 'sides' thus become essentially the same side, as is shown in a somewhat convoluted way in the chorus of 'One of Us Must Know':

> But, sooner or later, one of us must know
> You just did what you're supposed to do
> Sooner or later, one of us must know
> That I really did try to get close to you (L 225).

This song too is about the breaking up of a relationship, and blame is again refused. The chorus provides valid excuses for both 'you' and 'I,' and looks forward to the time when mutual understanding will be acknowledged. But *which* one of us is 'one of us'? The 'you' presumably already knows that she just did what she was supposed to do while the 'I' already knows that he really did try to get close to her. Besides, as the author of the song, 'I' already knows what 'you' knows; and as the posited audience of the song, 'you' will know (sooner or later) what 'I' is telling her that he knows. In other words 'one of us' is already 'both of us'; 'you' and 'I' are implicated in each other.

This reciprocity is traditionally expressed in the images of mirrors and reflections, a motif that takes on particular importance in *Renaldo and Clara*. In 'Tomorrow Is a Long Time,' the traditional sense is conveyed in its negative form. The singer's separation from his 'own true love' is shown by his inability to see his reflection or hear his footsteps (L 42). The implication is that the woman's presence would enable him to see his reflection, since she would herself be the true mirror. Conversely, in 'Mama, You Been on My Mind,' the presence of an actual mirror cannot compensate for the singer's absence:

> When you wake up in the mornin', baby, look inside your mirror.
> You know I won't be next to you, you know I won't be near.
> I'd just be curious to know if you can see yourself as clear
> As someone who has had you on his mind (L 159).

The potential for the lovers changing positions is clearly formulated at the end of 'To Ramona.' After almost a complete song of giving advice to Ramona, the singer concludes: 'And someday maybe, / Who knows, baby, / I'll come and be cryin' to you' (L 136). Here the reciprocity is the basis for greater understanding and sympathy between the two lovers, but in 'Positively 4th Street' the same exchange of positions is evoked only to be twisted into a vicious attack:

> I wish that for just one time
> You could stand inside my shoes
> And just for that one moment
> I could be you
>
> Yes, I wish that for just one time
> You could stand inside my shoes
> You'd know what a drag it is

To see you (L 211).

In these songs, reciprocity and ambivalence are signs of a connection between 'you' and 'I' that runs deeper than the separation announced by the pronouns. Here as elsewhere the 'you' is a projection of the self, and the mirror reflection is again one of eye and I. 'Denise' is another song in which the woman acts as the mirror:

Denise, Denise,

You're concealed here on the shelf.

I'm looking deep in your eyes, babe,

And all I can see is myself (L 157).

But if he sees himself in Denise's eyes, and if Denise is concealed, then he too is concealed, and what he both sees and shows is his concealment. Dylan returned to this paradox in 'The Man in Me': 'The man in me will hide sometimes to keep from bein' seen' (L 295). Again there is the sense that the I is doubled and that this doubling involves a concealment of the self. But the self is concealed *in me*: so this 'me' is the outer surface visible to the world. The self is a mask. In 'The Man in the Long Black Coat,' Dylan linked the motifs of the mask and the eyes as a mirror of concealment: 'He looked into her eyes when she stopped him to ask / If he wanted to dance—he had a face like a mask' (OM).

What Dylan sees in Denise is his reflection, his I in her eye (or in the plural, his I's in her eyes). In the love songs, neither 'you' nor 'I' can stand completely alone. When Dylan sings that 'You're the other half of what I am' (L 350), he is not simply overstating a compliment; he is acknowledging an inner dynamic which gives added dimension to all his love songs, especially those in which he stages his relationships to Suze Rotolo and Sara Dylan.

The degree to which Dylan's early love songs were based on his affair with Suze Rotolo was apparently widely acknowledged around Greenwich Village. Bob Spitz records that 'friends familiar with his domestic situation felt embarrassed by such a public disclosure'; one unnamed friend 'found it difficult to sit through [Dylan's] performances "because the stuff he was doing was so transparent and Suze wasn't around to defend herself"' (200). This is not an unreasonable point: it has always been true that poets and artists get the unfair advantage of being able to tell their side of the story while the women subjects of their poems are denied a voice. For a popular singer, this may happen night after night in front of large

85

audiences, which may even include the person being addressed. What can Sara Dylan have thought, listening to the agonized Rolling Thunder performances of 'You're a Big Girl Now'?

For an audience wider than the immediate circles of 1962 Greenwich Village folkies, the biographical reference would not have been identifiable, and in many songs there is no direct reference to Suze Rotolo. It is widely assumed that 'Don't Think Twice' is about her, but nothing in song's text openly acknowledges that connection. The song is so generalized that it could be about any relationship on the verge of breaking down. In other songs, references to Suze are presented in passing. In 'Down the Highway,' for instance, Dylan sings:

> Yes, the ocean took my baby,
>
> My baby took my heart from me.
>
> She packed it all up in a suitcase,
>
> Lord, she took it away to Italy, Italy (L 55).

The specificity of 'Italy' points directly to the circumstances of Suze Rotolo's departure for Perugia. For a brief moment it stages the real; it brings into the song the intertext of Dylan's life.[3]

The reference to Suze is more oblique in 'Boots of Spanish Leather,' though the displacement of Italy to Spain is a fairly minimal gesture of disguise. The staging in this song is more apparent in its use of the formal conventions of the ballad, with the alternating verses presenting a dialogue between the two lovers. The effect is more objective and depersonalized, as if Dylan seeks to distance his pain by casting it in quasi-dramatic form. To a great extent this distancing works, though an element of self-pity can still be sensed. The woman is portrayed as shallow and insensitive while the man (by implication, the singer himself) is loving and suffering. But the situation is not quite so clear-cut.

'Boots of Spanish Leather' derives much of its force from its title. On the first hearing, a listener who has read the title on the album cover is kept in suspense, waiting for its occurrence in the song, already suspecting the impending betrayal through the protestations of the early verses. On subsequent hearings the title confirms and emphasizes the complex sense of betrayal with which the song ends: not only has the woman betrayed her lover, he has betrayed himself. By asking for 'Spanish boots of Spanish leather' (L 99), he has abandoned his lofty ideals and cynically acquiesced in the value system he attributes to her. He does not ask for a casual souvenir but for an expensive item; he is making her pay, literally, for her infidelity. In staging this exchange, Dylan does not place himself in an entirely favorable light. His final gesture is in equal measure one of genuine grief, one of bitterness, and one of mean-spirited pettiness.

This divided response is also apparent in the most direct and undisguised of the songs about Suze, 'Ballad in Plain D.' Despite the 'Ballad' in the title, this song fails to achieve any of the fictional distance of 'Boots of Spanish Leather.' The 'Plain D' is plain Dylan, naked and exposed: the first word of the song is 'I,' and in performance it is held like a long, drawn-out cry. The almost painful directness of the song is evident in the clumsiness of some of the writing. 'Ballad in Plain D' contains what is arguably the worst line Dylan ever wrote: the description of Suze as 'A magnificent mantel-piece, though its heart being chipped' (L 142). Other lines, however, give a precise rendering of the language of bitter, repetitive arguments.

The bitterness is reserved mainly for 'her parasite sister,' who lives on Suze's creativity like a parasite or like a false mirror image. Part of the song's weakness is that it seems too obviously an act of revenge against this overdrawn character. When the singer describes himself as 'nailing her [the sister] to the ruins of her pettiness,' the pettiness is just as much his own, and he is the other whom she is reflecting.

Suze is presented as a passive victim and compared to a lamb or a child. This idealization of the woman is two-edged: it deprives her of adult status and the responsibility for her actions. The singer is not so much her lover as her guardian. This tendency to see women as childlike, and thus to condescend to them, shows up in several Dylan songs: think of 'she breaks just like a little girl' (L 231) and 'You're a big girl now' (L 356).

'I' is the most complex character of the three. While 'Ballad in Plain D' is clearly an attempt at self-justification, it also admits his share of the blame. This ambivalence shows in the lines 'Myself, for what I did, I cannot be excused, / The changes I was going through can't even be used,' in which, of course, the changes *are* used simply by being mentioned, even though the ostensible meaning is to refuse the mitigation they offer.

To the extent that he blames himself, he also recognizes the degree to which he reflects the 'parasite sister': they are in effect parasites on each other, and the song is as much about his relationship to her as about his love for Suze. This alignment is presented in the tableau of 'Her sister and I in a screaming battle-ground. / And she in between, the victim of sound.' It is even more evident in a revision Dylan made in the text printed in *Lyrics*. On the record he sings, 'I gagged in contradiction, tears blinding my sight'; in *Lyrics* this line appears as 'I gagged twice, doubled, tears blinding my sight' (L 143). The revised form empha-sizes the doubling of the I: but the doubling is with *the sister*, not with 'the victim of sound.'

Even for a listener unaware of any biographical details, 'Ballad in Plain D' is plainly a highly personal song. It attempts to stage the breakup of Dylan's rela-tionship with Suze Rotolo, but too many elements remain unresolved for the stag-ing to succeed. Only in the last stanza does Dylan attempt to achieve some degree of distance from the events, by reverting to a traditional ballad formula. On the one occasion when the song recurs in Dylan's work, as part of the soundtrack for *Renaldo and Clara*, the distance is achieved by using not Dylan's own recording but a performance by another singer, Gordon Lightfoot. In that context, doubled as quotation, 'Ballad in Plain D' is more effective.

In none of these songs, however explicit, does Suze Rotolo's name appear in the text (though her photograph is featured on the cover of *The Freewheelin' Bob Dylan*).[4] The name is included, however, in '11 Outlined Epitaphs' as 'beautiful Sue,' who is 'the true fortuneteller of my soul' (L 114). She is compared to a frightened fawn (an echo of the lamb in 'Ballad in Plain D'), and she is also associ-ated with silence: 'there is no love / except in silence.' This association is interest-ing, since it recurs in other songs that are clearly *not* about Suze. 'Queen Jane Approximately' posits as the ideal lover 'somebody you don't have to speak to' (L 201); and in 'Love Minus Zero / No Limit,' which most commentators take as an early song for Sara because of its Zen-like qualities, 'My love she speaks like silence' (L 167).

Silence is always the condition of the 'you' in love songs: by definition the addressee cannot speak. In *Tarantula* Dylan wrote that 'there is no Second Person' (T 134). The mode of address elides the Other while invoking her. The question that closes 'Sad-Eyed Lady of the Lowlands'—'Should I leave them by your gate, / Or, sad-eyed lady, should I wait?' (L 239)—can never be answered. It does not close the song but leaves it open to a choice without resolution.

'Sad-Eyed Lady of the Lowlands' has often been dismissed as gorgeous but meaningless, the final excess and decadence of Dylan's self-indulgent piling up of psychedelic images. Michael Gray, for example, calls it 'sexy, fur-lined wallpaper' (158). But in the context of my argument here, the song is very interesting: not so much for the vexed question of who it was written for[5] as for its dramatic play of 'I' and 'you' triangulated with a pervasive 'they.'

The verses contrast the mystical sad-eyed lady (who I admit almost disappears in the haze of images that surround her) and a hostile third party, variously identified as kings of Tyrus, farmers, businessmen, or simply a generalized 'they.' As if reacting against the lady's lack of definition, 'they' repeatedly try to pin her down, to define and possess her: in the words of the recurring lines of the song, to bury, carry, outguess, impress, kiss, mistake, persuade, employ, and destroy her. But the lines' very repetition and their obsessive refrain 'who among them? ... how *could* they?' begin to imply subversively that the singer too is obsessed by these same desires. 'They' want the dark, suppressed side of what the 'I' wants.[6]

The song's triangular structure is repeated and compressed in the chorus:

> Sad-eyed lady of the lowlands,
>
> Where the sad-eyed prophet says that no man comes,
>
> My warehouse eyes, my Arabian drums,
>
> Should I leave them by your gate,
>
> Or, sad-eyed lady, should I wait?

Here the 'prophet' mediates as a third party between the lady and 'I,' but all three are connected in terms of eyes. The lady and the prophet are assigned the same adjective, 'sad-eyed,' while 'I' offers as his tribute a whole warehouse full of I's.[7] All three thus can be seen as aspects of the same sad-eyed I.

In Dylan's singing of the choruses, the singular 'prophet' sometimes becomes the plural 'prophets.' Similarly, there is more than one possible Biblical source for this line. Of the Hebrew prophets, the one who most extensively preached against Tyrus was Ezekiel:

> The word of the Lord came again unto me, saying,
>
> > Son of man, say unto the prince of Tyrus,
>
> ....
>
> > I will bring strangers upon thee, the terrible of the
> > nations: and they shall draw their swords against the

beauty of thy wisdom, and they shall defile thy brightness.

They shall bring thee down to the pit, and thou shalt

die the deaths of them that are slain in the midst of the

seas (Ezekiel 28:1-2, 7-8).

After its destruction, Ezekiel prophesies, Tyrus will become 'a place for the spreading of nets in the midst of the sea' (26:5). Babylon was the 'terrible of the nations' that God brought upon Tyrus, and Babylon in turn was denounced by the most sad-eyed of the Hebrew prophets, the lamenting Jeremiah:

The sea is come up upon Babylon: she is covered with

the multitude of the waves thereof.

Her cities are a desolation, a dry land, and a wilderness,

a land wherein no man dwelleth, neither doth any son of

man pass thereby (Jeremiah 51:42-43).

The 'lowlands,' where the sad-eyed lady remains inaccessible, are a place where 'no man comes' / 'wherein no man dwelleth'; they are a 'desolation,' the result of destruction by the sea. 'The sea is come up upon Babylon,' and Tyrus is 'a place for the spreading of nets in the midst of the sea.' These Biblical associations also echo the traditional British folk song 'Lowlands,' in which 'the lowlands of Holland' refers paradoxically to the sea, to the treacherous sandbanks on which fishermen (those who spread their nets) foundered their boats. In the folk song it is the ghost of a dead sailor who returns from the Lowlands to inform his loved one of his death: 'The cold sea weed was in his hair, / Lowlands, Lowlands away, my jo.' Reciprocity is again at work: in 'Lowlands,' the *man* is the ghost, but in Dylan's song the *woman* lives in the Lowlands and has a 'ghost-like soul.'[8]

Both lovers, then, may be cast in the role of a dead sailor. Another verbal echo in the chorus evokes a different long-lost sailor, namely Odysseus. When Odysseus blinds the Cyclops, he escapes by giving a false name: No Man. Under this evasion he conceals his identity, in the same way as Robert Zimmerman is concealed by the alias Bob Dylan. As No Man, then, Bob Dylan can come where no man comes, into 'a land where no man dwelleth'; as Odysseus, he can reach his sad-eyed lady, offer her his warehouse I's, and wait by her gate for the answer that the song cannot give him. My love she speaks like silence, and the track fades out on a harmonica solo.

However one resolves the question of biographical reference in 'Sad-Eyed

Lady of the Lowlands,' there can be little doubt that the love songs Dylan wrote in the 1970s take as their major focus his relationship with Sara. What one can read in these songs, looking back at them over the retrospective sweep of a decade, is the narrative of that relationship: in Ingmar Bergman's phrase, 'Scenes from a Marriage.' They move from the idyllic presentations of mutual love in *New Morning* and *Planet Waves*, through the increasing stress of *Blood on the Tracks* and *Desire*, to the breakup of the marriage in *Street Legal*. Of course, it is a one-sided picture. We hear only Dylan's version of what was going on, and the songs are not always free of self-pity and special pleading. But at their best they are strikingly intense and vivid portraits of the singer's emotional state, and as such they fulfill a major traditional function of lyric poetry.

The *critical* interest of these songs, however, does not lie in any attempt to piece together a biographical account of what 'really' happened between Bob and Sara. The question is not so much how close Dylan is to the protagonist of these songs as how much distance he can achieve. For example, in the first phase of this narrative, he had to tackle the problem of writing straightforwardly happy love songs in a noncliché manner about a stable and reciprocal relationship. It's all too easy to write about unhappy love—My baby left me and I'm standing here alone in the rain without an umbrella—or to write songs that take revenge on abandoned lovers. One great cliché of Dylan criticism has been that he only writes well when he's angry—which is why most listeners find it easier to respond to the familiar venom of *Blood on the Tracks* than to the daring simplicities of *Planet Waves*.

In writing this kind of love song, Dylan was continually on the edge of cliché. At his best he would use a conventional phrase but somehow hit it slightly off-center, so that it's not quite the way a listener would expect. For example, 'Something there is about you that strikes a match in me' (L 345) evokes but avoids 'meets a match' by substituting the unexpected 'strikes,' which in turn suggests a pun on 'match,' so that the finding of an equality also flares like a new flame.

More extended examples run through 'You Angel You.' The opening phrase —'You got me under your wing' (L 348)—echoes 'I got you under my skin' as well as literalizes the 'angel' cliché by insisting on the physical reality of the 'wing.' As Dylan sings the song on *Planet Waves* (the lines are revised in *Lyrics*), he continues:

'I just walk and watch you talk / With your memory of my mind.' The walk/talk rhyme is sheer cliché, but this version twists it around so that the lines collapse all the categories of separation. Talking is watched, not listened to; *her* memory is of *his* mind. Then comes 'You know I can't sleep at night for trying' where 'trying' substitutes a realistic observation (there are times when you can't get to sleep for thinking about it) for the expected and half-heard 'crying.' The next line—'Never did feel this way before'—insists on the uniqueness of the experience even as it leads into a phrase that is anything but unique: 'If this is love then gimme more.' And again the cliché is literalized as the line continues with 'and more and more and more and more.' The statement in 'You Angel You' is not at all complex, but the verbal wit is very precise. It may lack the flamboyance of, say, 'The motorcycle black madonna / Two-wheeled gypsy queen' (L 175), but it certainly lacks nothing in subtlety.

Not all the songs on *Planet Waves* manage to maintain this distance. Large parts of 'Wedding Song' remain, verbally, utterly banal,[9] though the beauty of the tune and the urgency of the performance redeem it. In retrospect one can sense a desperation in this song; the singer protests too much, and the overstatement of his case betrays some uneasiness about its validity. While much of *Planet Waves* is devoted to the celebration of this 'wedding,' the album is shot through with flashes of doubt and uncertainty. 'Something There Is About You' stages a vivid autobiographical image—'Rainy days on the Great Lakes, walkin' the hills of old Duluth' (L 345)[10]—and attempts to associate the present love with the past. But at the same time the singer insists: 'I could say that I'd be faithful, I could say it one sweet, easy breath / But to you that would be cruelty and to me it surely would be death.'

Such premonitions take center stage in *Blood on the Tracks*, in which almost all the love songs are full of anxiety, jealousy, and the fear and sorrow of separation. Even the most carefree and cheerful of them, 'You're Gonna Make Me Lonesome When You Go,' says 'when,' not 'if.' Most of these songs project this emotional turmoil into a quasi-fictional setting. This is most clearly seen in 'Idiot Wind,' in which a highly personal statement is prefaced by a piece of blatant fiction: 'They say I shot a man named Gray and took his wife to Italy, / She inherited a million bucks and when she died it came to me. / I can't help it if I'm lucky' (L 367). Both 'Tangled Up In Blue' and 'Simple Twist of Fate' also weave autobiographical elements into apparently fictional structures. 'If You See Her, Say Hello' assumes that the separation has already occurred and projects a future attitude of rueful acceptance and quiet sorrow. When the singer says (in one of Dylan's most brilliantly concise lines), 'Sundown, yellow moon, I replay the past' (L 369), he is already 'replaying' the future. But all these scenes are 'replayed': staged and projected as if they were on film and thus distanced from the singer's immediate and painful experience.

After the fictional flourish of its opening, 'Idiot Wind' becomes an increasingly bitter and recriminatory portrayal of separation. The 'you' of the song is blamed for not knowing the singer better and for the 'corrupt ways' that have 'finally made you blind.' But again the separation is not absolute, and the song carries a subtext of hints at the merging of this 'you' and 'I.' The final verse states, 'I kissed goodbye the howling beast on the borderline which separated you from me': once the beast is kissed goodbye, it no longer guards this border, so the 'you' and 'me' can merge into the 'we' of the final chorus. The vicious invective of 'You're an idiot, babe. / It's a wonder that you still know how to breathe' is modified to 'We're idiots, babe. / It's a wonder we can even feed ourselves.' Nothing is forgiven, but the singer is prepared to accept a share of the guilt and responsibility.

'Idiot Wind' became progressively fiercer as it went through its various versions. By the time of the Rolling Thunder recording preserved on *Hard Rain*, it had become a rant, with very little room for this acknowledgment of complicity. But its earliest form is different. Several songs on *Blood on the Tracks* were recorded twice. The original tapings of September, 1974, were later replaced on the album by versions recorded in December. The September 'Idiot Wind' is much softer, more forgiving and sympathetic, not so much in the words as in the performance.[11] When Dylan sings, in lines deleted in the released version, 'You close your eyes and part your lips, and slip your fingers from your glove, / You can have the best there is, but it's going to cost you all your love, / You won't get it for money,' the words may be sardonic and angry, but the voice is almost unbearably tender. The singer offers freely all the love it's going to cost.

The song that depends least on any fictional distancing is 'You're a Big Girl Now.' This is a song (like 'Ballad in Plain D' or 'Wedding Song') that seems to have slipped past all disguises to an almost embarrassing directness. These songs appear at times to reveal more than the singer intends or is aware of. Take, for instance, these lines, which show the singer desperately trying to come to terms with his lover's newly asserted independence:

> Time is a jet plane, it moves too fast
>
> Oh, but what a shame if all we've shared can't last.
>
> I can change, I swear, oh, oh,
>
> See what you can do.
>
> I can make it through,
>
> You can make it too (L 356).

The singer appears to accept his share of the responsibility for what has gone wrong, and promises to change. At the same time he hints that 'Time' is really to blame, and he shifts the burden of responsibility quickly back onto the woman by demanding that she match his offer. But if he was wrong in the first place, why should she have to change as well? Nor can the song resist gestures of self-pity:

> Oh, I know where I can find you, oh, oh,
>
> In somebody's room.
>
> It's a price I have to pay
>
> You're a big girl all the way.[12]

The title phrase itself betrays, perhaps unconsciously, the singer's paternalistic condescension. As in 'Ballad in Plain D,' the woman is more a daughter than a wife. How many women of the mid-1970s would take kindly to being congratulated on their maturity in the phrase 'You're a big girl now'?

These problems are especially evident in the performances of the song during the Rolling Thunder tour. The version on *Hard Rain* is extremely long: seven minutes, as opposed to the four and a half on the *Blood on the Tracks* recording, though no words have been added. Dylan sings with excruciating slowness, dragging out the pauses, wringing every drop of emphasis from the words. It's like witnessing a confessional psychodrama played out on stage in front of an audience— an audience which on many occasions included Sara.

'You're a Big Girl Now' reveals a deep division in the singer's attitude. On the one hand he is trying to come to terms with the changes in his relationship; on the other hand his language remains within the patterns of paternalistic condescension. The 'big girl' is no more real, no more human, than the 'sad-eyed lady.' This division is intensified on *Desire*, which takes as its main theme the crisis of patriarchy.

Desire is full of images of disempowered men, of dead or dying fathers. Hurricane Carter in prison; the dead Joey Gallo, and Joey Gallo's father, who 'had to say one last goodbye to the son that he could not save' (L 384); the dying narrator of 'Romance in Durango,' who can no longer protect the woman he loves—all are instances of traditional male power thwarted and denied. The father in 'One More Cup of Coffee' may 'oversee his kingdom / So no stranger does intrude,' but he cannot keep his voice from trembling when he 'calls out / For another plate of food' (L 381). In 'Oh, Sister,' Dylan invokes the traditional power of the Patriarchy in its ultimate form as a sanction against the woman's challenge:

> Our Father would not like the way that you act
>
> And you must realize the danger.
>
> ....
>
> And is our purpose not the same on this earth,
>
> To love and follow His direction? (L382)

But for women who are familiar with the feminist analysis of patriarchal power and the way that it works through traditional religious images, such appeals no longer carry their old authority. In later chapters I will return to this image of the dead father and examine it in more detail; in the present context it serves mainly as background for the most undisguised of Dylan's love songs, 'Sara.'

'Sara' openly flaunts the autobiographical references that Dylan had so often kept oblique or hidden. This is not an innocent tactic: the factual references are used to establish the singer's credentials and build up sympathy for his position. We get intimate glimpses of Bob, Sara, and the kids at play, on a beach, on holiday in Portugal. And we get Dylan writing his image into his history:

> I can still hear the sounds of those Methodist bells,
>
> I'd taken the cure and had just gotten through,
>
> Stayin' up for days in the Chelsea Hotel,
>
> Writin' 'Sad-Eyed Lady of the Lowlands' for you (L 390).

But how accurate is this paraded autobiography? 'Sad-Eyed Lady of the Lowlands' was recorded in February, 1966. No Dylan biography mentions him undergoing any 'cure' around this time. Both Spitz and Heylin claim that 'Sad-Eyed Lady' was written or at least completed in the studio at Nashville. And despite Dylan's statement, there are still those who believe that the song had more to do with Joan Baez than with Sara. In other words what is presented as authoritative autobiographical fact is open to some question: again what is important is that the life is *staged*, presented in dramatic terms as part of a performance.

From one point of view, the performance is simple and predictable: the oldest trick in the patriarchal book, emotional blackmail by way of the kids.[13] In the late 1970s such an approach was likely as anachronistic and counterproductive as saying 'you're a big girl now' or 'Our Father would not like the way that you act'—but does the singer of this song realize that? Between the verses the repeated appeals to Sara surround her with a strange array of epithets: 'Sweet virgin angel, sweet love of my life ... Radiant jewel, mystical wife ... Scorpio Sphinx in a calico dress ... Glamorous nymph with an arrow and bow.' In phrases like these, one sees again the inability to come to grips with the woman as a real, other person. In the verses she is trapped in the traditional role of motherhood; in the choruses she is lost in a haze of romantic abstractions.

From another point of view, 'Sara' repeats the mythological drama staged in the other songs on *Desire*. The references to the children stress Dylan's position as a father whose authority has failed; his voice too 'trembles' as he calls out to his errant wife. And Sara, as the 'mystical' wife, takes on the characteristics of Isis, who could be both virgin and mother, with her saintlike face and ghostlike soul.

The problem presented *in the songs* (and we have no way of knowing how close this is to the problems that existed in real life) is that the singer has no way of reconciling these divisions. Whether Sara is portrayed as a mother or a mother-goddess, she does not appear in the songs as a human being met as an equal. Like the addressee of *any* song, 'Sara' is denied speech (she has to speak like silence). This imbalance is always present in love songs, but in Dylan's songs it is accentuated by the consistent idealization of the woman. Only in *Renaldo and Clara* does she have a chance to appear in her own right, but even there she was hedged around by the fictional structures of the film. Ultimately, her response could only be made outside the songs, though the songs anticipate it. It is clearly feared and foreseen even in the lines which plead against it: 'Sara, oh Sara, / Don't ever leave me, don't ever go.'

But she did leave, and on *Street Legal* Dylan provides a concise summary of the separation. The last three songs on the album act as a mini-trilogy replaying the past. The first, 'True Love Tends to Forget,' is a tender, rueful, slightly ironic look at the fading away of the love once so joyfully celebrated:

> I'm getting weary looking in my baby's eyes
> When she's near me she's so hard to recognize.
> I finally realize there's no room for regret,
> True love, true love, true love tends to forget (L 411).

The old motif of looking in the lover's eyes/I's, as in 'Denise,' is repeated here to stress the extent of the separation. If she is 'so hard to recognize,' then so is what he must see in her eyes: his reflection. The chorus holds onto the phrase 'True love' for as long as it can, repeating it three times and stretching out the long vowel of 'True,' in an exact formal expression of the way the singer also has held onto true love for as long as he can, but now he recognizes, in the last few quick, clipped syllables, that true love 'tends to forget.'

The second song in the sequence, 'We Better Talk This Over,' takes the separation a stage farther. It replays some final discussions but from the resigned acceptance that the affair is over. Some lines are still bitter and angry: 'I feel displaced, I got a low-down feeling / You been two-faced, you been double-dealing' (L 412). There is perhaps a hint of reciprocity in these lines, with the singer 'displaced' into the position of the other. There is even a distant pun between 'dealing' and 'Dylan': Sara and Bob were, as a couple, 'double-Dylan,' but then Bob, as the ghost of Bobby Zimmerman, was a 'double-Dylan' all by himself. At another point in this song, the unlikelihood of the lovers getting together again is compared to 'the sound of one hand clappin'.' The image not only recalls Sara's interest in Zen but also reinforces, in the very absence of the second hand, the lost ideal of reciprocity.

Much of the bitterness is contained in this song, however, by two factors. First, the tune is jaunty and cheerful, seemingly in opposition to the mood of the words. Secondly, the writing is witty, twisting colloquial phrases to new uses and making full use of Dylan's virtuoso rhyming:

> Why should we go on watching each other through a telescope?
> Eventually we'll hang ourselves on all this tangled rope.
>
> Oh, babe, time for a new transition
> I wish I was a magician
> I would wave a wand and tie back the bond

That we've both gone beyond.

The artist's delight in the creation of this intricate, witty song has already taken him some way beyond its pain.

Some way: for the pain returns in the final song, the epic 'Where Are You Tonight? (Journey Through Dark Heat).' Again, this song interweaves autobiographical references (the 'nickels and dimes' of the divorce settlement) with openly fictional elements (no one has ever suggested that Sara's father was 'A full-blooded Cherokee') (L 413). The singer is now definitively alone: 'There's a woman I long to touch and I miss her so much but she's drifting like a satellite.' The situation is abnormal, a disruption of how things should be. A 'satellite' does not normally 'drift' but moves in a regular orbit round a fixed center. The woman is something that has strayed from its appointed course around the central point traditionally occupied by the man. At the very moment that the song laments the woman's departure, the image reinstates the imbalance between the two lovers which may have contributed to that departure in the first place.

At other points the singer recognizes that this conflict is also, as always, an internal one: 'I fought with my twin, that enemy within, 'til both of us fell by the way.' Before, this recognition reinforced the lovers' reciprocity, but in this song it begins to lead in a different direction. The language of 'Where Are You Tonight?' is more generalized and symbolic than in most of Dylan's love songs of the 1970s; the internal conflict again takes on a social dimension. The 'long-distance train' of the first line already looks forward to the 'slow train coming' of the following album.

But it *is* also a farewell to Sara, and the song rises to a great emotional climax of cathartic release. The final chorus sums up and puts an end to the narrative that all the love songs of the 1970s had told:

> There's a new day at dawn and I've finally arrived.
> If I'm there in the morning, baby, you'll know I've survived.
> I can't believe it, I can't believe I'm alive,
> But without you it just doesn't seem right.
> Oh, where are you tonight?

And there, for some time, the matter rested. During the period of his religious albums, Dylan occasionally returned to the conventions of the love song, but they were intricately mixed in with the gospel idiom. 'Precious Angel' for instance is simultaneously a love song with a strong erotic content and an extended warning of imminent Armageddon:

> You're the queen of my flesh, girl, you're my woman, you're my
>   delight,
> You're the lamp of my soul, girl, and you torch up the night.
> But there's violence in the eyes, girl, so let us not be enticed
> On the way out of Egypt, through Ethiopia, to the judgment
>   hall of Christ (L 426).

Like several songs of this period, 'Precious Angel' may have been addressed to Mary Alice Artes, who was partly responsible for Dylan's conversion to Christianity. So the love song cliché of the 'angel,' which Dylan had reworked in 'You Angel You,' is here returned to its religious context, but with all its erotic associations intact.

The love songs of the mid-1980s are mostly rather mediocre, vapid pieces like 'Emotionally Yours' (L 498). Only occasionally do they have a real edge to them, and then it is of anger and confrontation, as in the brilliant and highly charged 'Something's Burning, Baby' (L 499). But in the 1989 album *Oh Mercy*, Dylan returned to the height of his powers, in the love song as in other modes.

Again there is a mixture of idioms. 'What Was It You Wanted?' could be read as a love song, an extended reprise of 'It Ain't Me, Babe,' but also as the singer's response to the demands of his audience or his God. Similarly, 'Shooting Star' may speak to a woman who is irrevocably lost—'Guess it's too late to say the things to you that you needed to hear me say' (OM)—or it may address, like 'Blind Willie McTell,' another dead singer (possibly Roy Orbison). It too contains a concise and chilling evocation of the Apocalypse. The reciprocity of Dylan's early love songs returns: the opening line, 'Seen a shooting star tonight, and I thought of you,' moves logically in the next verse into 'Seen a shooting star tonight, and I thought of me' (OM).

The purest love song on the album, and one of the most moving Bob Dylan has ever written, is 'Most of the Time.' (The temptation to read this song biographically, as a cry of the heart back over the years to Sara, is irresistible.) The song operates by a simple ironic reversal. The singer declares that he is all right, in control ('I can deal with the situation ... I can survive and I can endure'), and that he longer thinks of his lost love ('Don't even remember what her lips felt like on mine'). But each declaration is undercut by the repeated phrase 'most of the time' (OM). What he feels like the rest of the time is never directly described, but as the protestations of his imperviousness multiply and grow more and more desperate, the simple understatement of the song accumulates into a massive overstatement:

> Most of the time she ain't even in my mind
> Wouldn't know her if I saw her, she's that far behind
> Most of the time I can't even be sure
> If she was ever with me, or if I was ever with her...
> I don't compromise and I don't pretend
> I don't even care if I ever see her again
> Most of the time

Dylan voice is quiet and restrained, belied by the surging emotion of the musical backing. It's a love song of such intensity and purity that the listener is totally swept up into its tenderness and its pain. Quite simply, it breaks your heart.

C H A P T E R   S I X
RENALDO AND BOB

The image on screen is of a face in white pancake makeup leaning into the microphone with the tense urgency of a steel spring. The lips are drawn back almost in a snarl; the eyes move in and out of the shadow of a wide-brimmed hat, and they gaze searchingly into the darkness and into the light.

Who is this singer? What is his alias this time? One answer would be that it's Bob Dylan, filmed in documentary style during a 1975 concert of the Rolling Thunder Revue. Another answer would be that it's the fictional character Renaldo, the central figure in the long, complex, and multilayered movie *Renaldo and Clara*. Renaldo, of course, is played by an actor called Bob Dylan— and the film is directed by someone who is also called Bob Dylan. I and I and I.

Not many people have had the opportunity to see *Renaldo and Clara*. Although Dylan clearly regards this film as a major part of his work (he spent over a year editing it), it remains the most difficult and inaccessible of his texts. Unlike the record albums, it is not in public circulation. Since its critical and commercial failure, prints are scarce, and most viewers have access only to poor-quality videotape copies on which the rich colour patterns can only be guessed at. Moreover, its four-hour length makes even a single complete viewing a daunting prospect. Most film audiences are not trained in maintaining such a long attention span, especially for a film that offers little in the way of linear plot and continuity but relies instead on a nonlinear pattern of associations in which connections must often be made between scenes widely separated in time.

Renaldo and Clara is a complex text, full of allusions and connections that often depend upon information not made explicit in the film itself. So it is very helpful to approach the film with a guide such as that provided in Stewart P. Bicker's privately printed pamphlet, *The Red Rose And The Briar: A Commentary on*

Bob Dylan's Film 'Renaldo and Clara' (1984).[1] I have also made extensive use of comments by Dylan himself, especially his 1977 interview with Allen Ginsberg.[2]

To some extent it is a weakness of the film that some of the points Dylan makes in the interview, points that are crucial to a viewer's understanding, could not be gathered from the film itself by even the most perceptive audience. Repeated viewings will elucidate the symbolic meanings of most characters, but when Dylan says that Ramon, who appears with 'Mrs Dylan' in scenes 36 and 38, is the ghost of her dead lover,[3] nothing in the scene as filmed gives the slightest hint that Ramon is supposed to be dead. Yet the idea of dead lovers and ghosts is, as I will show, thematically important to the film.

'You wanna stop time,' Dylan told Ginsberg, 'that's what you wanna do. You want to live forever, right Allen? Huh? In order to live forever you have to stop time.... We have literally stopped time in this movie' (10). The major way in which Dylan attempts to stop time in *Renaldo and Clara* is by abandoning the linear progression of plot and narrative, a technique relatively common in 20th century literature: Ginsberg cites the 'cut-up' novels of William Burroughs and the collage method of Ezra Pound's *Cantos* as analogues (7, 32). Nonlinear narrative is also present in much avant-garde cinema and in the work of such directors as Jean-Luc Godard and Alain Resnais, but it is foreign to mainstream American cinema. It could be argued that such methods are fiercely resisted by the medium of film, whose very existence depends upon its temporal movement through the projector, the succession of images upon the screen. There are fragments of plot in *Renaldo and Clara*, but they often appear in a scrambled order. For example, scene 60 breaks off at precisely the point where scene 6, part of the same sequence in the New York offices of CBS records, begins; similarly the subplot of Lafkezio and the traded horse would appear in chronological order as scenes 72, 68, 74.

The effect is that the scenes are laid out spatially rather than temporally. The viewer is invited (eventually, after several viewings) to see all the scenes existing in the same timeless moment and to make connections between them not in terms of their chronological sequence but in terms of imagistic associations which crisscross the temporal divisions. Ginsberg[4] describes the film's composition in just these terms:

> It's like a tapestry. What he did was, he shot about 110
> hours of film, and he looked at it all. Then he put it all on

index cards, according to some preconceptions he had when he was directing the shooting; namely themes; God, rock 'n' roll, art, poetry, marriage, women, sex, Bob Dylan, poets, death, maybe 18 or 20 thematic preoccupations. Then he also put on index cards all the different characters, all the scenes, the dominant colours blue or red, and certain other images that go through the movie, like the rose and the hat and American Indians, so that finally he had an index of all of that. And then he went through it all again and began composing it thematically, weaving in and out of these specific compositional references. So it's compositional, and the idea was not to have a plot but to have a composition of those themes.

This method is not original to Dylan. What Ginsberg describes is the classical Modernist method of early 20th century art. But few American film directors have attempted to apply the method as consistently and radically as Dylan does in *Renaldo and Clara*—and none, of course, has been able to rely on such a rich body of intertext on which to base this collage as the entire corpus of Bob Dylan's songs. What Ginsberg does not emphasize in his analysis is the pervasiveness of music in the film (55 musical selections are listed in the closing credits, 22 by Bob Dylan). To extend the tapestry metaphor, the music, with all its manifold associations outside the film, provides the warp through which the weft of Dylan's index-card composition is drawn. Nobody but Bob Dylan could have made this film, not so much because of its time-shuffling technique as because of its peculiar structure, which required that the central actor already be a figure of mythic proportions outside the film.

One brief sequence illustrates the kinds of transitions that Dylan arranges out of his index cards. Scene 89 is part of the central sequence in the latter part of the film in which Renaldo (played by Bob Dylan) is confronted by two women, Clara (Sara Dylan) and the Woman in White (Joan Baez). The sequence plays back and forth between the real identities and histories of the actors and the fictional roles of the characters. Scene 89 ends with the Woman in White looking at Clara and demanding, 'Who is she?' Whereupon we cut directly into scene 90, Bob Dylan on stage singing, 'Sara, oh Sara / Sweet virgin angel, sweet love of my life.' The biographical reference could scarcely be more blatant, but as the scene ends the camera shifts to the character called 'Mrs Dylan' (played by Ronee Blakley), who is standing on stage, wearing a large red hat, which recalls the hat Renaldo wears throughout the movie. Scene 91 then returns to the sequence begun in scene 11 in which a CBC reporter, told that 'You'll recognize Bob, he's got a hat on,' mistakes Ronnie Hawkins for Bob Dylan. In scene 91 Hawkins and Blakley reappear, playing the roles of Mr and Mrs Dylan. So in quick succession, 'Bob Dylan' has been split into the character of Renaldo (89), the man on stage who sings of Sara (90), and a fictional character played by Ronnie Hawkins (91). Scene 92 returns to the shots of David Blue playing pinball, which have been regularly interspersed ever since scene 3. In 92 Blue first tells us that Bob Dylan is a myth ('You know what a myth is? It's a myth!') and then that Bob Dylan is not a myth ('He lives like a human being. He's a wife and family, you know what I mean, it's ridiculous'). And with the mention of wife and family, scene 93 cuts back into the sequence of scene 89 with Renaldo and Clara (Bob and Sara Dylan) making love on a bed. So in this sequence, four totally different times and narrative lines have been woven together into a continuous collage on the myth and reality of Bob Dylan's marriage.

What is obvious from this sequence is that *Renaldo and Clara* deals in parallel images that reflect and double each other. Indeed, doubling or duality is the central obsessive gesture of the film. Everything in *Renaldo and Clara* happens at least twice: every reference, gesture, and name finds its double at another point in the structure.[5]

For example, two scenes deal with palm-reading: in 81 Scarlet Rivera is reading Renaldo's hand while in 83 Mama Frasca reads the palm of The Father (played by Allen Ginsberg). Each scene in turn contains doubles: 'You have a duality in your life,' Scarlet tells Renaldo (one of the film's great understatements) while Mama Frasca tells The Father, 'You have been married twice.' ('Well, sort of,' responds Allen Ginsberg!) Similarly, two different scenes repeat the motif of barred entrance. In 21 a security guard (Mick Ronson) blocks the way of Bob Dylan (Ronnie Hawkins) while in 60 Renaldo (Bob Dylan) is refused entrance to the CBS offices.

Doubles also appear within individual scenes. Scene 23 features two street-preachers haranguing the crowds on Wall Street: the two preachers not only double each other's gestures, one of them repeats exactly the arm gesture of a statue of George Washington behind him. The preachers reappear in scene 52, in which intercutting makes it appear as if Renaldo in Toronto can see them in New York—thus doubling the U.S. and Canada.

The film moves freely back and forth between these two countries, and even between two languages, as in the bilingual line delivered in scene 52: 'Not pour moi, monsieur; c'est un mistake.' In scene 94 The Father translates the Stations of the Cross from French into English for Renaldo's benefit. The scene concerning Hurricane Carter (58) insists repeatedly on the *two* witnesses who have contradicted their testimony against him. Prominent in the background of this scene is a cinema, Harlem's Apollo, which is showing *Earthquake*, thus implicitly echoing two natural disasters.[6]

Doubling within single scenes is also accomplished by using mirror images. In scene 38, the angry dialogue between Ramon and Mrs Dylan, the camera begins by shooting through the bathroom mirror, pulls back, and follows the couple into the bedroom, where a second mirror is prominent on the wall. In one bordello scene (78), The Father is offered 'a mirrored room' in which he can watch the proceedings. Other forms of mirroring are more indirect. In two scenes (46 and 92), we catch glimpses of a second camera crew filming and being filmed. Scene 103, in which Dylan and Baez are on stage singing together, is followed in the first shot of 104 by Renaldo and Clara looking at a newspaper photograph of Dylan and Baez on stage singing together.

Characters' names are also doubled.[7] Most intriguing in this regard is the name David Blue. Blue appears as a kind of chorus throughout the film, and his witty, articulate reminiscences of Greenwich Village in the early 1960s are among its most enjoyable scenes. But 'Blue' also keys the colour coding of the film: the concert sequences especially are all shot with a strong visual emphasis on red and blue. These colors combine patriotically with Renaldo's whiteface stage makeup in, for instance, the tight close-up of him singing 'Tangled Up In Blue' (106). 'Blue,' like 'Dylan,' is an assumed name: David Blue was originally David Cohen. *David* Cohen is then doubled by *Leonard* Cohen, who makes several phantom appearances in the film. The women in the bordello (Anne Waldman, Denise Mercedes, and Linda Thomases) are referred to collectively in the credits as 'Sisters of Mercy,' the title of a Cohen song. It is one of these women who offers

Allen Ginsberg 'a mirrored room' (78), recalling the line 'Suzanne holds the mirror' from Cohen's song 'Suzanne,' which is sung in the film by Joan Baez (101).[8]

Doubling is the key gesture of *Renaldo and Clara*. All details of the film reflect each other in intricate patterns of cross-reference and allusion. At the center of these doublings stands the multiply doubled figure of Bob Dylan himself. He is both outside the film, as its director-editor, and inside it, as an actor. As actor he is both the character Renaldo and the man who sings Bob Dylan's songs on stage. As Renaldo he has to confront Bob Dylan's history in the shape of characters played by Joan Baez and Sara Dylan; as Renaldo he also dreams the whole film (113) as if he were Bob Dylan, its director-editor. Doubling is thus the technique by which *Renaldo and Clara* stages Bob Dylan, enabling him to tell the story of himself—the story that begins, as always, 'I is another.'

It begins on stage. In the film's first shot, we see the cast of the Rolling Thunder Revue singing 'When I Paint My Masterpiece.' The choice of song already points both to the visual nature of the film (a song about painting opens a film about singing) and to its ambition. *Renaldo and Clara* advertises itself as Bob Dylan's masterpiece. The song's third line—'You can almost think that you're seein' double' (L 300)—introduces the motif of doubling. In fact what Dylan sings in this performance is 'You can almost think that you're seein' *your* double,' placing the audience squarely in front of the film's mirror. The screen in *Renaldo and Clara* always acts as a mirror. Dylan says that Renaldo 'looks right at you through the mirror' (Ginsberg 23).

The audience does see double. In the first place, who is singing? Dylan insists that the singer on stage is not Bob Dylan but the character Renaldo, played by Bob Dylan. When Ginsberg asked, 'Who's Bob Dylan [in the movie]?', Dylan replied, 'Nobody's Bob Dylan. Bobby Dylan's long gone' (28). The audience's awareness of this fiction must, however, be combined with their nonfictional awareness that what they are seeing is concert footage of actual Rolling Thunder shows. The effect of this doubling is that the real 'Bob Dylan' of the concert footage is appropriated by the image of the fictional 'Renaldo,' who sings his songs for him.

The audience sees double, secondly, because Dylan/Renaldo in that opening shot is wearing a mask. In *Rolling Thunder Logbook*, Sam Shepard gives a detailed account of the mask-effect:

> Tonight Dylan appears in a rubber Dylan mask that he'd
> picked up on 42nd Street. The crowd is stupefied. A kind
> of panic-stricken hush falls over the place. 'Has he had
> another accident? Plastic surgery?' Or is this some kind of
> mammoth hoax? An impostor! The voice sounds the same.
> If it is a replacement, he's doing a good job. He goes
> through three or four songs with the thing on, then
> reaches for the harmonica. He tries to play it through the
> mask but it won't work, so he rips it off and throws it back
> into the floodlights. There he is in the flesh and blood!
> The real thing! A face-lift supreme! It's a frightening act
> even if it's not calculated for those reasons. The audience
> is totally bewildered and still wondering if this is actually
> him or not (114).

As a dramatist Shepard responds to the theatricality of the gesture and gives a brilliant analysis of the effect it might have on an audience who are being told that they are seeing double. Other accounts, however, describe it not as a Bob Dylan mask but a Richard Nixon mask, and both the film and the photograph in Shepard's book tend to confirm this.

Two other points about the mask are perhaps more important than whether it was really possible to buy a Bob Dylan mask on 42nd Street. The first is the date: this concert was filmed on Halloween, 1975, so the scene in the film deliberately recalls the 1964 Halloween concert at which Dylan made his famous remark about wearing a Bob Dylan mask.[9] So again the character on stage, Renaldo, inherits and wears Bob Dylan's history, and the audience sees double. Secondly, whether of Dylan or Nixon, the mask is *transparent*. It does not really hide the face beneath it. Like the Classical *persona*, the mask not only disguises but also gives expression to the man who wears it. In this sense the mask is, in fact, *Renaldo*. And through Renaldo's transparent mask, the audience sees the face, the other mask, of Bob Dylan.

'Bob Dylan,' however, is a character in the film, played by Ronnie Hawkins. We see him mainly in two contexts: one of mistaken identity and one of seduction. In scenes 11 and 91, a CBC reporter in Toronto naively mistakes Ronnie Hawkins for Bob Dylan, and the Hawk plays the scenes to the hilt. Asked what he thinks of

Bob Dylan, he replies, 'A hero of the highest order,' to which the reporter can only respond, 'Why do you say that about yourself?' A more subtle variation on mistaken identity occurs in scene 21, in which Dylan/Hawkins finds his way barred by a Security Guard played by Mick Ronson in a thick Yorkshire accent. The Guard refuses to believe that Ronnie Hawkins *is* Bob Dylan and tells him, 'I don't know you from Adam.' In these scenes identity becomes a fluid and arbitrary concept more dependent upon other people's recognition than on any intrinsic truth.

'I don't know you from Adam,' says the Guard, 'so off you pop' (21). The colloquial English phrase echoes, as a distant double, the American 'pop' as father, while 'Adam' recalls the first father. In the other scene involving 'Bob Dylan,' the unseen father plays a major role. Scene 12, which begins typically as a shot inside a mirror reflection, depicts 'Bob Dylan' attempting to persuade a young woman to accompany him on the upcoming Rolling Thunder Revue tour. 'You're a lovely young lady,' he tells her. 'We'll do things that kings and queens have never tried.' But she resists him, insisting that 'I have to get my father's approval.'

There are several ways of extrapolating the significance of this scene. One is to follow the appearances of the woman whom 'Bob Dylan' is trying to seduce. The credits refer to her simply as 'The Girlfriend,' and Dylan says that 'she's the one figure of real Truth in the movie.... She's actually the one person in the movie thinking more of Renaldo than of herself' (Ginsberg 24). As such she continually challenges Renaldo. In scene 15 she tells him, 'Looks like every time you look at me, you turn away'—a comment on Renaldo's shifty gaze, which never directly faces the camera.

The Girlfriend is also connected with the film's religious imagery. In scene 17 she spreads her arms in a crucifix and says to Renaldo, 'Stand and bear yourself like the cross and I'll receive you.' This statement is followed by a shot of the crucifix in the Lowell Cemetery (18). The Girlfriend's obedience to her absent father thus may be seen as religious obedience to the Father, in contrast to the woman addressed in 'Oh, Sister': 'Our Father would not like the way that you act' (L 382).

By contrast, the figure of The Father, played by Allen Ginsberg, is fully involved in the sexual scenes in the bordello. Scenes 44 – 46 amount to a full-scale erotic parody of Christian iconography. In scene 44 Mama Frasca (herself a parody of the Mother) is singing a song called 'God and Mama,' which invites the listener: 'Why don't you kneel / Pray Jesus / And you'll cry.' While she sings, Joan Baez is trying on Mama's wedding dress. The white dress prefigures Baez's later appearance as the ghostly Woman in White and, of course, suggests virginity. Scene 45 shows a marble statue of the Virgin Mary (in the same cemetery as the crucifix mentioned above). But scene 46 takes us to the brothel, where The Father (Allen Ginsberg) jovially oversees preparations for the deflowering of the Son (David Mansfield), who wears only a pair of ludicrous angel's wings. Father, Son, and Virgin thus form a parodic trinity (further emphasized, of course, by Ginsberg's publicly avowed homosexuality).

In other scenes the religious imagery is more seriously presented. In scene 94 Ginsberg the Father, instructs Renaldo the Son, by translating for him the Stations of the Cross in the Lowell cemetery. The statues shown in the earlier scenes reappear as Renaldo lights a candle for the Virgin and stands beside the crucifix. The identification of Renaldo/Dylan as a Christ-figure is strongly suggested. At the beginning of the film, in scene 4, Renaldo had responded to the question, 'You running from the law?' by claiming, 'I am the Law.'[10]

This discussion of religious imagery began by looking at the line 'I have to get my father's approval,' spoken by The Girlfriend to the fictional 'Bob Dylan.' I now return to this character and *his* fictional wife, 'Mrs Dylan,' played by Ronee Blakley.[11] In the same way as the lead singer in the concert footage is both Renaldo and Bob Dylan, Ronee Blakley appears on stage both as Mrs Dylan and as herself. In scene 39 she delivers a strong performance of Ronee Blakley's song 'Need a New Sun Rising.' The title evokes not only the rising of the Son (Christ) but also the ending of Dylan's 'Romance in Durango,' in which the dying Ramon tells his doomed lover that 'We may not make it through the night' (L 386). The point of this reference is that Blakley has just appeared as Mrs Dylan in the prior scene with a character called Ramon, whom Dylan describes as the ghost of her dead lover.

This ghostly appearance links the fictional 'Mrs Dylan' to the Sara Dylan for whom Dylan claims he wrote 'Sad-Eyed Lady of the Lowlands.' As I noted in the previous chapter, the title of the song evokes the traditional British ballad, 'The Lowlands of Holland,' in which the ghost of a dead lover appears to a woman. In *Tarantula* the ghost was described as 'more than one person' (T 120). In the film, too, the appearance of a ghost sets up multiple echoes. 'We've all had a lot of friends who died,' says Mrs Dylan to Renaldo in scene 98, and *Renaldo and Clara* is full of their ghosts.[12]

One major theme of the film, for instance, is dead poets. English Romantic poets are evoked through Ginsberg's singing of Blake in scene 30[13] and through references to the graves of Keats and Shelley in scene 84. This scene, in which Ginsberg also recalls leaving a copy of his book *Howl* on Baudelaire's grave, takes place at a writer's grave (Kerouac's) in a cemetery that bears the name of yet another poet (Lowell). Kerouac also bears a double name: the English 'Jack' and the French 'Ti Jean' inscribed on his tomb. At the end of this scene, Renaldo declares his desire to be buried in an unmarked grave, free of names.

Ghosts are also alluded to in the songs, especially in Joan Baez's performance of 'Diamonds and Rust' in scene 71, which begins with the line 'Here comes your ghost again.' The song is widely assumed to have been written about Bob Dylan: a response to what Baez took to be the portrait of her 'ghost-like soul' in 'Sad-Eyed Lady of the Lowlands.' The latter song appears on the soundtrack of *Renaldo and Clara* in scene 104 in ambiguous reference to both Joan Baez and Sara Dylan. It begins as accompaniment to the last exit of The Woman in White (Baez) and continues in the background of a conversation between Renaldo and Clara (during which, incidentally, Renaldo is standing in front of a mirror!).

The Woman in White herself is described as a ghost. When Ginsberg asked about her, Dylan responded by referring to her not as a person but as 'it': 'It's the ghost of Death—Death's ghost. Renaldo rids himself of death when she leaves'; she/it is 'The Supreme Ego, White Death' (18). But there is a further paradox here, for if Death is to have a ghost, then Death itself must be dead. In that sense the Woman in White represents that which survives beyond death, the woman who lives on.[14]

If Dylan's description sounds like a negative role in which to cast Joan Baez, remember that there are several scenes in the movie in which The Woman in White is clearly played by Sara. During the whole sequence in which The Woman in White rides in an open, horse-drawn carriage through snow-covered streets, there is a deliberate confusion of roles. In the first few shots, she is clearly Sara/Clara, but when she arrives at her destination she is Baez.[15] The ghost then, returned from the Lowlands of death, is both Joan Baez and Sara Dylan—as well as Ramon, the lover of 'Mrs Dylan.'

These equivocal references point to the central obsession emerging in the second half of *Renaldo and Clara*: what I have called the 'staging' of Dylan's private life as public spectacle. Casting Joan and Sara in fictional roles provides a certain distancing effect, which enables Dylan to talk openly about the parts these two women have played in his life. If pressed too far he can always retreat into the assertion that they are only fictional characters. But the audience knows (and Dylan knows that the audience knows) that these actresses *are* Joan Baez and Sara Dylan, and the audience inevitably has a certain voyeuristic curiosity in watching them enact in public their private claims on Bob Dylan. *Renaldo and Clara* exploits this voyeurism in much the same way as Hitchcock often relied on the baser instincts of his audience; we should, rightly, feel uncomfortable with our own fascination.

We also may feel uncomfortable with some things that Dylan, as director of the film, does to the women. Several long sequences take place in a 'sporting house' (37), a bordello which Dylan refers to as 'Diamond Hell' (Ginsberg 22). Despite this title it is presented in the rosily idealized manner of cinematic fantasies about whorehouses. The provocatively undressed women displayed for the camera, including Joan Baez and Sara Dylan, are referred to as the 'Sisters of Mercy': an allusion not just to the Leonard Cohen song but also to that song's use on the soundtrack of Robert Altman's *McCabe and Mrs Miller*, which features a similarly romanticized brothel. Both Sara and Joan have commented rather bitterly on the reductiveness of these scenes. 'After all the talk about goddesses,' said Sara, 'we wound up being whores.' Similarly, Baez complained, 'we looked around for these mystical, powerful, life force scenes, we ended up playing a bunch of whores' (both comments cited in Bicker 51).

The women, however, take their revenge in several unscripted, improvised scenes in which they confront Renaldo, and it is to Dylan's credit (as director and editor) that these scenes, in which he generally comes off rather poorly, were retained in the movie. In the first of these scenes, 71, Joan Baez, possibly in character as The Woman in White, confronts Renaldo in a bar. Larry Sloman contends, via an interview with Mel Howard, that Baez had planned this confrontation without Dylan's knowledge: 'there was so much she wanted to say and ask him but ... she was afraid and he was so elusive.... And we talked about the fact that maybe the way to get him pinned was to do it on camera where he wouldn't back down' (300). Howard and Sloman characterize Dylan's response as 'stunned but ... brilliant.... Dylan is funny and turns what could have been maudlin into something really inspired' (301). Describing the same scene, Sam Shepard is only slightly more cautious:

> This is turning into either the worst melodrama on earth
> or the best head-to-head confessional ever put on film.
> Dylan is dancing around, soaked in brandy, doing his best
> to dodge the Baez kidney punches. She just stands there,
> planted, hoisting one-liners at him like cherry bombs.
> Producers are wincing in the background. Musicians are
> tittering. Cameras are doing double time (68).

Well, maybe you had to be there. On film the impact is considerably more muted, partly because the cameras are *not* doing double time: that is, the scene is shown from only one camera viewpoint, focussed on Baez, so Renaldo/Dylan's face is never clear. There is no cutting back and forth to articulate a full interaction between the two characters.

The main question that Baez poses in this scene—'What do you think it would have been like if we'd got married?'—brings the staging of Dylan's private life clearly to the center of the film. It makes sense only in reference to the close relationship Dylan and Baez had shared ten years before, the relationship broken by Dylan's marriage to Sara. Dylan simply evades the question—'I don't know'— and turns it back against her—'I haven't changed much, have you?' Baez has nowhere to go; she gives a sick grin and answers, 'Maybe.' But while she answers, her hands are switching their brandy glasses on the bar. Perhaps Dylan gave his definite answer much later, in the editing process, in which this scene is intercut with Baez singing 'Diamonds and Rust' and is immediately followed by a scene in which Renaldo trades The Woman in White to an escaped convict for a horse.

This confrontation may have been unplanned, but the other major scene between Renaldo, Clara, and The Woman in White is very elaborately set up. It is prepared for by a long series of intercut shots in which The Woman in White, played by both women in turn, drives through a snow-covered city and eventually enters a room where Renaldo and Clara are together. The scenes that follow unite many disparate themes of the movie.

We first see Renaldo and Clara talking to each other in the privacy of their bedroom (87). It is the first time that their names have actually been spoken in the movie, and no sooner are the names mentioned than the possibility of changing them comes up. 'We'll be famous,' says Clara. 'Renaldo and Clara. Maybe I should change my name, huh?' The immediate allusion may be to Robert Zimmerman changing his name in order to become famous, but the comment also points to the whole web of doubled names throughout the movie. Scene 88 cuts back to the brothel, where Baez and Sara appear in their other roles as Sisters of Mercy, but again the fictional stages the biographical when Baez, as if picking up Clara's comment from the previous scene, asks Sara, 'Did you ever have another name? One time I was involved with somebody, I think there is a possibility he was involved with you.'

Scene 89 returns to the bedroom and to the entry of The Woman in White, who looks at Clara and demands of Renaldo, 'Who is she?' I have outlined earlier in this chapter the quick sequence of cuts that follow from this question: Dylan/Renaldo on stage singing 'Sara' (90); Ronee Blakley as 'Mrs Dylan' (91); David Blue saying, 'He's a wife and family, you know what I mean, it's ridiculous' (92); and back to the bedroom (93). In scene 93 the two women openly compete for Renaldo's affection or even attention. Clara offers to take off his vest and scratch his back; The Woman in White writes him love letters. (On the soundtrack Bob Dylan and Joan Baez are singing a duet of 'The Water Is Wide,' a traditional song about the separation of two lovers.) Clara appears to win this round: 'She can't give you what I can give you, Renaldo,' she says, and The Woman in White departs, announcing that she is going to Honduras. As she leaves, Clara fires a sweetly innocent parting shot: 'Are you sure you've got the right room?'

But in scene 95 The Woman in White returns, and now the two women begin to join forces against Renaldo, if only to force his decision. 'I can't share any longer,' The Woman in White declares. Trying to pacify her, Renaldo finds himself quoting Bob Dylan: 'Now, wait a minute, no reason to get excited' might be followed by 'the thief, he kindly spoke' (L 252). 'You have to tell me something,' says The Woman in White, and Clara modifies this to 'You have to tell us *both* something.' Renaldo promises to tell the truth, and The Woman in White asks, 'Do you love her?' Pinned, Renaldo gives an answer that is either simply evasion or the closest thing to 'the truth' that Renaldo or Bob could ever come up with: 'Do I love her like I love you? No. Do I love you like I love her? No.'

113

After a brief cutaway to the band on stage, the sequence resumes in scene 97 with Clara and The Woman in White comparing notes. 'He never gives straight answers,' says Clara, accurately enough. 'Evasiveness is all in the mind,' protests Renaldo. 'Truth is on many levels.' To which both women reply in unison, 'Horseshit.' 'Has he always been like that?' Clara asks, and The Woman in White replies, 'For the ten years I've known him.' 'Has he ever given you a straight answer?' 'Not to my recollection.' The dynamics of the scene have now shifted completely. The two women are no longer in competition with each other but have joined in a tacit exclusion of Renaldo. Trying to get back in, Renaldo declares, 'I'm a brother to you both'—thus recalling the song 'Oh, Sister' and its invocation of patriarchal authority. But Clara defuses the threat by remarking simply, 'Then we'll be a family.'

Again the mood of the scene changes. It is as if the players, juggling their private and fictional worlds, are trying out various modes and resolutions. After a few interpolated scenes, scene 102 returns to the bedroom, where Clara poses the same question to The Woman in White: 'Are you in love with him?' Her answer seems direct enough—'Yes, I was in love with him'—but the past tense makes it just as evasive as Renaldo's. Clara now returns to the offensive: 'She's cold, Renaldo, you don't want a cold woman.' She mocks The Woman in White for being a virgin. But one of the interpolated scenes (99) had shown Sara Dylan, playing a Sister of Mercy, telling Allen Ginsberg, 'You all want the virgin.'

At the end of scene 102, The Woman in White finally leaves, and Renaldo and Clara embrace. Scene 103 cuts to Dylan and Baez on stage singing 'Never Let Me Go,' an obviously ironic title. The newspaper photograph of this duet leads back to scene 104, in which Clara repeats her statement, 'She's cold, Renaldo ... she's probably barren.' 'You don't even know her,' Renaldo protests; but Clara answers, 'I know her. We're like sisters.' Thus the evocation of 'Oh, Sister' is repeated, this time by Clara, to a very different purpose than Renaldo's previous evocation. The shot of The Woman in White leaving the house is then accompanied on the soundtrack by the beginning of 'Sad-Eyed Lady of the Lowlands.'

By the end of the sequence, then, the status quo has been restored: Renaldo is again with Clara, and The Woman in White (Death's ghost) has been banished. Renaldo has won the whole confrontation, and he has done so by doing nothing. As John Herdman comments:

> Renaldo ... controls situations through his very passivity.
> He seems to be played upon, tugged emotionally from
> Sara by the Woman in White ... and then tugged, physi-
> cally, back again; he appears like a little child, smothered
> and overwhelmed by the attentions of his rival lovers, yet
> in the end it is they who are manipulated by him, who ask
> him questions which he will not answer, who seek from
> him what he withholds. Clara may have his body, but nei-
> ther of them has his soul (141).

There is no resolution to this sequence, nor obviously can there be any conventional closure to a film as diffuse and wide-ranging as *Renaldo and Clara*. The
staging of Bob Dylan's private life as public psychodrama is only one aspect of the
film, albeit the most important one, but in this analysis I have scarcely touched on
the political aspects of *Renaldo and Clara*, such as its concern for the American
Indian, the campaign for Hurricane Carter, or the evocation of the Puritan history
of New England.

Closure, in the conventional sense, requires a more traditional structure,
with a central character to hold the film together. Renaldo, however, is too vague
and undefined as a fictional character to achieve this. 'Renaldo is everybody,'
Dylan told Ginsberg. 'Don't you identify with Renaldo?' (11). But it is hard to
identify with 'everybody.' What *does* hold the film together is not Renaldo but Bob
Dylan, not the actor but the singer. Dylan's music, recorded in the intense and
passionate performances of the Rolling Thunder Revue, continually grounds
Renaldo and Clara in emotional reality. That reality is both *inside* the movie (in the
songs we see on stage) and *outside* it (in the songs' independent existence). So
Renaldo and Clara cannot have a center in the traditional manner. Any center is
immediately split and doubled, and consigned to the play of doubles that forms the
texture of the movie. The center is both inside the film and outside it; it is both
Renaldo and Bob, I and I.

CHAPTER SEVEN
SHOUTING GOD'S NAME

When, in the autumn of 1979, Bob Dylan announced his conversion to born-again Christianity and released *Slow Train Coming*, reactions varied from shocked disbelief to perverse delight that Dylan had again succeeded in doing the utterly unexpected. The move caused an instant reevaluation of his previous work, and the religious elements that run throughout his songs acquired new prominence and relevance. What was surprising was not so much the commitment to a religious world view as the rigid, dogmatically based form in which that view had been adopted. Almost immediately followers of Dylan began to question how long he could be content within the bounds not just of his new faith but of the rhetoric that it employed and enforced.

Certainly, that rhetoric was the most distressing feature of the religious albums. While Dylan was able to adopt the conventions of Gospel *music* and shape them into an idiom that remained recognizably his own, he was less successful at manipulating the words, verbal formulas, and clichés of fundamentalism. The results show in some very slack writing: compare, for instance, the brilliance of his juxtaposition of 'Lincoln County Road or Armageddon' (L 420) in 'Señor,' just a few years earlier, with the lame and predictable 'Are you ready for Armageddon?' (L 450) on *Saved*. Or take a line like 'He unleashed His power at an unknown hour that no one knew' (L 437), where the last phrase is a redundant repetition and there only to fill out the rhyme. Or consider the tortured, clumsy syntax of the chorus to 'Covenant Woman':

> I just got to thank you
> Once again
> For making your prayers known
> Unto heaven for me

And to you, always, so grateful

I will forever be (L 444).

Dylan has always been capable of letting the occasional weak or awkward phrase slip by: he has never been a perfectionist in his lyrics. But in these three albums, the proportion of poor writing is so great that it can only be attributed to the constraints that Dylan evidently felt, the constraints of a religious orthodoxy with a strongly formative rhetorical code. For the first time in his career, Dylan seemed prepared to accept, without questioning, not just an established view of the world but also the verbal forms in which that view had to be expressed.

One of the most striking aspects of *Slow Train Coming* was its return to the themes of social critique so prominent in his work in the early 1960s. At that time, the conventions of folk music provided Dylan with a recognizable stance from which such criticism could be made: the stance of the 'protest singer,' in the tradition of Woody Guthrie and Pete Seeger, rooted in the Labor movement and continuing in the Civil Rights and Anti-War movements of the 1960s. That tradition leant moral authority to Dylan's early songs. The songs did not represent merely the dissatisfaction of an isolated individual; they were based on a cohesive social and political movement. When Dylan stepped away from what he rightly saw as the coercive demands of folk-protest purity, he moved to a different political and moral stance, which was individualistic to the point of anarchism.[1] Songs such as 'Desolation Row' seek their moral authority not in any communal vision but in the uniqueness of the writer's perceptions. Their moral guarantee is found at the limit of the singer's nerve, and nerves. With *Slow Train Coming*, Dylan returned to a communally based position, one considerably older than the protest-singer's but not entirely dissimilar to it: the prophet's.

The songs on *Slow Train Coming* offer acerbic comment and satirical criticism of rock 'n' roll stars and scientists, Karl Marx and Henry Kissinger, 'Adulterers in churches and pornography in the schools,' American dependence on 'foreign oil' and 'Counterfeit philosophies,' 'woman haters' and 'Spiritual advisors,' 'grain elevators ... bursting' in the midst of starvation, 'unrighteous doctors dealing drugs,' and all those who 'talk about a life of brotherly love' without knowing 'how to live it' (L 423, 431, 432, 436). These topics are generally consistent with the kinds of social positions and causes that Dylan had previously championed. But their association with the language of born-again Christianity gave them, in

the American context, a more right wing inflection than many of Dylan's old sup-
porters were entirely comfortable with. There is, especially in 'Slow Train,' an
unpleasant element of jingoism or even racism (see the reference to the 'Sheiks'
with their 'nose rings' (L 436)). But Dylan was usually able to avoid the more
obnoxious excesses of right wing fundamentalist Christianity.[2] His position might
more accurately be described as populist than reactionary.

These topics are also fairly *general* targets, and their generality shields them
from much potential dispute. (We might all agree that pornography should not be
taught in schools; the difficulty arises when we try to specify which particular texts
are pornographic.) The religious albums offer no individual portraits or case histories as vivid or compelling as 'Ballad of Hollis Brown' or 'The Lonesome Death
of Hattie Carroll.' Rather, they use the generalized rhetoric of 'Blowin' in the
Wind' or 'The Times They Are A-Changin'.'

Generality is characteristic of the prophetic stance. Although the prophet
may preach against particular kings or sinners, he appeals always to universal principles. He attacks not so much the individual as the type; the moral concern is
always a *public* one. This point is illustrated by 'Political World,' the opening song
on *Oh Mercy*. When CBS planned to release a video of the song featuring photographs of political leaders, Dylan protested that despite its title, it wasn't 'political' at all. And he is right, insofar as 'political' refers to party politics or to specific
social problems with practical solutions. 'Political World' is not concerned with
Democrats against Republicans or with fiscal policy and subsidized housing; it
deals in abstract terms with a world where 'Wisdom is thrown into jail' and 'peace
is not welcome at all' (OM). Like 'Blowin' in the Wind,' it offers no solutions and
no political program for working toward solutions. Its stance is prophetic: a generalized moral criticism that encompasses the political but is based on religious
principles. The listener need not share these principles to agree with the criti-
cisms, but it is still the implied religious position that gives the prophetic stance its
resonance and authority.

Precisely because it appeals to the authority of religious truth, the prophetic
stance must also be deeply concerned about false prophets. One common target of
the religious songs is the 'preacher with … spiritual pride' (L 423). 'Man of Peace'
warns that Satan in disguise 'Could be the Führer / Could be the local priest' (L
482). Dylan echoes here his earlier distrust of 'corpse evangelists'—a phrase that

occurs in the same song as his self-criticism: 'Fearing not that I'd become my enemy / In the instant that I preach' (L 139). The irony is that the Dylan of *Slow Train Coming* is preaching: he may at times be preaching against preachers, but he is preaching.

The dogmatism of this preaching is most evident in the absolute judgments that it delivers: 'Ya either got faith or ya got unbelief and there ain't no neutral ground' (L 426). This is a world governed by absolute moral imperatives: 'You're gonna *have* to serve somebody, / Well, it may be the devil or it may be the Lord / But you're gonna *have* to serve somebody' (L 423, my emphasis). The choice is a clear-cut binary opposition in which the opposed terms, Lord and devil, are pre-defined. So it is no choice at all. 'Gotta Serve Somebody' may appear to be a disturbing song, challenging its listeners to examine and renew their beliefs and commitments, but at another level it does not challenge at all. It offers the security of a moral world in which decisions have already been made for you.

This absoluteness also derives from the context of Apocalypse. Moral judgments are absolute because they are all potentially the Last Judgment:

> Well, your clock is gonna stop
> At Saint Peter's gate.
> Ya gonna ask him what time it is,
> He's gonna say, 'It's too late' (L 39).

These lines come from a very early song ('I'd Hate To Be You on That Dreadful Day,' written in 1962), and they indicate the pervasiveness of the Apocalypse theme in Dylan's work. His songs are full of visions of the end of the world, from 'A Hard Rain's A-Gonna Fall' (also 1962) to 'When the Night Comes Falling from the Sky' (1984) and 'Shooting Star' (1989):

> It's the last temptation, the last account,
> Last time you might hear the Sermon on the Mount,
> Last radio's playin'... (OM).

In the 1960s this urgency could be attributed to the Apocalypse that could be immediately envisioned in the secular form of nuclear war. While clearly obsessed with this prospect, Dylan responded in a positive fashion, refusing to accept its inevitability passively. In 'Let Me Die in My Footsteps,' he rejects the fall-out shelter—'I will not carry myself down to die'—and somehow transforms the song into a celebration of 'every state in this union' (L 21-22). Similarly, the singer in 'Hard Rain' is not silenced by imminent destruction but proclaims his resolve to 'stand on the ocean until I start sinkin'' (L 60). In 'Talkin' World War III Blues,' Dylan even exorcises the spectre of nuclear war with cheerful black comedy.

Not all the Apocalyptic songs are secular, however. Both 'I'd Hate To Be You on That Dreadful Day' and 'Quit Your Low Down Ways' envisage the Last Judgment in Gospel song terms, while 'When the Ship Comes In' celebrates a vengeful Apocalypse in specifically Biblical imagery:

> And like Pharaoh's tribe,
>
> They'll be drownded in the tide,
>
> And like Goliath, they'll be conquered (L 101).

Street Legal, the last of the 'pre-Christian' albums, also contains many premonitions of Apocalypse: 'Changing of the Guards' proclaims that 'Eden is burning' (L 404) while 'Señor' extends its narrative from history to eternity, 'from Lincoln County Road to Armageddon' (L 410).

In *Slow Train Coming*, however, Apocalypse takes the center stage of Dylan's imagination. The title itself is a powerfully suggestive image of a doom that is both inevitable and unpredictable. But Apocalypse is not to be feared. As in the songs of the 1960s, the album challenges listeners to declare their allegiance (to the devil or the Lord) and take action: 'When you gonna wake up and strengthen the things that remain?' (L 432).[3] The singer and his 'precious angel' are called 'to the judgment hall of Christ' (L 426), and the record closes by triumphantly anticipating the time 'When He Returns' (L 439). One could see these songs as fulfilling the moral imperative of 'Hard Rain': the singer should bear witness in the final days and know his song well before he starts singing.

Absolutism of judgment, however, has a less positive side. There is often an unpleasant sense that Dylan is gloating over the fall and punishment of the unbelievers. The singer who proclaims 'I'd hate to be you on that dreadful day' must be self-righteously sure of where he will stand, and the song seems to take an almost sadistic delight in the other's doom. Vengefulness is again evident in *Slow Train Coming*, especially in lines like the horrific 'Can they imagine the darkness that will fall from on high / When men will beg God to kill them and they won't be able to die?' (L 426). As Aidan Day comments, 'the blackest feature of the imagining here is that it attributes to the highest light a power of the abysmal

dark' (107). There is great relish in this black imagining: listen to how in performance Dylan emphasizes the word 'able.' Several critics of Dylan's religious
albums have pointed out that their theology is notably lacking in Christian compassion and forgiveness.[4] The unregenerate are consigned to hell with gleeful
abandon.

The album's *pronouns*, however, are worth noting. As always, Dylan's use of
them is shifting and unstable in reference, with his use of 'you' especially problematic. The most unambiguous denunciations occur in the third person, referring to generalized classes of sinners or unbelievers: 'gangsters in power,' 'Masters
of the bluff and masters of the proposition' (L 432, 436). The use of 'you' is much
more various.

It is striking, for instance, how *seldom* the 'you' addresses God directly. Only
'I Believe in You' and 'What Can I Do for You?' maintain a dialogue with the
divinity for the whole song. It is as if Dylan feels too humble or unworthy to talk
to God directly; the songs never adopt the mode of prayer. Even 'I Believe in You'
is ambiguous, since much of it uses the language that might be addressed to a
lover—and the 'you' in 'Precious Angel,' 'Covenant Woman,' and 'In the Summertime' clearly refers to a woman whom Dylan regards as his spiritual guide.

The 'you' also may designate the targets of the preacher's denunciation, the
unregenerate others. Often, however, closer examination suggests that this 'you'
also refers to Dylan himself. Here again is the familiar theme of this book: I is
another, the mask of the divided self. When Dylan sings 'take off your mask' (L
437), he clearly addresses himself, attempting to present himself in a unified form,
without disguise, before the throne of Judgment. But the internal division continues and is as evident in these songs as it is anywhere else.

This point has been most strongly argued by Aidan Day, who contends that
the religious songs reflect a split 'within the lyric-speaker's own identity. Time and
again it is a conviction of his own depravity which traumatizes the speaker of these
lyrics' (99-100). This interpretation is most plausible in songs in which the 'you'
conflicts with an 'I': that is, when the speaker is still struggling with those aspects
of himself that cling to the old ways and are reluctant to accept the submission of
the new faith. The old ways are often those of riches and fame, 'The glamour and
the bright lights and the politics of sin' (L 459). The song from which this line is
taken—'Dead Man, Dead Man'—is a particularly good example. The 'you' is not

only a generalized sinner ('Uttering idle words from a reprobate mind') but also, more immediately, someone who has power over the 'I,' someone who *can* 'take me down to hell.' This 'you' is thus interchangeable with the 'I'—'The ghetto that you build for me is the one you end up in'—or more accurately with the I's dark, unregenerate side. This self-identification is further suggested by the chorus: the phrase 'Dead man,' with the accent always on the first word, distantly echoes the name 'Dylan,' and the last line provides again the central pun of identity: 'Dust upon your eyes' / your I's.

The question of the chorus, 'When will you arise?', thus becomes urgent and self-directed: 'Do you have any faith at all? Do you have any love to share?' Aidan Day argues that the song reflects 'a certainty of alienation from grace that is … close to despair,' and that the chorus's questions are 'weighted in favor of the darkest answer' (101). But the very fact that the questions continue to be asked with such urgency implies that they are still open.

Another interesting use of split pronoun reference occurs in 'Property of Jesus.' The dramatic situation of a Christian being mocked by nonbelievers is one that Dylan frequently identifies as his own. But here the protagonist is presented in the third person as 'he': 'He's the property of Jesus / Resent him to the bone' (L 456). His antagonists are presented as 'you,' but the singer is able to move imaginatively inside 'your' viewpoint: 'Stop your conversation when he passes on the street, / Hope he falls upon himself, oh, won't that be sweet.' Dylan's identification in this song is thus split between the 'he' and the 'you,' both of whom project possible positions for the unspoken 'I.'

Another ambiguous use of 'you' occurs in 'Gonna Change My Way of Thinking':

> Stripes on your shoulders,
> Stripes on your back and on your hands,
> Swords piercing your side,
> Blood and water flowing through the land (L 428).

John Hinchey sees in these lines 'the particular combination of diffidence and evasiveness of an "I" disguised as a "you"' (32). This interpretation, which I find possible but by no means definite, assumes that such sufferings are the singer's. In Biblical terms, the piercing of the side out of which blood and water flow refers to the passion of Christ (John 19:34). The redemptive quality of the suffering comes from Jesus, but if the 'you' were to be understood as self-directed, then the singer takes that redemptive quality on himself.

This would not be the only time that Dylan, even before his born-again incarnation, has hinted at his identification with Jesus. (As Robert *Zimmerman*, after all, he was already a carpenter and the son of a carpenter.) Michael Gray writes:

> From *Blood on the Tracks* onwards, we are given parallel after parallel between Dylan and Christ: both charismatic leaders, both message-bringers to their people, both martyrs because both *get betrayed*. In retrospect, it is as if Dylan eventually converts to Christianity because of the way he has identified with Christ and understood His struggles through his own (202).

The Christ with whom Dylan most often identifies is the suffering Christ: Christ on the cross, Christ 'in the garden' of Gethsemane (L448). (Of all the religious songs, 'In the Garden' is the one he has most often performed in concert.) There are no Dylan Christmas songs, and references to healing and miracles are scarce. Dylan's Christ is overwhelmingly the dying and the resurrected Lord.

In the previous chapter, I referred to the Crucifixion images in *Renaldo and Clara*: to such scenes as Ginsberg's translation of the Stations of the Cross, the girlfriend's admonition, 'Stand and bear yourself like the cross and I'll receive you,' and the repeated shots of the Crucifix in Lowell Cemetery.[5] The Crucifixion is also directly evoked in such songs as 'Sign on the Cross' (1967) and 'Shelter from the Storm' (1974). In the latter Dylan presents himself as a sacrificial victim who wears a 'crown of thorns' and says, 'In a little hilltop village, they bargained for my clothes' (L 360-61).

In passages like this it seems that Dylan is appropriating Christ's image in much the same way as he did those of Lenny Bruce or Blind Willie McTell. Jesus is another mask of the self, or mask of the other, one of many possible models for Dylan's continuously shifting sense of his identity. Before 1979 this was primarily an aesthetic gesture, a way of incorporating a complex and culturally overdetermined reference (Christ) into the play of masks and mirrors that made up Dylan's multiple 'self-portraits.' After 1979 the gesture of identification could not be made in such explicit terms, since it would be, for a true believer, blasphemous. With the possible exception of the lines from 'Gonna Change My Way of Thinking,' Dylan in the religious albums never directly refers to himself as Christ—but the shadow of Christ's image hangs over them, and there is always this potential identification to be made.

It is not until *Oh Mercy* that Dylan again presents a direct allusion to himself as Christ, and when it occurs the allusion is as much to Judas as it is to Jesus. These two characters are so closely linked in Dylan's imagination that they seem like twins, each other's mirrors or ghosts: I and I. When the 1966 heckler yelled 'Judas!' at a Dylan whom he had presumably seen previously as Jesus, he showed how easy it is for the two figures to be conflated in the one person.

Judas and Jesus appear together in 'Masters of War' and also in 'With God on Our Side,' which notes that 'Jesus Christ / Was betrayed by a kiss' and poses the question of 'Whether Judas Iscariot / Had God on his side' (L 93). This is a difficult theological point. In some sense Judas *is* carrying out God's will by making the Crucifixion possible. Many modern presentations of Judas, such as Martin Scorsese's controversial film *The Last Temptation of Christ*, see him not as pure evil but as an idealist trying to force Jesus' hand, to make him declare his divinity.

The identification of the two figures finds literal expression in the oath 'Judas Priest,' which is in origin a euphemism for 'Jesus Christ.'[6] In Dylan's 'Ballad of Frankie Lee and Judas Priest' (L 252-4), the two characters intricately implicate each other. Some commentators have suggested that Frankie Lee, since he clearly opposes Judas, should be seen as a Christ-figure. The grounds for this identification are slight: an ambiguous reference to Frankie's 'deceased' father (God is dead?) and his dying 'of thirst' (echoing Christ's words on the cross). Frankie Lee would be a very secular Christ: he borrows money, he confesses to 'foolish pride,' he is a gambler, he 'soon [loses] all control,' he dies raving, and there is no suggestion of salvation or resurrection. Conversely, several of Judas Priest's actions *are* Christ-like: he lends money generously, he lives in Paradise, and he holds his dying friend in his arms. The reversal is not complete, however. Frankie Lee is still innocent, and Judas and the house he inhabits are still very sinister. The song's only conclusion is that 'Nothing is revealed,' so the two characters' links to each other remain as mysterious as they are profound. Like Pat Garrett and Billy the Kid, 'they were the best of friends,' and Judas Priest carries in the euphemistic echo of his name the ghostly alias of Jesus Christ.

Judas reappears on *Oh Mercy* in 'What Was It You Wanted?' In this song the speaker is the object of multiple and unreasonable demands from an unspecified 'you,' who may be a fan, a lover, God, or, of course, Dylan addressing himself. But at one point the 'you' is unmistakably Judas: 'What was it you wanted / When you were kissing my cheek?' (OM). We are again in Gethsemane. This is the same kiss (Matthew 26:48-49) with which Judas betrayed Christ in 'With God on Our Side'; the watchers in the shadows are the waiting soldiers whom Peter attacks in 'In the Garden.' And Dylan, the recipient of the kiss, is Christ.

'What Was It You Wanted?' is followed immediately by 'Shooting Star,' with its reference to 'the last temptation,' which may be a reference to Scorsese's film of Kazantzakis' novel *The Last Temptation of Christ*. The film would have been of interest to Dylan not only in its emphasis on the Crucifixion but also in its dramatic focus on the relationship between Jesus and Judas. At one point Judas angrily demands of Christ, 'What good are you?' Again, *Oh Mercy* has a direct echo: in 'What Good Am I?' Dylan presents a searching self-examination of his effectiveness as a Christian. But if the title phrase is indeed a direct quotation from the film, then the song is not so humble, for it again casts Dylan in the role of the Saviour.

Between 'What Good Am I?' and 'What Was It You Wanted?' the perhaps timely warning of 'Disease of Conceit' intervenes. The split within the self is here clearly identified and denounced: 'seein' double' is a symptom of the disease, one which 'Gives you delusions of grandeur, and an evil eye' (OM). If identifying with Christ is a delusion of grandeur, then the evil eye/I again evokes Christ's doubled counterpart, Judas, who waits with his kiss in the following song.

Thus the general themes of Dylan's religious work lead into one other. His prophetic social critiques lead to the absolute judgments of Apocalypse; judgment of others leads to judgment of the self and the self-directed 'you' of some lyrics; and the 'you' in turn takes on the characteristics of both Jesus Christ and his linguistic shadow, Judas Priest. Far from being a monolithic mass of dogmatic certainties, the songs reveal much ambiguity, internal division, and complexity. Nevertheless, it is true that *Slow Train Coming* and especially *Saved* are inhibited by the clichés of a rhetoric that is fundamentally opposed to ambiguity, division, and complexity. Some fascinating songs occur at the end of this period, however, as Dylan begins to reintroduce a more symbolic or even surrealist vocabulary.

In 'Every Grain of Sand,' for instance, there is still a strong reliance on divine power and mercy, but that providential presence figures less in images of a conventional God than in a generalized, almost pantheistic vision. The mood is even reminiscent of 'Lay Down Your Weary Tune': the singer is aware of 'every leaf that trembles ... every sparrow falling ... every grain of sand' (L 462). The Biblical source (Matthew 10:29-31) stresses God's presence—a sparrow 'shall not fall on the ground without your Father'—but the song's context is more secular—'I am hanging in the balance of the reality of man.'

These images point to a universal sense of unity, in which even the scattered grains of sand are gathered up in the singular act of counting. By contrast, the protagonist of the song, whose sense of his sinfulness excludes him from this unity, is presented in images of fracturing and internal division. The singer is separated not only from the divine unity but also from himself. In the first stanza he hears 'a dyin' voice inside me,' and in the second he compares himself to Cain, his brother's murderer. He seeks for a 'mirror of innocence on each ... face.' The mirror would declare his wholeness and self-knowledge, but this insight would have to come not from within himself but from his reflection in the face of the other. These doubled images are themselves divided: the mirror is 'broken' and each face is 'forgotten.' Another traditional image of self-possession, the proper name, also comes from outside him, and its site is the 'doorway of temptation.' In the last stanza he says, 'I hear the ancient footsteps like the motion of the sea / Sometimes I turn, there's someone there, other times it's only me.' Like the 'shadow' in 'Mr Tambourine Man,' this 'someone' is and is not the singer himself. It is the doubled projection of his self-division (the Abel to his Cain or Jesus to his Judas), which separates him from the innocent self-possession that exists 'In every leaf that trembles, in every grain of sand' and leaves him, uncertain and sinful, 'hanging in the balance.'

'Every Grain of Sand' uses looser, more imagistic language than most of the other religious songs, but it remains quite comprehensible. The same cannot be said for the extraordinary trio of songs recorded for *Shot of Love* but not included on the released album: 'Angelina,' 'The Groom's Still Waiting at the Altar,' and 'Caribbean Wind.'[7] Here the language becomes frankly surrealistic, and none of the three songs has any clearly demarcated line of argument or narrative. Characters and pronouns come and go with bewildering nonspecificity, and they move in a landscape of unexplained symbols and bizarre juxtapositions. Nevertheless, the concerns are still clearly religious; it is as if Dylan had transported his new ideas back into the landscape of 'Desolation Row.' The three songs are closely linked, so it may be useful to point to the elements they share.

First, all three songs are set in an atmosphere of violence, which mixes contemporary political references (especially to Central and South America) with the language of Apocalypse. 'Angelina' contains a remarkable couplet: 'Tell me, tall men, where would you like to be overthrown / In Jerusalem or Argentina?' While 'Argentina' might be simply a convenient rhyme for 'Angelina,' the geographical-political reference recurs in 'The Groom's Still Waiting at the Altar' as part of an even more remarkable rhyme: 'What can I say about Claudette? Ain't seen her since January, / She could be respectably married or running a whorehouse in Buenos Aires' (L 464). South America is obliquely evoked in another song of this period, 'Trouble,' whose reference to 'stadiums of the damned' (L 461) recalls the murderous events of Salvador Allende's overthrow in Chile. The reference to 'killing nuns and soldiers ... fighting on the border' (L 464) points to the death of American nuns in El Salvador in 1980. 'Caribbean Wind' is more general in its pictures of violence—'famines and earthquakes and train wrecks and the tearin' down of the walls' (L 466)—but its title returns us to the Central American region and to the 'Tales of Yankee Power' Dylan had previously attacked on *Street Legal*.

In the released version the wind is strictly Caribbean, blowing between Nassau and Mexico. In the earlier concert version, it also 'blows hard from the Valley Coast to my back yard' and 'howls from Tokyo to the British Isles.' Specific areas of political tension, like Central America, are broadened out to the universal violence of the Apocalypse. The geographical setting of 'The Groom's Still Waiting at the Altar,' 'West of the Jordan, East of the Rock of Gibraltar,' is the traditional site of the final battles of Armageddon, which are witnessed by the singer in 'Angelina': 'I see pieces of men marching, trying to take heaven by force, / I can see the unknown rider, I can see the pale white horse.'[8] 'Caribbean Wind' warns that all things are being brought 'nearer to the fire.' The end of history is prophesied in 'The Groom's Still Waiting at the Altar': 'I see the turning of the page, / Curtain risin' on a new age.'

But although the end is announced, it is also delayed. Apocalypse is at hand but not yet here; the groom is at the altar but still waiting. Almost ten years later, in the greatest line from *Oh Mercy*, Dylan announced that the wait would be extended further: 'time is running backwards, and so is the Bride' ('Ring Them Bells,' OM). References to the groom and the bride are based on the Song of Solomon, which is alluded to in the opening lines of 'Caribbean Wind'—lines that also contrive to unite Rome and Jerusalem, Milton and Dante, with a virtuosity of intertextual reference that Dylan had not shown since 'Desolation Row':

> She was the rose of Sharon from paradise lost
> From the city of seven hills near the place of the cross.
> I was playing a show in Miami in the theater of divine comedy (L 466).

The Rose of Sharon appears in the Song of Solomon (2:1), which has been the subject of a long tradition of allegorical interpretation as an account of 'the "mystical union" between Bridegroom and bride, between Christ and the soul' (Pelikan 128). This union culminates in the celebration after the defeat of Satan: 'Let us be glad and rejoice ... for the marriage of the Lamb is come, and his wife hath made herself ready' (Revelation 19:7). If, however, the Groom is still waiting at the altar, then the final battle of Armageddon has not yet been won; and if time and the bride are running *backwards*, then we are moving catastrophically further away from victory.

Traditional Christians have always recognized that this interpretation presents the 'danger' of 'eroticism': 'The Song is after all still a love poem and a very explicit love poem at that, even if one reads it as an allegory; and the allegory can easily revert to the very eroticism it is intended to transcend' (Pelikan 130). But Dylan seems unconcerned about such danger: all three songs openly court the erotic. Each centers on a particular woman, though the shifting of names and pronouns keeps her identity indeterminate. The violence of the songs' political landscape extends into their view of sexual relations: 'Angelina' evokes 'the combat zone' not only in the military sense but also in reference to the notorious red-light district of Boston. The combat zone is dominated by the 'furnace of desire,' whose flames are fanned by the Caribbean winds. Just as the 'ships of liberty' must remain 'distant,' so this desire must remain unfulfilled. Lovers are always at cross-purposes: 'Don't know what I can say about Claudette that wouldn't come back to haunt me, / Finally had to give her up 'bout the time she began to want me.' Claudette may end up as a bride or a whore: the singer has no way of knowing her, and his futile words are like the ghosts of their relationship.

This composite but unknowable woman, like the woman in 'Precious Angel,' is a religious messenger, who 'Told about Jesus, told about the rain,' but she also unites this evangelical mission with the political one: 'She told me about the jungle where her brothers were slain.' The songs are full of messengers, both good and evil. In 'Caribbean Wind,' 'Every new messenger brings evil report' while the singer in 'The Groom's Still Waiting at the Altar' 'Got the message this morning, the one that was sent to me.' The noun 'angel' means 'messenger,' so this motif links 'Precious Angel' to the longing expressed in the name's repetition in the chorus: 'Angelina—Oh, Angelina—.'9

The shifting images of the women in the songs are matched by a familiar indeterminacy in the identity of the singer. 'Angelina' presents him as characteristically divided within himself ('My right hand drawing back while my left hand advances') or possibly divided among several separate characters ('Your best friend and my worst enemy is one and the same'—that is, me). The most drastic internal split comes in the concert version of 'Caribbean Wind':

Stars in my balcony, buzz in my head, slayin' Bob Dylan in my bed,
Street band playin' 'Nearer My God to Thee.'

Here the singer, Bob Dylan, witnesses his death and hears the hymn played at his funeral. The hymn's title is echoed in the chorus, 'Bringing everything that's near to me nearer to the fire.' Near to *me*, then, is also nearer to *Thee*, suggesting again the implicit identification of Dylan with Christ. The fire is the fire of Hell, 'the flames in the furnace of desire,' but also perhaps the refining and purifying fire of God's love. 'In God's truth,' Dylan promises the woman in 'Angelina,' 'tell me what you want and you'll have it of course.' The satisfaction of desire is possible then, but only when the request is made 'In God's truth.'

Having said so much, however, I admit that a great deal in these three songs still resists interpretation. What is one to make of the allusion to Ezekiel in 'Pass the tree of smoke, pass the angel with four faces'? These visions are never resolved into the possibility of communication. Perhaps this sense of noncommunication led Dylan to see these songs as incomplete and thus to withhold their release. But the strength of his vocal performance provides even the most incomprehensible lines of 'Angelina' with an emotional intensity that does, in a broader sense, 'communicate' to the listener. Certainly these three songs, for all their problems, are among the most fascinating he has written.

The reintroduction of a symbolic vocabulary in the *Shot of Love* outtakes paved the way for the more controlled use of imagery on *Infidels*, especially in 'Jokerman' and 'I and I.' 'Jokerman' is very much in the mold of 'Angelina' or 'Caribbean Wind,' a series of surrealistic flashes that can only be reconciled around the central figure of the Jokerman with a good deal of difficulty and ambiguity.[10] The song shows to its best advantage in the video, where the quick cutting of visual images from a wide variety of paintings and photographs corresponds admirably to the collage method of the lyrics.

'I and I' is a more complex song, which may stand as the summation and climax of this period of Dylan's work. The song has a double focus, enunciated by its title and its chorus. In the secular context, 'I and I' is the definitive image of what I have called 'the mask of the divided self': the double, ghost, alias, or shadow that always intervenes in the supposedly unified human subject. In the theological context, the chorus speaks, as we shall see, of the unspeakable Name of God.

The song begins with an intimate confession: 'Been so long since a strange woman has slept in my bed' (L 480). The woman is immediately idealized and thus, rather like the sad-eyed lady, denied the individuality in human frailty that the first line claims for Dylan himself: 'In another lifetime she must have owned the world, or been faithfully wed / To some righteous king who wrote psalms beside moonlit streams.' The Biblical allusions suggest both David, composer of the Psalms, and Solomon, author of the Song of the Bridegroom and the Bride.[11] Dylan would then be associated with these two divinely inspired singers. But the song also disclaims this identification. The singer is not, after all, 'faithfully wed' to this strange woman, and in the second verse he tries to avoid her rather than face the challenge she might pose by waking up and wanting him to talk. He says he has nothing to say: a disclaimer that goes all the way back to 'I know I ain't no prophet / An' I ain't no prophet's son' (L 27). The paradox of anti-art persists, however, for the whole song indicates by its very existence that he does have something to say.

The third stanza invokes 'the worthy,' who can 'divide the word of truth.' This phrase comes from Paul's Second Epistle to Timothy, 2:15, which the King James Version gives as 'rightly dividing the word of truth.' The *New English Bible* gives a simpler translation, 'be straightforward in your proclamation of the truth,' but the older wording is intriguing in its suggestion that truth *can* be divided and that the Word of God is *not* indivisible. The idea of division is certainly central to the song. In the next line Dylan tells how he has learned 'to see an eye for an eye and a tooth for a tooth.' His phrasing again plays variations on the commonly accepted sense. Instead of demanding punishment by *taking* an eye for an eye, 'to see an eye for an eye' means accepting the other for what or who it is. And, especially in the context of the chorus, the pun is unavoidable: 'to see an I for an I.'

The fourth stanza provides a wonderful imagistic vignette of two men in a railway station 'waiting for spring to come, smoking down the track.' Note how 'smoking' could apply grammatically either to the men or, more ominously, to spring. The slight echo of *Slow Train Coming* is picked up in a remarkably mild and even friendly invocation of Apocalypse: 'The world could come to an end tonight, but that's all right.' The source of this acceptance is in the singer's confidence that the woman will still be waiting for him when he returns.

He does not rest, however, in that security. The last verse finds him again on the road, traveling through darkness even at noon. The division of the self is asserted at the level of language—'Someone else is speakin' with my mouth'—and countered at the level of faith—'but I'm listening only to my heart.' The singer presents himself as a humble Christian servant, who has 'made shoes for everyone … while I still go barefoot.' But this humility is tempered by the sudden intrusion of the phrase 'even you,' which introduces into the song an unidentified second-person addressee. 'Even you' seems to imply an enemy, someone for whom he might not be expected to make shoes; but the 'you' is also an enemy who has been forgiven, who has been seen as an I for an I rather than having an eye extracted for an eye. 'Barefoot' also disturbingly echoes the 'barefoot servants' who observed the onset of Apocalypse in 'All Along the Watchtower' (L 252).

The verses present, then, a drama typical of the religious songs: a protagonist who feels a double division, split within himself and separated from God, but who yet struggles toward a higher unity. The chorus evokes this absent God in terms that paradoxically combine division and unity.

The term 'I and I,' as I have said, may be taken in a secular context, referring to the essential alienation within every human consciousness. In a religious context the immediate source of the phrase is in the Jamaican cult of Rastafari. As Tracy Nicholas explains:

For the Rastafarians, the most powerful and significant

letter of the alphabet is also a word and a number: 'I.' I is part of His Imperial Majesty's title—Haile Selassie I. It is the last letter in Rastafari. 'I' is so important that a Rasta will never say 'I went home,' but would say instead 'I and I went home,' to include the presence and divinity of the Almighty with himself every time he speaks. 'I and I' also includes bredren, who also say 'I and I.' In this simple way, through language, Rastafari is a community of people all the time.... 'I and I,' then, reminds the Rastafarian of his own obligation to live right and at the same time, it praises the Almighty (38-39).

'I and I' is thus a way of naming God while naming one's self. It asserts the immanence of the divinity, His presence in every moment of self-awareness and speech. These secular and religious senses may then be ironically juxtaposed: 'I and I' testifies simultaneously to unity and separation.

Dylan takes irony a step further by the additional juxtaposition of the Rasta term with the line 'One says to the other, no man sees my face and lives.' The Biblical source is Exodus 33:20, in which God says to Moses, 'Thou canst not see my face: for there shall no man see me, and live.' In contrast to Rastafari this view of God is one of absolute separation: far from including Him in every utterance of 'I,' it asserts that man can *never* see God, never draw close to Him. The implied but unspoken reconciliation of these two views would come in Christianity, in the Incarnation of the absolutely Other as human.

Dylan's line, however, contains an element not present in Exodus: the phrase 'One said to the other.' An orthodox reading would see this as God (the One) speaking to man (the other), but there is also a strong suggestion, given the *divided* name of the divinity as 'I and I,' that 'One' and 'the other' are both aspects of God and that God, like man, suffers a divided identity.

What is going on here is a very complex collage of *the names of God*. 'I and I' is the Rasta way of naming God both as unity and division. In the Old Testament the only name that God gives Himself is 'I AM THAT I AM' (Exodus 3:14), a formulation which declares the indivisibility of God but can only do so by again simultaneously doubling the 'I.' It is I AM THAT I AM that transliterates roughly as Jehovah, or Jaweh, or JWH, as in 'John Wesley Harding'. God's *name* is unknowable and unutterable. An orthodox Jew will not even write out the word 'God' but spell it 'G-d.' 'I and I Am That I and I Am' is thus a name for the unnameable. In 'Political World,' Dylan sings 'You climb into the frame / And shout God's name / But you're not even sure what it is' (OM). 'I and I' is his most serious and complex attempt to be sure of that name and to name it in song.

CHAPTER EIGHT
THE NAME OF THE FATHER

The end of the previous chapter brought together the outlaw John Wesley Harding and the possibility of reading the initials of his proper name as an unspoken name of God the Father. Here I wish to pursue this conjunction of motifs—the outlaw, the name, the father—especially as it occurs in Dylan's narrative songs. The best place to start is with the song 'John Wesley Harding.'

Dylan commented on this song, in a 1969 interview, in a typically casual and self-deprecatory manner:

> I had the song 'John Wesley Harding,' which started out to be a long ballad. I was gonna write a ballad on ... like maybe one of those old cowboy ... you know, a real long ballad. But in the middle of the second verse, I got tired. I had a tune, and I didn't want to waste the tune, it was a nice little melody, so I just wrote a quick third verse, and I recorded that.
>
> But it was a silly little song... (quoted in Miles 85).

However accidentally the effect may have been produced, the impression, as Dylan acknowledges, is one of reduction. 'John Wesley Harding' sounds like the remains of a longer song. It is almost reminiscent of an exercise in structuralist narratology, like Joseph Campbell analyzing the components of myth or Vladimir Propp reducing Russian folktales to a sequence of 31 narrative 'functions': hero meets obstacle, hero finds helper, hero overcomes obstacle. We are given not so much a fully developed outlaw ballad as a selective invocation of the semiotic codes of outlaw ballads, a skeletal series of the basic narrative gestures of the genre.

Stanza two, for example, offers several such gestures toward narrative, but each one immediately withdraws into equivocation and incomplete specification:

> 'Twas down in Chaynee County,
> A time they talk about,
> With his lady by his side
> He took a stand.
> And soon the situation there
> Was all but straightened out,
> For he was always known
> To lend a helping hand (L 249).

The particular name 'Chaynee County' appears to promise a documentable historical incident, but the biographies of the 19th century outlaw John Wesley Hardin do not mention it.[1] The 'situation there' remains undefined and unexplained; instead the song merely asserts that it is well known, 'A time they talk about.' Repeatedly, Dylan evades responsibility for his narrative by attributing it to rumor and general report. The effect is to cast some doubt on Harding's character: we are not told unequivocally that he never hurt an honest man but only that 'he was never *known* / To hurt an honest man' (my emphasis).

Similarly, 'took a stand' seems decisive and courageous until one examines the implications of its juxtaposition with 'his lady by his side.' As Michael Gray comments, 'Within the cowboy ethic, the hero should neither have needed his lady by his side to give him his courage nor have placed her inside the dangerzone' (36). What the song grants to its hero with one hand it takes away with the other. The situation is 'straightened out,' as it should be by a hero, but then the equivocation of the 'all but' cancels this accomplishment. The song raises multiple questions—what *is* the situation? what is *not* straightened out?—but rather than answer them, it takes refuge in cliché: 'To lend a helping hand.'

Such narrative ambiguities are common in Dylan's songwriting. It is notoriously difficult to make out exactly what goes on in songs like 'Black Diamond Bay' or 'Tweeter and the Monkeyman.' At times, as in 'John Wesley Harding,' the difficulty is due to the gaps and ellipses in the story; at other times the narrative is buried or implicit, as happens in 'Señor (Tales of Yankee Power).'

Much critical attention to 'Señor (Tales of Yankee Power)' has focused on reading it as either a religious or a political allegory. In view of its 1978 composition date, immediately before Dylan's religious conversion, John Herdman writes that 'It seems reasonable to assume that the Lord is being addressed here' (109). Alternatively, if you take the subtitle seriously, a political reading seems more likely: the song is about American imperialism, especially in Central America.[2] The song invites such allegorical interpretations with its overtly symbolic language—'the last thing I remembered before I stripped and kneeled / Was that trainload of fools bogged down in a magnetic field' (L 410)—but there is also surely a straightforward narrative level to the action.

We infer from his use of 'Señor' that the speaker of the song is a Central American, possibly a Mexican, employed by a 'Yankee' to accompany him as a guide or hired gun on some unspecified mission. The line 'do you know where she is hidin'?' suggests that they are looking for a woman, possibly the Yankee's wife or daughter, while the line 'their hearts is as hard as leather' suggests that the two of them face the prospect of tough adversaries, possibly kidnappers holding the woman. The narrative is so sketchy that most of these problems cannot be solved, but enough of a narrative exists that they can be *posed*. At first the speaker is merely puzzled and ignorant: he does not know where they are going or how long they will be riding. As the song proceeds, however, he becomes more committed and even eager for the fight to begin:

> Señor, señor, let's disconnect these cables,
> Overturn these tables.
> This place don't make sense to me no more.
> Can you tell me what we're waiting for, señor?

This suggested narrative makes grim sense as a political allegory. American imperialism imposes itself through hired surrogates like the Nicaraguan Contras, who eventually become more eager and more bloodthirsty than their sponsors, and who adopt the cause of 'Yankee power' as their own. I am much less convinced that the religious allegory works.

'Señor' is the most oblique of Dylan's narrative songs, conveying its story line through hints and implications. More often the ambiguity of Dylan's narratives depends on the technique noted in 'John Wesley Harding,' the omission of causal connectives. John Herdman bases a fascinating analysis of 'Tangled Up In Blue' on the proposition that Dylan deliberately intends to mislead his audience. Herdman argues that various stanzas of this song refer to *different* women, whereas the listener is led to suppose, by the undifferentiated use of the simple pronoun 'she,' that the references are to the same character (see Herdman 55-58). It is true that Dylan's use of pronouns is always tricky (and in the next chapter I will make a similar argument in relation to 'Brownsville Girl'), but I remain unconvinced by Herdman's argument. For me the song continues to make more sense if the women are all the same character. Nevertheless, the possibility of the argument points to the indeterminacy of Dylan's narrative (or *anti*-narrative) techniques.

In attempting to describe these techniques, critics have frequently resorted to analogies from cinema, and it is often tempting to think of the songs as potential scripts for fast-paced, if somewhat discontinuous, films. Aidan Day, for instance, uses the idea of montage in his comments on 'Tangled Up In Blue':

> the narrative is organized less around a simple sequential
> structure than built up cumulatively by a principle of
> montage. It is possible to reconstruct from this montage a
> single, straightforward story. But the disturbance of
> sequential structure simultaneously gives rise to elements
> in the text which resist accommodation within such a
> reconstruction (52).

Another cinematic technique that Dylan uses frequently is the jump-cut, the abrupt transition from one scene into the middle of the next, eliding causal connections. In 'Tweeter and the Monkeyman,' for instance, the fourth stanza begins with the title characters 'cornered' by the 'undercover cop,' cuts to Jan taking a gun and leaving her husband, and then cuts back without explanation to 'The undercover cop was found face down in a field / The Monkeyman was on the river bridge using Tweeter as a shield.' Did Jan kill the cop or had the Monkeyman already escaped before she got there? Against whom is Tweeter used as a shield? The song doesn't say.

It is important to insist that the point *is* that the song doesn't say. There are clear dangers in attempting any definitive statements of what 'actually' goes on. It is not as if the events of these narratives have ever existed in any form outside the songs. The 'story' exists *only* in the words and performances of the songs, and these words include, as Day notes, elements that resist clear reconstruction. Indeterminacy remains the basic characteristic of all Dylan's major narratives, and there is no appeal beyond it.

Indeterminacy affects not only the plot but also the nature of the fictional characters. John Wesley Harding remains elusive and undefined, known only through rumor and negations: in these respects he is, of course, very similar to Bob Dylan. Dylan's presentations of his own identity are always haunted by this indeterminacy. The self-created figure of 'Bob Dylan' is a 'Wanted Man' (L 279), the unnamed and unnamable object of multiple desires. As a 'wanted man,' he has frequently presented himself in the role of outlaw or thief. 'I am a thief of thoughts,' Dylan wrote (L 112), discussing his intertextual indebtedness to previous singers. Lenny Bruce was 'some kind of robber' (T 54). Dylan casts himself in this role in satirical songs like 'Positively 4th Street'—'If I was a master thief' (L 211)—and even in love songs. 'Sad-Eyed Lady of the Lowlands' presents his relationship to his lover as that of a thief to a parole officer, although the terms of the relationship have been subtly inverted: 'Now you stand with your thief, you're on his parole' (L 240).

The outlaw figure's attraction is that he stands for the romantic outsider, the ultimate individualist, who stakes his destiny against the forces of society and conformity. When Dylan sings that 'to live outside the law, you must be honest' (L 233), he reflects what David Pichaske calls 'the myth of the moral outlaw':

> The outlaw springs from and champions the huddled
> masses, living among them, protected by them from pur-
> suing agents of the law, somehow more moral in his
> excommunication (and more admirable by virtue of his
> relative cunning and leanness) than the forces of 'justice'
> which hound and, invariably, kill him (43).

John Wesley Harding is a 'moral outlaw' in the tradition of Woody Guthrie's 'Pretty Boy Floyd,' or at least he would be if the equivocations of the song's language did not cast some doubt over his character. While the traditional American outlaw ballad celebrates the outlaw's clever evasion of justice, Dylan concentrates more on *un*successful outlaws. John Wesley Harding 'was never known / To make a foolish move,' but again this invulnerability is a matter of report to which Dylan is unwilling to commit himself. Almost all his other outlaws *do* make foolish moves, and many of them die for it. As early as 1962, 'Rambling Gambling Willie' tells the story of a successful gambler who 'had twenty-seven children, yet he never had a wife' (L 11). Willie uses his winnings to support his children, but at the end of the song, holding Wyatt Earp's 'dead man's hand' of eights and aces, he is shot, presumably leaving his twenty-seven children to their fatherless fate.

In the 1965 'Outlaw Blues,' Dylan sings:

> Ain't gonna hang no picture,
> Ain't gonna hang no picture frame.
> Well, I might look like Robert Ford
> But I feel just like Jesse James (L 168).

The singer identifies with Jesse James, not as the successful bank robber, but with Jesse James at the moment when he is shot in the back by Robert Ford while he is hanging a picture on the wall of his room. It is interesting to note, however, that the song hints at a double identification: not only with the dead outlaw but also with the universally despised figure of the traitor who killed him. In the theme song that he wrote for Sam Peckinpah's *Pat Garrett and Billy the Kid*, it is again the hunted, dying outlaw that Dylan chooses to identify with: 'Billy, don't it make ya feel so low-down / To be shot down by the man who was your friend?' (L 335).[3]

Many features of the outlaw song that I have been discussing so far—the indeterminate narration, the equivocal 'hero'—find their fullest expression in 'Lily, Rosemary and the Jack of Hearts' (L 364-6). This song is characteristic of the elliptical, elusive nature of Dylan's narratives. The events of the story go by in a rapid succession of cinematic cuts, some of which are jump-cuts, omitting sections of the narrative which the listener must attempt to reconstruct in retrospect. The most startling of these jump-cuts elides the central event of the story, the killing of Big Jim. This elliptical narrative, with a few nicely ambiguous phrases, prevents the listener from ever being completely certain what has happened.

The usual problems of narrative indeterminacy are compounded, because there are two slightly different versions of this song. The version released on *Blood on the Tracks* omits one stanza, which is included both in the earlier studio recording and the printed *Lyrics*. As we shall see, the extra stanza makes a crucial difference to the reading of the narrative.

The song begins by suggesting that one story is already finished. An unspecified festival is over, and 'Anyone with any sense had already left town.' The characters who are left, about whom *this* story will be told, are those without sense, those whose actions are driven more by their passions than by reason. We are then given the strange detail of 'the drillin' in the wall,'[4] which will be mentioned again in stanza 8. Not until the song's end can this be retrospectively identified as a clue pointing to a bank robbery. The robbery is always in the background, like a sound on the edge of consciousness. The Jack of Hearts may lead the gang, but he takes no part in the actual robbery, though he has presumably planned it. The Jack of Hearts is always defined in this song by a curious mixture of presence and absence: as the second last stanza puts it, 'The only person on the scene missin' was the Jack of Hearts.' On the scene and simultaneously missing: the Jack of Hearts is always there but not there, leader of the gang but not participating in the looting of the bank, present but absent from the scene of the murder.

Even his introduction into the song is shadowy and uncertain. When 'he' first appears we are told not that he *is* the Jack of Hearts but only that he looks *like* the Jack of Hearts. This equivocation is repeated in the next stanza, when 'he moved into the corner, face down like the Jack of Hearts.' The character's similarity to the Jack is defined in terms of disguise or absence. He is *like* the Jack of Hearts *because* his face cannot be seen. He fully enters into the song only after the third stanza, in which Lily's drawing of the card in the poker game evokes him, creates his presence, draws him into the textual reality.

The same three stanzas concisely introduce the other leading characters. Lily performs in the saloon (we are never told whether she sings or just dances) and loses at poker. Big Jim is the local mine owner, a figure of wealth and power, complete with bodyguards, who mysteriously vanish for the rest of the song.[5] Rosemary lives outside town, presumably at Big Jim's mansion, and she is initially subservient to him, whispering apologies for being late. It seems probable that Rosemary is married to Big Jim and that Lily is his mistress.

The elusive nature of the Jack of Hearts is stressed as Big Jim stares at him:

'I know I've seen that face before,' Big Jim was thinkin' to himself,
'Maybe down in Mexico or a picture up on somebody's shelf.'

Again the Jack of Hearts is defined by his likeness, which can never quite be pinned down. In narrative terms it is most likely that the 'somebody' who keeps the Jack's picture is Lily, who has definitely known the Jack of Hearts in the past, but nothing excludes the possibility that it also might be Rosemary.

Lily's cabaret performance is not directly described. Instead it is replaced by a series of foreboding images: the arrival of the hanging judge, the continuation of the drilling in the wall, Rosemary staring at her face reflected in a knife. These images come together at the climax of the song, so it is interesting that they stand in for *Lily's* performance. Although she seems the most innocent of the characters, it is Lily who first conjures up the Jack of Hearts, and it is Lily's song or dance that prefigures the tragic conclusion.

Stanza 10 is set in Lily's dressing room after her performance, and she is talking to the Jack of Hearts. Her tone is friendly but not passionate. She assumes that he has come to see her because he is down on his luck, and she warns him not to touch a freshly painted wall. Her most emotional comment, 'I'm glad to see you're still alive,' is not exactly a declaration of love.[6] Lily appears less interested in the Jack of Hearts than he is in her. She tells him that he looks like a saint: in what sense? that he looks dead, emaciated, ascetic, beatific? As always, the Jack of Hearts is not quite *there;* he is present in the room but doesn't say anything.

We now approach one of the major ambiguities of the song. The next stanza tells us that the backstage manager is getting worried and trying unsuccessfully to get help from the judge. As he does so, 'the leading actor hurried by in the costume of a monk.' Who exactly *is* 'the leading actor'? It might be Rosemary, though it is more likely that she would be called an 'actress,' or it might be Big Jim on his way to Lily's dressing room to confront her and the man he suspects is visiting her there. But neither Rosemary nor Big Jim has any reason to wear the disguise of a monk; the only person who consistently appears in disguise is the Jack of Hearts. But here a further question arises: in which *direction* is this character 'hurrying by'? Toward Lily's dressing room or away from it? The answer must surely be away from it: where else would the Jack have had the opportunity to put on the costume of a monk? He could scarcely have done so sitting at a table in the saloon. But if this is the case, then the Jack of Hearts *has already left* Lily's dressing room before Big Jim arrives. What then would be the reason for the murder? What would there be for Big Jim to see when he bursts in?

There is a narrative impasse here that the song never resolves. The identity of 'the leading actor' and the direction in which he hurries must remain unknown. The succeeding events only make sense if we can assume that the Jack of Hearts is still in Lily's dressing room. This is certainly what stanza 12 tells us: the Jack of Hearts is there with Lily's arms around him. Stanza 12, however, has a very equivocal status: Dylan omitted it from the revised take of the song which was released on *Blood on the Tracks*, but included it in the published *Lyrics*.

142

It is important to note here that if the Jack of Hearts is still in Lily's dressing room, in her arms, when Big Jim bursts in, then he has been, despite his apparent cleverness and invincibility, caught. Despite the song's assertions of the power, resourcefulness, and trickery of the Jack of Hearts, he has been trapped in the most elementary way: unlike John Wesley Harding, he has made a foolish move. He escapes Big Jim not through his own skill but through a woman's intervention. On the other hand, if he is 'the leading actor' and was *leaving* Lily's dressing room, then he has done what the Jack of Hearts always seems to do: slip away just in time, leaving his absence behind, on the scene and missing.

No wonder then that Dylan as narrator also steps back from the action and draws attention to the indeterminacy of the narrative: 'No one knew the circumstance but they say that it happened pretty quick.' The climactic events are presented in such spare terms that several interpretations are possible:

1. The dressing room door bursts open, and 'Big Jim was standin' there, ya couldn't say surprised.' He is not surprised because what he sees is, as he suspected, Lily in the arms of this strange man whom he has dimly recognized, the Jack of Hearts. Big Jim attempts to shoot the Jack of Hearts, but his 'cold revolver clicked'—clicked presumably because it is empty. And the only person who could have emptied it would be Rosemary. Rosemary, who is standing *beside* Big Jim, is the only person in position to stab him in the back. Thus the Jack of Hearts escapes from the situation entirely by virtue of Rosemary's efforts. This remains the standard, and the most likely, interpretation.

2. The dressing room door bursts open, and 'Big Jim was standin' there,' but the Jack of Hearts has already gone, 'in the costume of a monk.' But in this case surely Big Jim would be surprised, since he expected to find Lily with another man. So why would Rosemary have to kill him?

3. The door bursts open and Big Jim is standing there, *already dead*, already stabbed in the back by Rosemary. The gun clicks because he does not have time to fire it, only to pull back the hammer. In this case it doesn't matter whether the Jack of Hearts is still in the room.

4. The above all assume that Big Jim bursts open the door, but the song does not actually say this:

> The door to the dressing room burst open and a cold
>> revolver clicked.
>> And Big Jim was standin' there, ya couldn't say suprised....

Big Jim is standing *where?* If he is *already inside* the dressing room, then perhaps the Jack of Hearts bursts open the door, having returned after his previous visit. In this case the person in the best position to stab Big Jim in the back would be *Lily*.

Interpretations 2, 3, and 4 are all farfetched and require massive assumptions about what has been left out of the narrative. But the point is that the song is so elliptical that nothing in the text excludes any of these interpretations. At the central point of his story, Dylan is deliberately vague: 'No one knew the circumstance,' and Dylan accepts that limited viewpoint. He refuses the stance of the omniscient narrator.

Instead we jump ahead to the gang successfully completing the bank robbery and waiting for their leader, and then, even more drastically, to the hanging. The circumstances of the murder may be obscure, but that does not prevent arrest, trial, sentence, and execution following in a matter of hours. Rosemary is on the gallows,' probably for a crime she did commit, to save the Jack's life, but just possibly for a crime that he, or even Lily, actually committed. In either case Rosemary acts as a sacrificial substitute. In addition, Rosemary and Lily must have conspired to conceal the Jack's presence and participation. The Jack of Hearts is now most crucially 'the only person on the scene missin'.' Whatever Rosemary covers up for him, the Jack of Hearts makes no move to save her from the gallows. Lily may be thinking about him, but he is gone.

Lily's reflections in the final stanza[7] move beyond the particular characters and events of the drama to include more general topics:

> She was thinkin' 'bout her father, who she very rarely saw,
> Thinkin' 'bout Rosemary and thinkin' about the law.
> But most of all she was thinkin' 'bout the Jack of Hearts.

The figure of the father is closely associated with the idea of law in both religion and psychoanalysis. God the Father—Jaweh, JWH—decrees the Law to Moses on Mount Sinai. According to Freud, the father institutes the law by laying down the prohibition against incest. Jacques Lacan uses the French phrase 'le Nom du Père' to refer not only to the Name of the Father, which vests the law in the property rights of the proper name, but also to the prohibition (Nom/Non) which the father proclaims. For Lacan, the Name of the Father also institutes the symbolic realm of language.

The figure of the father is particularly important to Bob Dylan in the songs of the 1970s. As the bearer of an assumed name himself, he would, as I argued in Chapter Three, be very conscious of the problematic nature of the proper name, the patronymic. There are, of course, biographical reasons for the increasing prominence of the father-image—his father's death in 1968, the birth and rearing of his children, the instability of his marriage—but it also coheres with the deepest continuing obsessions of his writing. In the 1970s the image of the unsuccessful or dying outlaw fuses with that of the helpless, missing, or dead father.

As early as 1967, 'Tears of Rage' evoked the figure of the impotent father in its echo of *King Lear* —

> Oh what dear daughter 'neath the sun
> Would treat a father so,
> To wait upon him hand and foot
> And always tell him, 'No'?

—and immediately associated it with the outlaw—

> Tears of rage, tears of grief,
> Why must I always be the thief? (L 312)

Of the songs Dylan wrote for *Pat Garrett and Billy the Kid*, the most memorable, and the one he has returned to again and again in concert, is 'Knockin' on Heaven's Door.' In the film it accompanies the scene of Sheriff Baker's (Slim Pickens') death; but Baker's role as a sheriff rather than an outlaw is less important than his role as a dying *father*. The second verse makes the phallic implications unmistakable:

> Mama, put my guns in the ground
> I can't shoot them anymore.
> That long black cloud is comin' down
> I feel like I'm knockin' on heaven's door (L 337).

The killing of Sheriff Baker is a primal scene, the father's death. The scene counterpoints the killing of Billy, the 'Kid,' by his surrogate father, Pat Garrett. The father's killing (or castration) of the son is the feared event that the Oedipal scenario is intended to ward off. Oedipus meets his father, Laius, at the crossroads, and their fight is always to the death. In *Tarantula* 'boy dylan' is 'killed by a discarded Oedipus' (T 120). In 'Highway 61 Revisited' God the Father demands of Abraham (the name of Robert Zimmerman's father), 'Kill me a son' (L202). This is the primal scene of psychology, myth, and narrative, which has to be staged and restaged, in words Dylan later added to this song, 'just like so many times before.' Or, as the Mexican hired gun says to *his* surrogate father in 'Señor,' 'Seems like I been down this way before' (L 410).

On the album *Desire* (1975), the theme of the dying outlaw or father is omnipresent. Rubin 'Hurricane' Carter, accused of murder and 'falsely tried,' now 'sits like Buddha in a ten-foot cell,' the innocent outlaw, who 'could-a been' but now never will be 'champion of the world' (L 377), rendered impotent by a corrupt justice system. Joey Gallo, unconvincingly portrayed as a humane mobster, dies because he refuses to carry a gun in the presence of children. The idea of helplessness is extended to Joey's father, who 'had to say one last goodbye to the son that he could not save' (L 384). The unnamed protagonist of 'Romance in Durango' flees after accidentally killing a man named Ramon but is eventually shot down from ambush, leaving his beloved Magdalena unprotected. In 'One More Cup of Coffee,' Dylan sings, 'Your daddy he's an outlaw / And a wanderer by trade,' but the father's trembling voice undermines his patriarchal authority (L 381). Similarly, 'Oh, Sister' presents a rebellion against patriarchal authority: 'Our Father would not like the way that you act' (L 382). In 'Romance in Durango,' 'The face of God will appear / With His serpent eyes of obsidian' (L 386), but He will be visible only to the dying narrator. His serpent eyes are the I's of 'I and I': 'No man sees my face and lives.'

In 'Lily, Rosemary and the Jack of Hearts,' these obsessive images are present, but given the ambiguities of the narrative, they are dispersed among the various characters in inconsistent and indeterminate combinations. Who *is* Lily's father? Stanza 7 tells us that Lily comes from a broken home, but there is no other direct clue. It is possible that her father is the Jack of Hearts, an interpretation quite consistent with what she says to him in her dressing room and with her 'very rarely' seeing him. It is even barely possible that her father is Big Jim. The most obvious interpretation, noted earlier, of the relationships between Big Jim and the two women is that Rosemary is his wife and Lily his mistress. But, again, the song does not actually say this. Rosemary, we are told, was 'tired of *playin'* the *role* of Big Jim's wife' (my emphasis), a phrase that suggests equally the possibilities that she is or is not legally married to him. We are not told that Lily 'had Jim's ring' but that *'It was known all around* that Lily had Jim's ring' (my emphasis). Again Dylan refuses the stance of the omniscient narrator, reporting only the general opinion or gossip, which may or may not be true.

On a symbolic level, Big Jim certainly appears as Lily's father. He is a 'king' while Rosemary first appears 'looking like a queen without a crown.' Lily, on the other hand, 'was a princess, she was fair-skinned and precious as a child.' King, queen, princess: in this triangle, Lily is indeed 'precious as a child,' a daughter.

But the imagery of kings and queens also leads in the direction of playing cards. In the nursery rhyme, the Jack of Hearts is a thief, as he is in the song; more generally, jacks or knaves are the villains of the deck. The Jack of Hearts is one of two jacks (the other one is the Jack of Spades) presented in profile so that only one eye shows. One of Dylan's earliest songs, written in 1960, was called 'One-Eyed Jacks'; the singer appeals to a Queen and a Jack to 'forget my name' (quoted in Shelton 54). Already, the Jack is associated with the forgetting or disowning of the father's name. In *Tarantula* boy dylan is killed by a *discarded* Oedipus.

'One-eyed Jacks,' besides being a slang term for masturbators, is the title of a 1961 movie in which a traveling outlaw (Marlon Brando) falls in love with a young woman and must fight and eventually kill her father (Karl Malden), who is an outlaw turned sheriff. *One-Eyed Jacks* was based on a novel about Billy the Kid, and Steven Tatum reports that one scriptwriter was Sam Peckinpah, who had directed Dylan in *Pat Garrett and Billy the Kid* just a year or so before Dylan wrote 'Lily, Rosemary and the Jack of Hearts' (Tatum 133, 159). The major song that Dylan composed for the film, 'Knockin' on Heaven's Door,' was written for a scene in which a sheriff who is also a father is dying. The line of association—Jack of Hearts, one-eyed jacks, Billy the Kid, dying fathers—is unbroken.[8]

Each of the other characters is also associated with cards. We first see Lily engaged in a game of poker; she 'had two queens, she was hopin' for a third to match her pair.' What Lily gets, however, is not a third queen but the Jack of Hearts, which disrupts her hand just as the arrival of the 'real' Jack of Hearts disrupts the 'pair' of Rosemary and Big Jim. But in poker, one-eyed jacks are often wild cards. Being a wild card certainly suits the nature of the Jack of Hearts: both present and absent, both himself and something else. If Lily plays one-eyed jacks as wild, then the card she draws can indeed count as a third queen and give her a winning hand.

Rosemary also has her associations with cards: she is 'a queen without a crown.' No queen in the standard deck wears a crown. All have embroidered shawls over their heads. More significantly, almost every mention of Rosemary in the song draws attention to her eyes. On her first appearance she wears false eye-lashes, but as she asserts her independence from Big Jim her sight becomes clearer, and she loses her association with falseness. On her second appearance she looks at her image reflected in the knife which she later uses to kill Big Jim. When she appears beside Big Jim in the dressing room at the moment of the murder, she is 'steady in her eyes,' and on the gallows 'she didn't even blink.' In contrast to the shiftiness of a one-eyed jack, Rosemary sees herself and her actions directly and honestly.

Big Jim is described as a king, and he owns a diamond mine. Of the four kings in the standard deck, only the King of Diamonds is one-eyed member. Separated in suit from the Jack of Hearts, Big Jim is nevertheless linked to him by their one-eyed nature. So in a curious sense, Big Jim could be the father not only to Lily but even to the Jack of Hearts. As a one-eyed king he is associated mytho-logically with one-eyed Odin, father of the Norse gods, who sacrifices his eye to gain wisdom and power. The dying father-gods of myth are all sacrificial figures, often killed by their successors, whose deaths recur in cyclical patterns.

The central Dylan motifs of the outlaw and dying father are thus dispersed throughout the ambiguous narrative of 'Lily, Rosemary and the Jack of Hearts.' Big Jim, although not a particularly sympathetic character, nevertheless figures in the imagery as dead father and sacrificial victim. The idea of sacrifice is even clearer in Rosemary, whose death on the gallows allows Lily and the Jack of Hearts to go free. Rosemary dies an outlaw's death, like Christ, whom Dylan described a few years later as 'the Man who came and died a criminal's death' (L 426). But the main outlaw of the song, the Jack of Hearts, escapes. Depending on how you interpret the ambiguities of the relationships, the Jack of Hearts could be both a father (to Lily, or to the members of his gang) or a would-be son who kills the father of the woman he loves. Whoever 'the leading actor' of this drama is, he appears 'in the costume of a monk': that is, of a holy father whose law prevents him from ever becoming a real father. Fathers, sons, and sacrificed daughters are bound together by the social and psychological structures of 'the law.'

In the end, of course, the Jack of Hearts stands for Dylan himself. The Jack evades the Name of the Father by using an alias: we never know his 'real' name. He is constantly in motion and hard to pin down. Like John Wesley Harding, he is 'never known / To make a foolish move' (L 249). Yet he also is ambiguous: it can be argued that he *does* 'make a foolish move' when Big Jim traps him, and that he escapes only because of Rosemary's courage and self-sacrifice. At the end of the story, instead of riding in heroically to the rescue, he simply disappears. He is absence.

In the same way, Dylan is absent from the story he stages for us. The narrative preserves a strict impersonality, and at several key points it pulls back from omniscience, choosing to report only what 'was known all around' or what 'they say' but 'no one knew.' The elisions and ambiguities of the narrative create unsettling gaps in the familiar patterns of the conventional story and ultimately deny the listener any secure position vis-à-vis the fictional world. Unknown and undefinable, the Jack of Hearts constantly disappears into these gaps, and so does Bob Dylan.

THE ONLY THING WE KNEW FOR SURE ABOUT HENRY PORTER

The conventional wisdom of Bob Dylan criticism is that he has never reattained the peak of creative output and ability that he achieved in the mid-1960s. Everything he has done since *John Wesley Harding* has been held to exhibit a slow decline, and Dylan has been regarded as irrelevant to the culture of the 1970s and 1980s. Every now and then he is granted a 'comeback,' with albums like *Blood on the Tracks* or *Oh Mercy*, but the tone of this judgment is usually one of mild condescension and surprise that the old man is still alive.

I agree that Dylan's greatest single period of creative intensity lies in the mid-1960s, but, as should be clear even from the songs I have chosen to focus on in this book, I do not dismiss the later work. I would go as far as to say that even if we possessed only the work that Dylan has done *since* 1970 he would *still* rank as the greatest singer and songwriter of his age.

To be sure, the later work is uneven. There are many weak songs and marginal albums—but whenever you are tempted to think that Dylan has lost it entirely, he comes up with a song or concert performance that triumphantly reasserts his mastery. Typical of this unevenness is the 1986 album *Knocked Out Loaded*. The songs come from a variety of recording sessions and styles, and the result is a curious mishmash, most of which is not worth a second listening. But in the middle of the album is a masterpiece, a song that must rank among the five or six best songs Dylan has ever written, a song that by itself redeems the somewhat bleak period between *Infidels* and *Oh Mercy*.

'Brownsville Girl' is credited to Bob Dylan and Sam Shepard, and not the least intriguing thing about it is trying to figure out just who wrote what. The long, rambling lines have a kind of colloquial poetry that recalls Shepard's plays, but Dylan's half-spoken, half-sung delivery makes them entirely his. Shepard recalls that he and Dylan 'wrote [the song] together in the spring of 1985.... We spent two days writing the lyrics—Bob had previously composed the melody line, which was already down on tape' (interview 198). Shepard's memory may be at fault though, for Clinton Heylin claims that the earliest version of the song—at this stage called 'Danville Girl' or 'New Danville Girl'—was recorded 'in late November or early December' of 1984 (266). This version was intended for inclusion on *Empire Burlesque*, but Dylan decided against it. Reemerging as 'Brownsville Girl,' it was partially rerecorded in May, 1986, and issued in July of that year on *Knocked Out Loaded*. In the *Rolling Stone* interview, Shepard says that Dylan has 'already gone through different phases with the song' (198). It even appears that Shepard did not realize that 'Brownsville Girl' had been released.[1]

One previous attempt at a collaboration had not worked out. Shepard was hired as a writer for the Rolling Thunder tour, to provide dialogue for the film that Dylan was making on that self-consciously mythic journey. But Shepard soon found it absurd to think of creating a fixed script for such a wild, free-form improvisation as *Renaldo and Clara* was becoming. He left the tour, though he later produced one of the best written accounts of it in his *Rolling Thunder Logbook*.

Other affinities between Sam Shepard and Bob Dylan exist. Both came from the Mid-West and arrived in New York at age 19 (Dylan in 1961, Shepard in 1963). Both had assumed new names: Shepard's was adapted from his given name, Samuel Shepard Rogers. Dylan's productivity in the mid-60s (seven albums, scores of songs) was matched by Shepard's (sixteen plays staged in six years). A large photograph of an iconic Bob Dylan is a major prop in Shepard's *Melodrama Play* (1967), and Dylan is evoked in *The Tooth of Crime* (1972): 'The big ones. Dylan, Jagger, Townsend. All them cats broke codes. Time can't change that' (*Seven Plays* 209). Several of Shepard's early New York productions were directed by Jacques Levy, who worked as stage director on the Rolling Thunder tour[2] and co-wrote with Dylan most of the songs on *Desire*.

More recently, after the 'Brownsville Girl' collaboration, Shepard wrote a play about himself and Dylan. The title, 'True Dylan,' is an ironic twist on Shepard's own *True West*, and further questions the possible 'truth' of an assumed name. The subtitle—'A one-act play, as it really happened one afternoon in California'—plays between the rival claims of journalism and fiction. Much material appears to be biographical, with Dylan reminiscing about James Dean and his motorcycle accident, but strange, surrealist touches—mysterious music, an unseen car crash—give it, even in its most 'accurate' moments, the feel of a Sam Shepard creation.

However, the aspects of the Dylan/Shepard affinity with the most relevance for 'Brownsville Girl' are found in the film that constitutes the song's continuing intertext. 'Well there was this movie I seen one time,' the first verse begins, 'About a man riding across the desert and it starred Gregory Peck' (BG). Shepard recalls that 'The film the song was about was a Gregory Peck western that Bob had once seen, but he couldn't remember the title. We decided that the title didn't matter' (interview 198). 'Danville Girl' begins 'I wish I could remember that movie just a little bit better' (DG). Before making the revisions that led to 'Brownsville Girl,' it is likely that Dylan *did* remember the movie and may even have seen it again to refresh his memory. The film in question is *The Gunfighter* (1950), directed by Henry King. 'Brownsville Girl' adds details from the film, such as 'riding across the desert,' which were not present in 'Danville Girl,' and corrects its erroneous 'Sheriff' to 'Marshall.'[3]

Movie references occur repeatedly in the works of both Dylan and Shepard. 'I keep praying,' Shepard wrote, 'for a double bill / of / BAD DAY AT BLACK ROCK / and / VERA CRUZ' (*Motel Chronicles* 86)—two films that must have shown in 1954 at the Lybba Theater in Hibbing, Minnesota, owned by Bobby Zimmerman's great-grandfather and his brother, and named for Bobby's great-grandmother (see Shelton 28). Sam Shepard has become a highly successful movie actor, in *Days of Heaven, The Right Stuff, Country*, and his own *Fool for Love*. His screen image (sometimes treated straight, sometimes ironically) is very much that of the cowboy: the kind of part, say, that Gregory Peck played. Shepard is even the same physical type as Peck: long, lean, and hard. When the protagonist of 'Danville Girl' says that all he remembers of *The Gunfighter* is Gregory Peck and that 'everything he did in it reminded me of me' (DG), one might hear Sam Shepard talking. But one might equally hear Bob Dylan. During a 1971 visit to Israel, a reporter asked Dylan how he had spent his thirtieth birthday. He replied, 'We went to see a Gregory Peck movie—I'm quite a fan of his' (Shelton 414).

The Gunfighter begins with a shot of 'a man riding across the desert.' He is Jimmy Ringo (Gregory Peck), a notorious gunfighter pursued by his fame. In every town is a brash young kid eager to make a name for himself as the man who shot Jimmy Ringo; in the first sequence we see such a challenge and its fatal result. Followed by the dead kid's brothers, Ringo moves on to the next town, where he meets an old friend, now the town Marshall, and where he hopes to reunite with Peggy, the local schoolteacher, his old sweetheart and the mother of his child. Threatened by the avenging brothers and by *this* town's dumb kid, Hunt Bromley, Ringo delays his getaway until he can talk to his son and to Peggy, from whom he exacts a vague promise to see him next year. The Marshall disposes of the brothers, but as Ringo is riding out of town he is shot in the back by Hunt Bromley. In the climactic scene, which is described graphically and accurately by Dylan and Shepard, the townspeople begin to lynch the killer but are prevented by the dying gunfighter himself, who says:

> 'Turn him loose, let him go, let him say he outdrew me fair and square
> I want him to feel what it's like to every moment face his death' (BG).

The memory of the film persists throughout the song. By the end of the second stanza, Dylan remembers the movie less as one that he has seen than as one that he has taken part in: 'I can't remember why I was in it or what part I was supposed to play' (BG). In the third stanza the protagonist is

> standing in line in the rain to see a movie starring Gregory Peck ...
> He's got a new one out now, I don't even know what it's about
> But I'll see him in anything, so I'll stand in line (BG).

The last verse, like the second and third, returns to *The Gunfighter* in its closing lines, and offers a briefer plot summary:

> All I remember about it was it starred Gregory Peck,
> He wore a gun and he was shot in the back
> Seems like a long time ago, long before the stars were torn down (BG)

The final phrase has obvious apocalyptic overtones, but it also may refer to the decline of the Hollywood 'star system.' *The Gunfighter* was the product of the Hollywood studios (20th Century Fox in this case) in the 1950s, when stars like Gregory Peck were assigned to scripts as automatically as their fans concluded, 'He's got a new one out now, I don't even know what it's about / But I'll see him in anything, so I'll stand in line' (BG). In the 'new' and very different Hollywood, Sam Shepard writes a screenplay for the German director Wim Wenders (*Paris, Texas*, 1984)[4] or appears as an actor in a production of his play *Fool for Love*, directed by Robert Altman. One kind of star has indeed been torn down, but others have been erected in its place; the fans' worship is just as intense if no longer as unquestioning.

The question of fame, of stars and their audiences, is dealt with by Shepard in *The Tooth of Crime*. Its futuristic setting fuses the roles of pop star and gunfighter: the central character, Hoss, worries about his position on the charts and about the young 'Gypsies' who, like Hunt Bromley, are out to get him. 'Look at me now,' he says. 'Impotent.... Stuck in my image. Stuck in a mansion. Waiting. Waiting for a kid who's probably just like me. Just like I was then. A young blood. And I gotta off him. I gotta roll him or he'll roll me' (226). That could be Jimmy Ringo talking.

The potentially lethal nature of the rock star's audience is also a prominent topic in *Rolling Thunder Logbook*. Shepard relates in vivid detail Roger McGuinn's 'profound fear of being assassinated on stage ... imagining the hands of the gunman as they polished the barrel with a chamois skin and then the black barrel of the rifle sweeping the width of the stage trying to find the correct angle' (60). Later Shepard writes: 'Strange fear comes over me that the audience might actually devour Dylan and the band. It seems that close. I'm afraid for them' (119). And in a short section simply entitled 'Fans,' he writes: 'Fans are more dangerous than a man with a weapon because they're after something invisible. Some imagined "something." At least with a gun you know what you're facing' (89). In the *Rolling Stone* interview, Shepard is asked, 'How do you avoid the so-called powers of relentless and overintrusive fans?' He answers, 'Carry a gun! *[Laughs.]*' The laughter is surely uneasy.

Bob Dylan has always had an ambivalent attitude toward his fame and his audience, much of which is humorously summed up in the 1963 song 'Hero Blues.' Ostensibly about a young man protesting his girlfriend's attempts to turn him into a macho 'hero,' the song can also be an emblem of Dylan's attitudes toward his fans. The girl's ideas of heroism are formed by media and pop culture: 'She reads too many books / She got movies inside her head / She wants me to walk out running / She wants me to crawl back dead' (L 41). The song offers one comic ending—'You need a different kind of man, babe / You need Napoleon Boneeparte' *[sic]*—and then a more somber one—'You can stand and shout hero / All over my lonesome grave.' Jimmy Ringo's efforts in *The Gunfighter* to avoid just such a fate would strike a sympathetic note in Bob Dylan.

The first function of *The Gunfighter* as intertext in 'Brownsville Girl' is thus to point to the theme of fame, to the ambivalence of audiences, and to the vulnerability of the 'star.' *The Gunfighter* finds echoes in Shepard's *The Tooth of Crime* and in *Rolling Thunder Logbook*, which in turn bears witness to the intensity of these pressures on Bob Dylan. In 'Brownsville Girl,' the stars do not just fall: they are torn down.

But other elements of the Jimmy Ringo character are just as important for Dylan and Shepard: Ringo is a father, and as a father he is absent. *The Gunfighter* is understandably reticent about plot details, since it wishes to establish both that Ringo has been an outlaw and that Peggy is a virtuous 1950s heroine. But somehow they have been married and had a son. She is now living under an assumed name, working as a schoolteacher, and bringing up her son in ignorance of his father's identity—so much so that in playground gossip he even prefers Wyatt Earp to the legendary Jimmy Ringo. Only after his death does she identify herself as 'Mrs Ringo,' with little Jimmy adding, 'And his boy!' The final shot of the film shows a horseman riding back into the desert: Jimmy Ringo's ghost, like Lenny Bruce's, lives on and on. The final situation (mother and son reunited, father returning to the desert) is identical with the ending of Sam Shepard's *Paris, Texas*.

The theme of the absent father is found in several Shepard works, notably in *True West*, where the two brothers on stage refer continually to 'the old man' living as a recluse in the Mojave Desert. In *Fool for Love*, 'The Old Man' is also the stage directions' designation for the father, who is both present and absent throughout: 'He exists only in the minds of May and Eddie, even though they might talk to him directly and acknowledge his physical presence. The Old Man treats them as though they all existed in the same time and place' (15). *Fool for Love* sets up a complicated story in which the father is absent from two families in turn, keeping each in ignorance of the other. Presence in one necessarily implies absence in the other: 'I was gone,' he protests, 'But I wasn't disconnected' (74).

In the movie version of *Fool for Love*, the Old Man is played by Harry Dean Stanton, who also plays Travis in *Paris, Texas*.[5] Travis comes out of the Mojave Desert, reappearing after a four-year absence to reclaim his son and reestablish the family unit (or rather the mother-son unit) before disappearing again. During the crucial confrontation between Travis and Jane, the characters are both present and absent to each other, speaking by telephone through a two-way mirror. The mirror acts as screen within the screen, and the play of looks traversing it mirrors the role of the cinema spectator identifying with the camera as the apparatus of cinematic perception.[6]

In Shepard's plays the essence of the father's role is not just that he is absent but that his very absence has to be 'staged,' imagined, projected as a presence underlying the action. The play 'True Dylan' returns obsessively to the empty *sites* of death—the curve of the road where James Dean died, the back seat of the Cadillac where Hank Williams died—as places haunted by the felt presence of the absent dead: their ghosts.

In the previous chapter I outlined the conjunction of these motifs—the ghost, the outlaw, and the dying father—in Bob Dylan's songs, especially on *Desire*. Shepard's Rolling Thunder association with Dylan did not begin until shortly after *Desire* had been recorded, but at the time of the tour these were the most urgent Dylan compositions of which Shepard would have been aware. The central songs on *Desire*—'Isis,' 'Oh, Sister,' 'Sara'—work out themes and images which recur both in Shepard's plays and the later collaboration on 'Brownsville Girl.'

Most discussions of 'Sara' (including mine in Chapter Five) have focussed on its autobiographical nature and have seen the name Sara as referring unproblematically to Dylan's wife. However, Robert Shelton reports that 'Dylan joked on his Rolling Thunder tour ... that "Sara" was not necessarily about his wife, [but] perhaps about the biblical Sarah' (464). As 'joked' indicates, this suggestion has been treated with general hilarity, but I suggest that it is worth a closer look. Given the Oedipal play around the proper name, the patronymic, and the adoption of a pseudonym, it is intriguing that the son of Abraham Zimmerman should have married a woman called Sara.

In the Book of Genesis, Sarah is the wife of the patriarch Abraham. She bears him a son 'in his old age' (Genesis 21:2) when he might have been considered incapable of fatherhood. On two separate occasions, however, she is described not as his wife but as his sister, or rather she is asked to take on the *alias* of his sister. In Genesis 12,

> it came to pass, when [Abram] was come near to enter into
> Egypt, that he said unto Sarai his wife, Behold now, I

know that thou art a fair woman to look upon:

>Therefore it shall come to pass, when the Egyptians
>shall see thee, that they shall say, This is his wife: and they
>will kill me, but they will save thee alive.
>
>Say, I pray thee, thou art my sister: that it may be well
>with me for thy sake; and my soul shall live because of
>thee (Genesis 12:11-13).

The deception is undertaken for self-protection in a foreign land. As one commentator points out,

>Abram appears in the story in a very unfavourable light. In
>order to save his own skin, he tells Sarai to pass herself off
>as his sister. A marriage contract with a beautiful woman
>could always be arranged through her brother; a husband
>might have to be liquidated. The lie pays dividends. As a
>result of Sarai's presence 'in Pharaoh's household' [Abram]
>receives 'sheep and cattle and asses, male and female
>slaves, she-asses and camels' (Davidson 25).

Abraham, that is, has saved himself and made a profit by placing his wife in a dangerous position, in much the same way as John Wesley Harding placed 'his lady by his side' when he 'took a stand.' A later chapter of Genesis repeats the story in another setting but this time attempts to rehabilitate Abraham's reputation by claiming that his story is true, that Sarah really *is* his sister. In Chapter 20 Abraham is again in a foreign country and again gives Sarah to a foreign king:

>And Abraham said of Sarah his wife, She is my sister: and
>Abimelech king of Gerar sent, and took Sarah.
>
>But God came to Abimelech in a dream by night, and
>said to him, Behold, thou art but a dead man, for the
>woman which thou hast taken; for she is a man's wife....
>
>And Abimelech said unto Abraham, What sawest thou,
>that thou hast done this thing?
>
>And Abraham said, Because I thought, Surely the fear
>of God is not in this place; and they will slay me for my
>wife's sake.
>
>And yet indeed she is my sister; she is the daughter of

my father, but not the daughter of my mother; and she
became my wife (Genesis 20:2-3, 10-12).

Davidson's commentary is again illuminating:

Some modern scholars believe that behind the present
form of the story lies the memory of a type of marriage
involving a wife-sister relationship.... Such a marriage in
which the wife has the legal status of sister is said to be a
particularly solemn and binding relationship (25-26).

The curious situation described in the Genesis stories finds echoes in both
Bob Dylan and Sam Shepard. In Shepard's *Fool for Love*, for instance, the two central characters, Eddie and May, are lovers who are also brother and half sister in
the same relationship as that claimed by Abraham: they have the same father but
different mothers. Their situation on stage, under the eyes of their ghostly and
disapproving father, the Old Man, reflects the lines of Dylan's song:

Oh, sister, when I come to lie in your arms

You should not treat me like a stranger.

Our Father would not like the way that you act

And you must realize the danger (L 382).

The theme of filial disobedience reaches back to 'Tears of Rage,' in which
another daughter says no to her father; that daughter is described as "neath the
sun,' with the inevitable pun on 'son' (L 312). The appeal to the authority of 'Our
Father' desperately reasserts patriarchal privilege. But why should Dylan have
addressed this appeal to Sara as 'Oh, *Sister*' unless he was already thinking of the
Genesis story in which the wife and the sister are one?[7]

There are other possible mythological sources for the image of the wife as
sister,[8] the most important of which is the story of Isis. In Egyptian mythology,
Isis is the sister and wife of Osiris, who is the father of their child Horus. After Set
murders Osiris, Isis recovers his body from a tamarisk tree; later, when Set has
dismembered the corpse,

Isis patiently began another search for her husband's body
and, finding the parts one by one, preserved them carefully.... She found them all except the phallus, which Set
had cast into the Nile, where it had been eaten by the Nile
crab, which for this reason was accursed. But Isis modeled

another and reconstituted the body of her husband,
anointing it with precious oils. She thus performed the
rites of embalmment for the first time, and thereby
restored Osiris to eternal life (Ions 59).

Isis can restore Osiris, the dead father of her child, not only to life but to potency.
Her female power encompasses the male; it is she who creates the phallus. Isis is
the Great Mother Goddess, the primordial female figure whose worship, many
mythographers believe, preceded that of any male deity. 'The worship of Isis,'
writes Richard Cavendish in his book on the Tarot,

> spread beyond Egypt to become one of the major mystery
> religions of the Roman world. She was a great mother
> goddess, who had many aspects, forms and symbols.... She
> was the ideal and complete woman and the prototype of
> the human woman.... Just as Isis had brought Osiris back
> to life, so her mysteries promised immortal life after death
> to those initiated into them. The ceremonies of initiation
> included a mock death and resurrection.... There was
> probably also a 'sacred marriage' or sexual union of the
> initiate with a woman representing the goddess (74).

The Christian worship of Mary arose in part as a response to, or co-option of, the
cult of Isis. The Egyptian Isis was closely associated with the River Nile, whose
annual flood, on which Egypt's survival depended, was mythologically represented
as caused by the tears of Isis weeping for her brother/husband, Osiris (Witt, 14-
15). One legend of the Tarot pack is that the cards were used to divine the date for
the Nile flood. In the Tarot, Isis is represented by The Empress, whose image
from the Waite design appears on the back cover of *Desire* (see Cavendish 76-78
and Shelton 463).

Dylan approaches this powerful body of mythological material in the song
'Isis'; in the midst of his songs on dying fathers, he attempts to evoke the Mother.
But he does so with hesitation. Isis is not the protagonist of the song that bears
her name; the focus is Osiris. And Dylan stops short of the full implications of the
Isis cult, preferring to deal with her in safer terms as the goddess who was 'chiefly
revered as the faithful wife and mourner' (Ions 62).

'This song is about marriage,' Bob Dylan told a Rolling Thunder audience in Montreal, on the live recording of 'Isis' issued on *Biograph*.9 Ostensibly, the song is about a man who marries Isis 'on the fifth day of May' (L 378), and then departs on a strange journey with another man, attempting to recover bodies from a pyramid. When the other man dies, the protagonist buries him in the empty tomb and returns 'by the fourth' to renew his relationship with Isis. One might speculate on Jacques Levy's responsibility for shaping the mythological references into such a neatly symmetrical dramatic structure, but Dylan's awareness of the Isis myth is clearly documented. Sam Shepard's *Rolling Thunder Logbook* contains a page of 'Isis Notes,' referring to the 'voyage of soul after death' and 'trials by fire, water, sex' (140). Allen Ginsberg's liner notes for *Desire* invoke 'Isis Moon Lady Language Creator Birth Goddess ... Divine Mother,' while Dylan's own liner notes pray 'Isis and the moon shine on me' (L 392).

The key reference to the Isis myth in Dylan's song is the line 'She was there in the meadow where the creek used to rise.' Given the transposition of the myth into humbler terms, the Nile becomes 'the creek.' Its failure to rise invokes the failure of fertility, which, as in the Osiris myth or the Grail legends, calls for a sacrificial death and rebirth. In the song this ritual is accomplished by the protagonist and the stranger whom he meets: indeed the two characters may be two aspects of the same role, a doubling of the self as the dying father (sacrificial victim) and the reborn son (the bridegroom of Isis). The protagonist heads out to 'a high place of darkness and light [where] the dividing line ran through the center of town.' Here he undergoes a ritual purification ('wash my clothes down') and encounters his double as the 'man in the corner [who] approached me for a match' (with a possible pun on 'match'). The would-be grave robber then dies, and substitutes his body for the missing one (of Osiris), which he had hoped to steal. Reborn, 'different,' the son returns, completing the ritual cycle of the seasons and the year (from the fifth to the fourth) to reconsecrate his mystic marriage with Isis.

When he does, he might well address her, 'Oh, sister,' like Eddie to May in *Fool for Love*, like Abraham to Sarah, or like Osiris to Isis. There is even a further possibility of bridging these different mythologies. If Dylan had been reading Robert Graves' *The White Goddess*,10 he would have seen that Osiris is sometimes identified with the Greek god Proteus, and further that Proteus also may have been the mythological 'priest-king of Pharos' who 'married Sarah, the goddess mother of the "Abraham" tribe' (Graves 276-77). (Proteus, the shape-shifter, is certainly a god who suits Dylan's constantly changing personae.) The link through Proteus may be tenuous, but 'Oh, Sister' clearly identifies Isis with Sarah, and Osiris with both Abraham and his protean son. The clearest connection is simply in the tight sound pattern that unites the names: Isis, Osiris, Oh Sister, Oh Sarah, Desire.

In 'Isis,' then, the theme of the dying father is explicitly mythological, and just as the worship of Isis was subsumed by the cult of the Virgin Mary, just as the legends of the dying God (Atthis, Osiris) were gathered up into the Christian doctrine of the Resurrection, so too Dylan moved into his Christian phase, in which all the references to outlaws and dying fathers could be summed up in 'the Man who came and died a criminal's death.' The role of dying, sacrificial father thus mutates through Abraham and Osiris to Christ: in Dylan's songs it moves from Sheriff Baker putting his guns in the ground to the dying gunfighter of 'Danville Girl,' of whom Dylan remarks, 'everything he did ... reminded me of me' (DG).

Now it is time to return to 'Brownsville Girl' and the question of what actually *happens* at the narrative level. Sam Shepard offers the following account:

> It has to do with a guy standing on line and waiting to see an old Gregory Peck movie that he can't quite remember—only pieces of it, and then this whole memory thing happens, unfolding before his very eyes. He starts speaking internally to a woman he'd been hanging out with, recalling their meetings and reliving the whole journey they'd gone on—and then it returns to the guy, who's still standing on line in the rain (interview, 198).

This is a plot summary of the song considerably more coherent than any that can with any confidence be drawn from the text. 'Brownsville Girl' never develops a single, coherent narrative: rather it presents the fragments of several possible narratives, sometimes evoked and discarded within a line, whose relationship to each other remains unspecified. Dylan, Shepard continues, is 'a lot of fun to work with, because he's so off the wall sometimes. We'd come up with a line, and I'd think that we were heading down one trail over here, and then suddenly he'd just throw in this other line, and we'd wind up following it off in some different direction' (interview 200). This fragmentation and indeterminacy are present even in 'Danville Girl,' but most revisions Dylan made before 'Brownsville Girl' increase them.

The exceptions are the references to *The Gunfighter*, which are clearer in the later version.

The continuing protagonist is referred to only as 'I.' In the first stanza he recalls a relationship with a woman specified only as 'you.' Together they travel to San Anton and the Alamo, and then cross the border into Mexico, where 'you went out to find a doctor and you never came back' (BG). It is never specified whether she went to find a doctor for herself or the protagonist,[11] nor is any reason given for her failure to return. (The possible suggestion that the 'doctor' is an abortionist reinforces the idea of the father's failed authority.) The protagonist's response, more cautious than the average macho cowboy hero's, is 'I would have gone out after you but I didn't feel like letting my head get blown off' (BG), but he gives no reason why he might anticipate such a fate. This story line is then dropped, and the final lines of the first stanza present the protagonist riding in a car with a second woman ('she ain't you') while remembering the first.

The distinction between 'you' and 'she' is clear in the first stanza, but the rest of the song falls back into the indeterminate pronoun reference characteristic of Dylan. In the second stanza the protagonist again travels in a car with a woman, but whether she is the 'you' or the 'she' of the first stanza, or even a third character, is unspecified, as is the sequence of events. 'We' visit Henry Porter, or to be more precise, 'we pulled up where Henry Porter used to live' (BG). Henry is absent, though a woman, Ruby (possibly Henry's wife), says that he will be back soon. In Henry's absence the song focuses briefly on Ruby, her sense of despair and isolation, her wish to return home, yet also her world-weary realization that escape is impossible. The protagonist proclaims that he and his woman are 'going all the way, till the wheels fall off and burn,' but Ruby 'just smiled and said,"Oh you know some babies never learn"' (BG). The song then shifts back to memories of *The Gunfighter*, and we never do find out whether Henry shows up.

Stanza three opens with another compressed melodrama, set in Corpus Christi, whose name echoes the sacrificial theme of the dying god, in which the protagonist is caught in a crossfire and mistakenly arrested. He is rescued from his predicament by the perjury of yet another unnamed woman. Again she is referred to only as 'you,' but whether she is the 'you' of the first stanza is unspecified. By the end of the stanza, he is separated from her and 'standing in line in the rain to see a movie starring Gregory Peck' (BG).

Stanza four has very little narrative content. A few general remarks are addressed to 'you,' and Henry Porter makes a brief reappearance, only to be further consigned to the indeterminacy of the song: 'the only thing we knew for sure about Henry Porter is that his name wasn't Henry Porter' (BG). The line vaguely suggests criminality in that 'Henry Porter' might be, like the 'part I was supposed to play' (BG) in *Pat Garrett and Billy the Kid*, an alias. Again the later version increases the indeterminacy of the narrative: this disclaimer of Henry Porter's name and identity is not present in 'Danville Girl.' (The fourth stanza of 'Danville Girl' is almost completely different.)

Between each stanza, a chorus addresses a 'Brownsville girl' or a 'Danville girl,' also designated as 'you.' No particular significance can be attached to the choice of name. 'Danville' perhaps evokes the 'Danville train' robbed by Jesse James and ridden by Virgil Cain. Brownsville[12] seems intended to unify the geographical references—San Anton, the Alamo, Amarillo, Corpus Christi—along the border area between Texas and Mexico that has fascinated Dylan from 'Just Like Tom Thumb's Blues' (1965) to 'Señor (Tales of Yankee Power)' (1978). As a border town it stands *between* the various realms of history, fiction, and myth; its identity is marginal and indeterminate, like that of Bob Dylan or the narrator of the song.

It is possible that most of the women in the song—the 'you's of stanzas one through four, the companion in stanza two, and the 'Brownsville girl' of the chorus—are the same person, and that a chronology might be reconstructed to account for the events. This is evidently the way Sam Shepard sees the song. But it is equally possible that the song refers to four or five different women (in the same way that 'Tangled Up In Blue' does, according to John Herdman) and that the scattered events cannot be convincingly arranged into a logically sequential plot. The best response to the song is to leave the indeterminacy open and to accept that the construction of a conventional story is not one of its purposes.

However, while the various narrative fragments may not comprise a coherent plot, they are thematically congruent with each other and with the overriding intertext of *The Gunfighter*. While no male character except Jimmy Ringo is explicitly identified as a father, all share a sense of failure and helplessness. The image of the Western protagonist as a capable, independent cowboy hero is continually undermined, as it is in so many of Sam Shepard's plays. In the stereotyped

Western thriller, the male hero is supposed to rescue the damsel in distress, but the protagonist of stanza three, who 'didn't know whether to duck or run, so I ran' (BG), has to be rescued from jail by a woman perjuring herself. Conversely, in stanza one he *fails* to rescue her (or her counterpart), abandoning her to an unknown fate. A similar willingness of ostensible heroes to allow women to suffer for them has already been noted in 'John Wesley Harding,' 'Lily, Rosemary and the Jack of Hearts,' and even in the Biblical Abraham. The grand project of stanza two—'going all the way, till the wheels fall off and burn' (BG)—seems to fizzle out and be forgotten; by stanza four the protagonist is reduced to saying, 'Hang onto me, baby, and let's hope that the roof stays on' (BG). At the equivalent spot in 'Danville Girl,' he says 'Tell me about all the things I couldn't do nothing about' (DG). Henry Porter is identified by where he 'used to live,' by his absence, and by the falseness of his name.

Even Dylan and Shepard are involved in this general abdication of power. While many lines have a rough narrative poetry, there are also confessions of verbal creative failure ('if there's an original thought out there I could use it right now'), and the lyrical set piece of the song, the chorus, is a string of banal clichés: 'Teeth like pearls / Shining like the moon above.' Although Dylan sings these lines with great conviction and even joy, any critical study of the lyrics must conclude not only that they are bad but that they are *deliberately* bad: the song is, at its center, concerned with a failure of creativity, linked to the death of the father in *The Gunfighter* and the death of patriarchal authority more generally.

The father's death returns us once more to the Oedipus myth and the place it holds in contemporary theories of narrative. The pleasure of narrative, Roland Barthes speculates, is an Oedipal one: the drive 'to denude, to know, to learn the origin and the end'; so 'every narrative (every unveiling of the truth) is a staging of the (absent, hidden, or hypostatized) father' (*Pleasure of the Text* 10). The story of 'a discarded Oedipus' (T 120) becomes the model for all stories, for the act and impulse of story telling itself. The participant in narrative (the protagonist, the hero with whom the reader is invited to identify) moves toward a disclosure which is also a closure: the revelation of a truth that was there from the start, an ending that was in place before the beginning. 'All narrative,' writes Teresa de Lauretis, 'in its movement forward toward resolution and backward to an initial moment, a paradise lost, is overlaid with ... an Oedipal logic' (125). Oedipus desires the ending of his story, but simultaneously fears it, not only because the ending is intolerable (the father, unhidden, turns out to be the man he killed at the crossroads) but also because he suspects that there is no ending, only another beginning.

The movement of narrative is the movement of desire, and desire always reconstitutes itself in the very moment that any apparent or temporary goal is fulfilled. The ending of one story is always the beginning of another, even, in the case of Oedipus, the beginning of itself. Desire depends upon a lack, upon the felt or staged absence of its object. In language, meaning itself is absent: a sign constitutes itself by the absence of the thing signified, which is always deferred, usually to another sign, where it is deferred in turn. Desire seeks the foundation of meaning, the origin, 'the father,' even while knowing that the only constant is the search itself. Narrative stages the simultaneous presence and absence of that goal. The goal's absence is required for desire to be able to move toward it; but equally, its presence is required, if only as image, as re-presentation, to place it on stage in front of the viewer's eyes as a story.

Much of this theory of narrative depends on Freud and on the reworking of Freud by Jacques Lacan. In both Freud and Lacan, the father's role is central: his authority institutes the incest prohibition, thereby separating the child from its original (or in Lacan's term, Imaginary) union with the mother. Le Nom du Père (the Name of the Father, but also his Non, his negation) creates this separation, this lack, and thus creates in the Symbolic order both desire and narrative.

The Oedipus myth deals with the incest prohibition specifically in mother-son relations. The father's death in *The Gunfighter* and his abdication in *Paris, Texas* leave the mother-son pairing intact—yet with the implication in both cases that the son is left positioned to take over the role of the father, to act out the Oedipal fantasy of being both husband and son to his mother (in relation to Sarah, to be both Abraham and the son of Abraham). Elsewhere the theme of incest is deflected to the brother-sister relationship, as with Eddie and May in *Fool for Love* or Isis and Osiris in 'Isis.' The erotic implications of 'Oh, sister, when I come to lie in your arms' are immediately countered by the Nom/Non du Père: 'Our Father would not like the way that you act / And you must realize the danger.' This comes, after all, from an album called *Desire*.

Much of Dylan's later work is overshadowed by the figure of the failed, absent, or dying father. Even the invocation of Isis serves less to worship the

Goddess than to reinscribe the theme of the father. In the unfolding drama of Dylan's lifework, Christianity functions not only to replace the core of conviction in love, in himself as a father, which he lost in the breakup with Sara, but precisely to replace that image of the father with another that is simultaneously authoritative (the patriarchal God of the Old Testament, the lawgiver) and sacrificial ('the Man who came and died a criminal's death').

As lawgiver, as Abraham, the father is, in patriarchal mythology, the source, the point of origin. Travis in *Paris, Texas* buys himself a plot of land in Paris, Texas, because he believes it is where his parents first made love: it is mythically the site of his origin. But what he actually buys is a vacant lot: the place of origin has been vacated, emptied of both presence and meaning. Nor does he truly possess or inhabit even this waste land: he only carries its photograph, which is nothing more than a sign, a reference to something not present, something which in turn itself is absent and vacant. The meaning, the origin, is always somewhere else, like the wandering father in *Fool for Love*, whose presence in one family necessarily entails his absence in the other. The sanction of the sign, its guarantee of meaningfulness, lies not in presence but in absence, in deferral, in difference.

Travis has wandered in the desert, 'somewhere without language,' and his reintroduction to the Symbolic order is gradual and difficult (he does not speak for the first half hour of the movie). Yet 'every man has your voice,' Jane tells him, gazing at the mirror in which he is both present and hidden. Behind that mirror he, as everyman, is the ultimate sanction and authority of the male patriarchal order, for whom the woman, even the mother, is objectified spectacle, fantasized pornography. The mirror/screen, in which, in Lacan's psychology, the child begins the process of ego-identification, deflects and displaces all communication between them. In the film they never meet face to face.

Traditionally, the face of God is also hidden: 'no man sees my face and lives,' as Bob Dylan puts it in 'I and I.' The doubling that we have seen throughout Dylan's work splits the self as it splits the sign: the I that writes and the I that is written, presence and absence, signifier and signified are all divided by the gap that is the action of desire. The 'dividing line' of 'Isis' runs through not just 'the center of town' but through the center of the Author, between I and I: 'Everything he did in it reminded me of me' (DG). Alias: the name as other. In *Renaldo and Clara* Ronnie Hawkins plays 'Bob Dylan' while Dylan himself appears wearing a mask. 'The audience is totally bewildered,' Sam Shepard records in *Rolling Thunder Logbook*, 'still wondering if this is actually him or not' (114). In Shepard's 'True Dylan,' the Dylan character claims that 'You always know who you are' but immediately undercuts that certainty by adding, 'I just don't know who I'm gonna become' (64). And again: 'I don't think of myself as Bob Dylan,' Bob Dylan says on the liner notes to *Biograph*: 'It's like Rimbaud said, ' "I is another." ' 'Je est un autre.'

'Un autre' is also an 'auteur,' the figure of the Author whose Death was proclaimed by Roland Barthes. 'The Author,' Barthes writes, 'is thought to nourish the book, which is to say that he exists before it, thinks, suffers, lives for it, is in the same relation of antecedence to his work as a father to his child' (*Image-Music-Text* 145). What dies in the text is the figure of the father (the Author) as the ultimate or transcendental Signified. But, as Barthes remarks, our narratives continually restage that death, Oedipally killing the father all over again, just like so many times before. The absent father in Dylan and Shepard can never be entirely disposed of: like the Old Man in *Fool for Love*, he is gone but not disconnected. His absent presence must always be re-presented, as it is in 'Brownsville Girl.'

'Brownsville Girl' longs toward a point of mythical origin, which 'seems like a long time ago, long before the stars were torn down' (BG). Yet the ideal of paradise—before the apocalypse, before the fall—is itself an image (like Travis' photo of a vacant lot in Paris, Texas) and so is always already betrayed, infected by semiotic deferral. What happened 'a long time ago' is, after all, *The Gunfighter*, a movie that already enacts the drama of the dying father. The song too begins with this image, begins with the *end* of the film, and returns to it at *its* end, just as the end of Oedipus' story is the dis-closure of its beginning. The song's fragmented and indeterminate narrative breaks up the linear drive of story toward its ending, only to reinstate that drive, dispersed and disseminated across half a dozen subplots whose incompletions try repeatedly to evade the Oedipal ending, the impossible closure of desire. There is no paradise, prelinguistic or prenarrative: the serpent is always already in Eden, the story has always already begun.

All characters in 'Brownsville Girl,' including Jimmy Ringo and Gregory Peck, live in the time *after* the stars have been torn down. It is a time of failure and betrayal ('Way down in Mexico you went out to find a doctor and you never came back / I would have gone out after you but I didn't feel like letting my head get blown off'). It is a time of separation ('I can't believe we've lived so long and are still so far apart'), a time of absence ('Henry ain't here,' 'she ain't you') (BG). It is a time when the sign is irrevocably divided from its meaning: 'when I saw you break down in front of the judge and cry real tears / It was the best acting I saw anybody do' (BG). It is a time of desire.

In 'Brownsville Girl' the figure of God the Father as ultimate source and authority of meaning has been replaced by the figure of Henry Porter. About Henry Porter, we know where he 'used to live' but not where he is now. He is present in the song only as an absence and a promise of return, a Second Coming, which is never fulfilled. Like the Jack of Hearts, he is both 'on the scene' and 'missing'; like Proteus/Osiris/Bob Dylan, he is a shape-shifter, elusive and invisible. He is the absent father whose presence is necessarily staged; he is the God who has vanished from His creation, returned like Travis to the desert; he is the author who has become un autre. He bears the authority of the Name, but it is a Nom which is also Non: 'the only thing we knew for sure about Henry Porter is that his name wasn't Henry Porter' (BG). Named and unnamed, present and absent, central and marginal, he stands in the place of the impossible origin as a stand-in for the other absent presence in the song, the kid from Hibbing, Minnesota, the son of Abraham Zimmerman, who on his thirtieth birthday went to see a movie starring Gregory Peck and found that 'everything he did in it reminded me of me' (DG). I and I. After all, the only thing we know for sure about Bob Dylan is that his name isn't Bob Dylan. It's Alias.

169

UNDER THE RE(A)D SKY

At the time of this book's publication, Bob Dylan's most recent album of new songs is *Under the Red Sky*, released in the autumn of 1990. Rather than integrate references to it into the previous chapters, I have chosen to include this account of it as a Postscript.[1]

The first thing that struck me when listening to *Under the Red Sky* was how different it was from *Oh Mercy*. And that was good news—it took me back to the days when no two consecutive Bob Dylan albums were the same, when you could never tell from one album to the next which direction he would be heading. So if you approach *Under the Red Sky* expecting to hear *Oh Mercy*, you're going to be disappointed. But if you approach *Under the Red Sky* on its own terms, then you may find that it is a very strange, mysterious, and wonderful work. If I had to invoke any previous recording by Dylan to compare it with, I would say that to find a collection of songs like *Under the Red Sky* you have to go all the way back to *The Basement Tapes*.

Of course, there are similarities and continuities from *Oh Mercy*, perhaps slyly signaled by the appearance of the word 'mercy' itself, which sneaks into *Under the Red Sky* in the last line of the last song, like a signature signing off: 'may the Lord have mercy on us all.' But the differences are more immediately obvious. We move from the precisely controlled production values of Daniel Lanois to Dylan's more accustomed ragbag approach, with its stray assortment of superstar guests dropping in on individual tracks. *Under the Red Sky* never sounds as well crafted as *Oh Mercy*, but on the other hand it's much more fun. The difference in tone is obvious in the opening songs: after the solemn socio-religious statement of 'We live in a political world' comes the cheerful informality of 'Wiggle Wiggle.' Who would have thought a 'serious artist' like Bob Dylan would write a song with such a title? He's not just letting down his hair, he's letting down his pants.

The casual appearance may be deceptive though. Even 'Wiggle Wiggle,' which seems like a throwaway opening number, almost a joke song, is the product of extensive revision. If you listen to the versions of the song performed by Dylan on tour (for instance, at Toad's Place in January, 1990), you will note that apart from the title phrase not one line is the same as the track released less than nine months later.

Nevertheless, there is something very scattered and incomplete about the album. In contrast to the tight, well-made songs of *Oh Mercy*, these new songs wander all over the place. I tend to remember individual lines and images rather than whole songs, and often these lines stick out from their surroundings in quite incongruous ways. Take, for instance, the very striking little narrative

Once there was a man who had no eyes,

Every lady in the land told him lies,

He stood beneath the silver skies

And his heart began to bleed

The theme of blindness is important to the album, but what are these lines doing in the middle of 'Unbelievable'? How do they relate to the rest of the song? A blinded man suddenly shows up for four lines, and then disappears again; no connections are made. This use of the 'bridge' passage to effect a sudden shift of perspective is not new in Dylan's work: think back to 'Señor (Tales of Yankee Power)' or 'Going Going Gone' (L 410, 342). Often the power and mystery of such songs arise not so much from the individual line as from the juxtapositions of apparently unrelated images.

Similarly, though I love almost every line of 'Handy Dandy' taken by itself, I can't combine them into any coherent picture of the song's protagonist. At times he seems like Dylan ('controversy surrounds him'); at times he seems like Christ, living in that heavenly mansion where 'no thieves can break in'; at times he seems like a cheap gangster; at times he seems like an excuse for some easy rhymes on 'candy' and 'brandy.' The only thing that ties this song together is the exuberance of its music and Dylan's bravura delivery of its long, rolling lines.

By describing these songs as incoherent I am not necessarily finding fault with them but rather trying to describe the kind of writing that's going on. Coherence is only one kind of virtue. In the language of literary criticism, *Oh*

Mercy displays a modernist urge toward the perfect lyric while *Under the Red Sky* reaches for postmodernist indeterminacy and open-endedness. There is a sense of risk-taking in *Under the Red Sky*. Every line takes a deep breath and plunges reck-lessly in an unexpected direction:

> Hey! Who could your lover be?
> Hey! Who could your lover be?
> Let me eat off his head so you can really see!

It is this craziness, as well as the down-home barnyard apocalypse of a song like 'Cat's in the Well,' that reminds me of *The Basement Tapes*. Describing that album, Greil Marcus wrote of 'strange adventures and poker-faced insanities' in songs that 'seem to leap out of a kaleidoscope of American music no less immedi-ate for its venerability.' A line like 'Back alley Sally is doing the American jump' seems to come straight out of the ethos of *The Basement Tapes*. From folk songs to the blues, from nursery rhymes to traditional counting songs, *Under the Red Sky* is filled with echoes. Even the apparent casualness of its craft, after the highly pol-ished professionalism of *Oh Mercy*, suggests a deliberate courting of the naïf. This is Bob Dylan's Grandma Moses album.

Pop music itself is part of this eclectic range of sources. The title *Under the Red Sky* recalls an album by U2, *Under a Blood Red Sky*, while the cover image, a black and white photograph in a desert setting, further evokes U2's *The Joshua Tree*. Other echoes and borrowings abound. The main riff in 'Unbelievable' is similar to Robert Palmer's hit a few years ago, 'Simply Irresistible,' which ended up as a Pepsi commercial. The music of 'Handy Dandy' echoes everything from Dylan's 'Like a Rolling Stone' (in Al Kooper's organ) to 'Snoopy Hang On.' When 'Wiggle Wiggle' appeared at a few concerts in 1990, Dylan scholars were unsure whether it was an original composition or another obscure 1950s B-side dredged up from the memories of late night radio in Hibbing.

The blues are also evident, in the format of '10,000 Men' and 'Cat's in the Well.' (Perhaps 'Handy Dandy' is, after all, W.C. Handy.) And the blues' fondness for repeated lines shows up to stunning effect in the title song, 'Under the Red Sky,' a rhythmic *tour de force* in which the same lines are repeated at double speed. The effect of this repetition is one of simultaneous progression and stasis: a story is told, but the situation remains the same. It has both the linearity of narrative and the timelessness of myth.

The title song, 'Under the Red Sky,' also invokes the feeling of nursery rhymes, though in a totally perverse manner, in which all the conventions of the form are viewed through a veil of desperate black humour:

> Let the wind blow low, let the wind blow high,
>
> One day the little boy and the little girl were both baked in a pie.

The saccharine melody enables Dylan to sing these lines with a straight face, so that at first you don't quite believe what you're hearing. By substituting 'the little boy and the little girl' for, let us say, 'four and twenty black-birds,' Dylan simultaneously uses and parodies the original form of the nursery rhyme. The parody works by exaggeration or by *literalizing* the image. There is something uncomfortably specific about these lines, something that invites us actually to see and experience the cruelty which is often present in nursery rhymes but is usually glossed over. The same thing happens in a later song, when the nursery rhyme 'Ding dong dell, pussy's down the well' becomes 'Cat's in the well, the wolf is looking down....'

Nursery rhymes provide a major intertextual matrix for the text of *Under the Red Sky*. Simon McAslan has pointed out a series of echoes and direct quotations from *The Real Mother Goose*,[2] including such key phrases as 'Every lady in this land,' 'feed the swine,' and 'The bull's in the barn.' The 'ten thousand men' may recall the Grand Old Duke of York while a nursery rhyme entitled 'Boy and Girl' opens with

> There was a little boy and a little girl
>
> Lived in an alley,
>
> Says the little boy to the little girl,
>
> 'Shall I, oh, shall I?'

Compare Dylan's lines 'There was a little boy and there was a little girl / Lived in an alley under the red sky.' The nursery rhyme references are not, however, *simple* quotation. The black-comedy context of 'Under the Red Sky' parodies the supposed innocence of nursery rhymes by insisting on an uncomfortably literal reading of what might otherwise be passed over as a conventional image. This technique of literalization is also used in two other areas of popular culture present in *Under the Red Sky*: numbers and clichés.

In a few key songs, a stress on numbering is strongly characteristic of folk culture. '2 x 2' is the most obvious example: it takes the form of a traditional counting song, but again the form is pushed toward the edge of exaggeration and parody. If one takes the numbers literally, the pictures they produce become absurd and surrealistic: 'Ten thousand women all sweepin' my room.' Biblically, ten may be the number of perfection (ten Commandments, ten tribes of Israel), but equally it may be the number of retribution (ten plagues sent on Egypt). 'Thousand' is an intensifier, a higher degree of whatever the number signifies; seven is another number of perfection. But together (ten thousand men, each of them with seven wives) they go just too far. Seventy thousand wives? The arithmetic is too precise for this numerology to be taken seriously.

The same thing happens with cliché. Dylan continually takes words or phrases gone dead in conventional usage and sets them in new contexts that twist their meaning and force them back into life.[3] Some reviewers have complained that the language of *Under the Red Sky* is banal, but the point is precisely the banality and what is done with it. The reviewer in *Rolling Stone*, for instance, quoted with great disdain the couplet, 'They said it was the land of milk and honey / Now they say it's the land of money.' Taken by themselves, these two lines are banal, but the next line must be included too: 'Who ever thought they could ever make that stick?' Now the change in social values is something imposed, a con job, and 'make that stick' suddenly and ironically evokes the literal image of 'honey.' The promised land has become a sticky mess.

Sometimes Dylan deconstructs cliché by simple inversion: 'Beat that horse and saddle up that drum.' This is an old Dylan trick, as in 'he just smoked my eyelids / An' punched my cigarette' (L 228), but it puts both halves of the phrase in a new context and invites us to see them freshly. We get, for instance, an uncomfortably literal picture of someone beating a horse, which in turn echoes 'beating on a dead horse' in *Oh Mercy*; at the same time 'saddle up that drum' eerily foreshadows those 'ten thousand men' who are 'Drummin' in the morning, in the evening they'll be coming for you.'

Most obviously, the song 'God Knows' takes a phrase that all of us, God knows, use without thinking and, by sheer repetition, restores it to literal meaning, so that the song moves from the casual 'God knows you ain't pretty' to the entirely serious assertion of divine omniscience: 'God knows everything.' As another example, 'Truer words have not been spoken' is simple cliché; but when the rhyme adds 'or broken,' the entire phrase twists back on itself. 'Word' changes from its declarative sense, as a unit of meaning, to its performative sense, as a promise; and the truth, not only of this word but of all words, is questioned. 'Truer words have not been broken' is a tortuously difficult sentence to untangle, even syntactically: how many negatives and double negatives are in there? The same is true of 'None of them doing nothin' that your mama wouldn't disapprove.' Does she approve or doesn't she?

And what are we to make of that extraordinary line 'Cat's in the well, and the barn is full of the bull'? It seems almost a nonsense line, produced by internal alliteration and rhyme (barn/bull/full); at the same time it suggests the colloquial use of 'bull' as bullshit, another kind of nonsense. The farm does seem neglected —perhaps the barn is literally full of shit. The words also might suggest a very large bull, an unnaturally large and threatening animal. The song is full of such strange inversions of the natural order, and this oversize bull takes its place, with the wolf and the dogs, as an image of menace.

The verbal texture of *Under the Red Sky*, though appearing casual at first glance, is rich and rewarding. And, of course, no Dylan album is without the occasional startling, vivid, or beautiful image: 'Ten thousand men dressed in Oxford blue,' or 'Back alley Sally is doing the American jump,' or 'You're blowing down the shaky street.' I wouldn't trade the complete works of Bruce Springsteen for that single adjective 'shaky.'

But what do all these scattered effects actually *say*? Here I feel less certain: the album's apparently casual and scattered nature is part of its theme, and to propose a coherent thematic interpretation is to work against the directions suggested by the text. But two areas of investigation are possible for a thematic analysis of *Under the Red Sky*. One is very general—the continuing Dylan theme of apocalypse—and the other is more specific—the strange treatment of vision and blindness.

We live in a political world, and this is no less true of *Under the Red Sky* than of *Oh Mercy*. 'Unbelievable' speaks of social disintegration while 'T.V. Talkin' Song' burlesques the degeneracy of the media. Signs of impending catastrophe are everywhere: '2 x 2' is about Noah's flood while the 'fire next time' in 'God Knows' evokes both the Negro Spiritual ('God gave Noah the rainbow sign, / No more water, the fire next time'), and also James Baldwin's impassioned account of black experience in America. The only previous appearance in Dylan's work of 'ten thousand men' is the 'ten thousand talkers whose tongues were all broken,' in the apocalyptic 'A Hard Rain's A-Gonna Fall' (L 59).

In 'Under the Red Sky,' the impending catastrophe is imagined in ecological terms: the sky turning red, the rivers running dry. This 'red sky' has many possible sources and implications. Its field of play includes the album's cover photograph, which is in black and white. (Inside, the lettering of the lyrics, white on black, reverses the normal order.) Dylan squats on his heels in a desert landscape, one in which indeed the rivers have run dry, and the only things red (and read) in the sky are the letters of his own name. But the pose in the photograph is highly reminiscent of the inner sleeve photograph in *Infidels*, where Dylan also squats on stony ground and where the sky is red. In the background of the *Infidels* photograph, under the red sky, is the holy city of Jerusalem, the city of the end of time.

According to weather lore, 'Red sky at night, shepherd's delight; red sky in the morning, shepherd's warning.' This proverb is quoted by no less an authority than Jesus, who uses it to give his own 'warning,' in Matthew 16:1-4:

> The Pharisees also … came, and tempting desired him
> that he would shew them a sign from heaven.
>
> He answered and said unto them, When it is evening,
> ye say, It will be fair weather: for the sky is red.
>
> And in the morning, It will be foul weather to day: for
> the sky is red and lowring. O ye hypocrites, ye can discern
> the face of the sky; but can ye not discern the signs of the
> times?
>
> A wicked and adulterous generation seeketh after a
> sign; and there shall be no sign given unto it, but the sign
> of the prophet Jonas. And he left them, and departed.

Christ's warning speaks to a 'wicked and adulterous' generation, and this brings us back perhaps to 'Wiggle Wiggle.' The song appears to be a straightforward call for its audience to get out there and wiggle. But there are some uneasy lines: 'Wiggle till you vomit fire' doesn't sound like much fun. A line from the earlier version, 'Wiggle on the 4th of July,' suggests that it could even be a State of the Union message on America's wicked and adulterous generation. The 'big fat snake' in the last line is suitably ambiguous: the snake is a standard phallic symbol and a symbol of mystical wisdom, but he is also, of course, Satan. He is the animal *not* named in 'Man Gave Names To All the Animals.' On the album's cover photograph, what is Bob Dylan doing wearing snakeskin boots?

Satan also appears in 'Under the Red Sky' as the 'man in the moon.' Dylan has a thing about the moon; there's a 'blue moon' in 'Wiggle Wiggle' and a 'sanctified' moon in 'Unbelievable.' In 'License to Kill' he claimed that 'man has invented his doom, / First step was touching the moon' (L 473). Now this man, who not only touches the moon but is in it, causes the sky to turn red and the river to run dry. In 'God Knows'

> God knows there's a river,
> God knows how to make it flow,
> God knows you ain't gonna be taking
> Nothing with you when you go.

Again there is the association of water, either as flood or as drought, with death. For Dylan the 'political' world is always near its end. Consistently throughout his work he has been drawn to the eschatological vision of the final days; this is always what gives his songs their urgency, morally, socially, and theologically.

'Cat's in the Well' is the fullest statement of this apocalyptic vision, though typically, it is conveyed in terms of a barnyard fable. (It is pertinent to note that some 1990 Dylan concerts opened with an instrumental version of 'Old MacDonald Had a Farm'!) The repeated title phrase, besides echoing the nursery rhyme, suggests both the cat's helplessness and the potential pollution of the source of life. From the cat menaced by the wolf through increasing levels of generalization, 'The world's being slaughtered.' The 'natural' order of the barnyard has collapsed. Besides the comic yet menacing bull, the 'dogs are going to war' (another example of a literalized cliché): the animals are taking over. The human forces of order and salvation, whether matriarchal or patriarchal, are helpless. The 'gentle lady is asleep,' and this sleep is not just passive indifference but a condition of being under attack: 'the silence is a-stickin' her deep.' The father is equally ineffective, 'reading the news' while 'His hair's falling out and all of his daughters need shoes.' By the end of the song, disaster gathers: autumn closes in, and all that is left is a desperate prayer for mercy to an absent God.

The theme of vision and blindness may be approached through one of the lighter, more comic pieces, the 'T.V. Talkin' Song.' This is a cunningly balanced song: what it says about the dire effects of the media is carefully distanced through two levels of characterization. Much of it sounds like a rant, but the overstatement is acknowledged by the fact that the rant is placed in the mouth of a Hyde Park preacher, an admitted crank. It is further filtered through the divided conscious-ness of the narrator, who admits that 'My thoughts began to wander' yet still remembers enough of what he heard to narrate it to us. The preacher's attack on T.V. is covered and repeated on T.V. The medium co-opts its own criticism and appropriates it as entertainment. What in the end does the narrator really remem-ber: what he saw or what he saw on T.V.? What is at stake here is a problematic of *sight*. The preacher warns against letting your mind be soiled by 'something you can't see.' This is an odd warning against television, the primary visual medium of our time, but it presumably means that you don't *really* see things on T.V. True sight, clear moral vision, must be direct.

Yet curiously, heaven is also something you can't see:

God knows there's a heaven,

God knows it's out of sight.

Heaven as 'out of sight' is another play on cliché: in colloquial speech 'out of sight' means both wonderful and unbelievable, but heaven is also literally out of sight. It can't be seen, even on T.V. It has to be (seen to be) believed.

Not being able to see heaven, we are in effect blind: 'Two by two, they step into the ark, / Two by two, they step in the dark.' This numbered procession, attempting to escape the catastrophe of the flood, approaches heaven. 'Seven by seven, they headed for heaven, / Eight by eight, they got to the gate.' But here they stop, drink wine, and then drink it again, before the song retraces its steps to begin the numbering again. They have not passed through the gate of heaven; they are back down in the flood, in the dark.

Physical blindness, then, is a metaphor for spiritual blindness; yet, in another of the paradoxes in which this album abounds, it is often also a sign of prophetic insight. In the song 'Unbelievable,' 'there was a man who had no eyes....' This man could simply be the victim of the 'unbelievable' political world that surrounds him. But he may also be a blind prophet or poet, someone who is not believed: Homer, Tiresias, or Oedipus. Blind Oedipus was guided by his daughter, Antigone, but this man is betrayed even by his daughters: 'Every lady in the land told him lies.' This use of 'lady' looks forward to the sleeping 'gentle lady' of 'Cat's in the Well.'

Other connections multiply between these songs. In 'Cat's in the Well,' the father who reads the news is unable to provide his daughters with shoes, but in 'Under the Red Sky,' the 'little girl' is promised that 'Someday ... you'll have a diamond as big as your shoe.' But who makes this promise? Is it the singer, or is it the sinister 'man in the moon'? And how does it relate to the mysterious second bridge of the song?

This is the key to the kingdom and this is the town

This is the blind horse that leads you around

The 'key to the kingdom' should unlock heaven's 'gate' at which 'eight by eight' arrive. But if heaven is out of sight, does the 'blind horse' lead you toward it or away from it? Is agreeing to be lead around by a blind horse a sign of humility or a sign of the reversal of the natural order? And how does this horse relate to the horse being beaten, the dead horse of *Oh Mercy*, the pale horse of the Apocalypse?

Strangest of all is the line from '10,000 Men': 'Let me eat off his head so you can really see.' The singer appears to argue that the woman being addressed will only 'see' truly and clearly when she can look through her own eyes: at the moment she sees only through her lover's eyes, which the singer generously offers to remove. Perhaps the exact meaning is less important than the bizarre shock effect of the line, but it does imply an interchangeability of identity, eye and I.

Throughout this book I have argued that the metaphor of sight is central to Dylan's songs and that the double sense of eye and I is continuously at play. The references to sight and blindness in *Under the Red Sky* are not in themselves conclusive, but they indicate the persistence of these motifs in his work. Look one last time at the cover photograph: one eye open, one eye almost closed; the gaze that returns the camera's gaze is wary, suspicious, defensive. Retreating from a relationship in 'Born in Time,' the singer, who has always preferred the disguise of an alias, complains that it was 'too revealing.' What is revealed in *Under the Red Sky* is like heaven—it's out of sight.

As always, Bob Dylan leaves us with more questions than answers. In 1991, at fifty years of age, he remains as much an enigma as when he first assumed the alias 'Bob Dylan' more than thirty years ago. *Under the Red Sky* is, in my view, a triumphant reassertion of his creative power—but it is a very open-ended album, offering no firm conclusions except the always-present possibility of Apocalypse. *The Bootleg Series*, on the other hand, moves back into his rich history and revisits the past with an ironic eye: the title, an officially released bootleg, acknowledges the paradoxes of his legendary status. Where will he go from here? No one can say—and that unpredictability remains the root of our continuing fascination with him. Who else, appearing on the Grammy Awards at the height of the Gulf War, could have sung a song so mordant in its protest as 'Masters of War'? And who else would have dared to sing it in such an unrecognizable form? Bob Dylan has never advanced in a straight line; his most characteristic move has always been the sidestep. Hell, just call him Alias. That's what I do.

N O T E S

P R E F A C E   N O T E S

1. 'Hull Rust Mahooning Mine: a national historic landmark,' pamphlet distributed by the Hibbing Historical Society.

2. My account of this concert is based on the biographies of Scaduto, Shelton, and Spitz, and on comments passed on to those attending the 'Mixed Up Confusion' Bob Dylan convention in Hibbing, October, 1989.

C H A P T E R   O N E   N O T E S

1. See, for instance, the hostile reactions to Aidan Day's academic style in *Jokerman*. Robert Sandall in *The Sunday Times* (July 17, 1988) lambasted 'ardent and wordy intellectuals' who '[cart] Dylan's lyrics away to the library to subject them to a tortuously close textual scrutiny.' The issue was extensively debated in the correspondence columns of *The Telegraph*, 8 and 9 (October and December, 1982).

2. Theorists like Jacques Derrida would argue that there is, strictly speaking, no such thing as a fully self-present 'intention,' but that the structure of language ensures that intention is always divided and deferred. Given these limitations, however, Derrida still writes, 'The category of intention will not disappear; it will have its place, but from this place it will no longer be able to govern the entire scene and the entire system of utterances' (M 326).

3. See, for example, Stokes 390.

4. The mask also acted as a mini-megaphone, amplifying the actor's voice through the carved mouth hole. One etymological theory, now disputed, held that this was the origin of the Latin word for mask (per-sona: through-sound), and thus of the English word 'person.'

5. See *Biograph*, liner notes, side 7; the comment comes, ironically, on a song called 'Up To Me.' For a more detailed discussion of Dylan and Rimbaud, see Chris Whitehouse and John Bauldie, 'On the Heels of Rimbaud,' *The Telegraph* 24 (Summer, 1986), 47-64. The famous Rimbaud line—'Je est un autre'—appears in a letter to Georges Izambard, May 13, 1871.

C H A P T E R   T W O   N O T E S

1. Printed lyrics did appear in *Bob Dylan at Budokan* (1978), but this album was initially intended for Japanese release only. The lyrics are also printed on the sleeve of *Under the Red Sky* (1990).

2. See Clinton Heylin, 'Lyrics 1962-1985: A Collection Short of the Definitive,' in *All Across the Telegraph*, 229-242. The lists of omitted songs are also published in Heylin's *Stolen Moments*, 395-397.

3. Such considerations inevitably raise the question of the extent to which *Lyrics* presents an 'authorized' text. Can we be sure that Dylan made all these changes, or could they be the result of editorial decisions by other people? Researching this point for a Ph.D. dissertation, Craig Snow reports: 'Martha Kaplan, who worked on *Writings and Drawings* and *Lyrics 1962-1985* as an editor with Alfred A. Knopf, Inc., the publisher of both books, told me in a phone interview that "all material" came from Dylan and that the editors at Knopf dealt with him as they would with any author. Pressed further, she clarified her contention, pointing out that the material for the two books came "from [Dylan's] office," but the editors did not alter the text of the lyrics' (49). This still leaves open the possibility that someone else 'from [Dylan's] office' made editorial changes—but the likelihood is that the oddities of the *Lyrics* text can be attributed to Dylan himself.

4. Conversely, he has often chosen to release on official albums some less successful live performances. The *Dylan and the Dead* live album, for instance, contains a performance of 'Queen Jane Approximately' in which Dylan forgets the words and stumbles through one verse, whereas other concerts from the same tour featured the same song with no errors.

5. These examples are drawn from Bert Cartwright, 'Like a Dead Man's Last Pistol Shot?' *The Telegraph* 29 (Spring, 1988), 109-114. More recently, Christopher Tookey wrote that 'the voice—which seemed, confusingly, to be singing in Iranian—was definitely either his, or that of a very old Ayatollah who had recently sandpapered his vocal cords' (London *Daily Telegraph*, June 9, 1989).

6. For a good collection of cover versions, listen to *The Songs of Bob Dylan*, compiled by Michael Gray and Iain McLay, Start Records STDL 20 (1989). Among the better tracks on this album are 'Tomorrow Is a Long Time' by Elvis Presley; 'Just Like Tom Thumb's Blues' by Judy Collins; 'Absolutely Sweet Marie' by Jason and the Scorchers; 'This Wheel's On Fire' by Siouxsie and the Banshees; 'Seven Days' by Ron Wood; etc. The album does not include any translations of Dylan songs, but there are many of these, notably Dionysos Savopoulos's wonderful Greek version of 'All Along the Watchtower.'

7. The song Boone sings is 'I Almost Lost My Mind,' by Ivory Joe Hunter. Cohen also quotes the lines 'I went to see a gypsy / And had my fortune read,' which Dylan later adapted for his intertextual tribute to Elvis Presley, 'Went To See the Gypsy' (L 288).

8. Several other recordings of the early 1970s show similar effects: two takes of 'Forever Young' on *Planet Waves*, for example, and on *Self-Portrait*, two versions of 'Alberta' as well as of 'Little Sadie.' In the latter case, the very rough, emotionally expressive version, which pays a lot of attention to the meaning of the words, is entitled 'In Search of Little Sadie,' whereas the much smoother, jauntier take, in which the tragic narrative becomes merely the excuse for a cheery piece of music-making, has the title of 'Little Sadie.'

9. Similarly, when Dylan at this time sang 'It Ain't Me, Babe' (L 144), the context clearly implied that it ain't *me* you're looking for, babe—it's Him.

CHAPTER THREE NOTES

1. See *Limited Inc* (Northwestern University Press, 1988).

2. Gray's initial discussion is in *Song and Dance Man*, 279-281; it was repeated in the revised edition, *The Art of Bob Dylan*, 167-168. Gray's retraction is in *The Telegraph* 29 (Spring, 1988). Dylan's 'claim' was made only on the record label; the sheet music credited him only with the arrangement, and the words do not appear in *Lyrics*.

3. The facts about Dylan's Minnesota background as Bobby Zimmerman were first widely publicized in an article in *Newsweek*, November 4, 1963.

4. At the same concert, Joan Baez joins in the game. Introducing 'Silver Dagger,' the traditional folk song that had been the first track on her first album, she describes it as 'an old Bob Dylan song.'

5. See, for instance, 'Desolation Row,' which features Cinderella, Bette Davis, Romeo, Cain and Abel, the Hunchback of Notre Dame, the Good Samaritan, Ophelia, Noah, Einstein, Robin Hood, a jealous monk, Dr Filth and his nurse, the Phantom of the Opera, Casanova, Nero, Ezra Pound, T.S. Eliot, and the entire passengers and crew of the *Titanic*, as well as 'Lady and I' (L 204-206).

6. For a full account of this topic, see Karen Mills-Courts, *Poetry as Epitaph: Representation and Poetic Language* (Baton Rouge: Louisiana UP, 1990).

7. Appropriate as it is, the name 'Alias' was not invented by Dylan. *All Along the Telegraph* quotes a passage from Pat Garrett's *The Authentic Life of Billy, the Kid*: 'Billy's partner doubtless had a name which was his legal property, but he was so given to changing it that it is impossible to fix on the right one. Billy always called him "Alias"' (126). The historical Billy went by a variety of names which were or were not 'his legal property': William H. Bonney, Henry Antrim, Henry McCarty....

8. 'You may call me R.J., you may call me Ray' is quoted from the comedian Ray Johnson. These lines formed, as it were, his signature.

9. See Kamuf's comments on Jean-Jacques Rousseau: 'Rousseau wrote his *Confessions* to justify and authenticate a signature already circulating widely so that, at a certain point in his career ... his signature is entirely concerned with *countersigning* what has already been signed' (25).

10. These values of presence and communication seem to me to form the unspoken assumptions underlying Paul Williams' *Performing Artist*. My main disagreement with this fine book is that I don't think it sufficiently acknowledges how problematic these assumptions are.

CHAPTER FOUR NOTES

1. This question is also central to the work of Leonard Cohen. See especially *The Energy of Slaves* (1972), whose lines 'I can't write a poem anymore / You can call me Len or Lennie now / like you always wanted' seem quite strikingly to prefigure Dylan's 'You may call me Bobby, you may call me Zimmy' (L 424).

2. This effect is increased for a recorded song, which is always there to be played again. The 'eternal circle' is also a turntable.

3. During the 1989 tour, in the song 'Memphis Blues Again,' Dylan changed the lines 'Shakespeare, he's in the alley / With his pointed shoes and his bells' (L 228) to 'Shakespeare, he's in the alley / With his *tambourine* and his bells'—another association, perhaps, of the tambourine with a male Muse.

4. This stanza is often omitted in concert performances.

5. The terms of this discussion are those of Jacques Derrida, who defines all language as a 'trace' of an origin that can never be fully present. However, both 'shadow' and 'trace' do appear in Dylan's text as well.

6. See Bill Allison, 'She Belongs To Me: One Possible Hearing,' *The Telegraph* 19 (Spring, 1985), 58-70.

7. The extent of Dylan's knowledge of the more obscure backways of American popular song can be seen on *Down in the Groove*, in such selections as 'When Did You Leave Heaven?' (by W. Bullock and R. Whiting) or 'Ninety Miles an Hour Down a Dead End Street' (by H. Blair and D. Robertson). In the former, the treatment of the 'angel' cliché is reminiscent of Dylan's 'You Angel You' (L 348).

8. I exclude from this list the poem Dylan wrote as liner notes for *Joan Baez In Concert Volume II* (L 78-85). Most of this poem is an extended and rather heavy-handed compliment to Baez. She does not appear as an image for Dylan. Instead, the poem presents a series of romantic images of Dylan as 'a demon child ... a saddened clown ... an arch criminal who'd done no wrong ... a lonesome king ... a scared poet ... a rebel wild.' These images remain unconvincing, precisely because they are unmediated, and have not been reflected through the persona of another artist.

9. For a similar account of the paradoxes in these last lines, see Paul Williams, 34.

10. The argument of the poem takes the form of a vastly extended sentence: When you're in an extreme state (many parallel examples), and there's something you need (examples), you won't find it in these places (examples), but there are two places you can go to (the two final possibilities).

11. A few examples: 'Yes, I am a thief of thoughts' (L 112); 'If I was a master thief' (L 211); 'Now you stand with your thief, you're on his parole' (L 240); 'the thief, he kindly spoke' (L 252); 'Why must I always be the thief?' (L 312).

12. Biographically, Robert Zimmerman does have a brother—David—but the word is meant in a more symbolic sense.

13. It is also, ironically, the only original Bob Dylan composition to contain the word 'bootleg.'

CHAPTER FIVE NOTES

1. See Patrick J. Webster, who also claims that 'your friend in the cowboy hat' (L 244) is Jack Elliott.

2. Even a comic song like 'All Over You' plays with this ambivalence by exploiting the loving and vengeful senses of the same phrase: 'I'm lookin' forward to when I can do it all again / And babe, I'll do it all over you' (L 44).

3. Suze Rotolo sailed for Italy on June 8, 1962, and Dylan recorded 'Down the Highway' on

July 9 (Heylin 24-25). The second 'Italy' is added almost as an afterthought, a quizzical puzzlement at the woman's choice of destination. This doubling of 'Italy' was later to acquire an added irony, since in January, 1963, Dylan also went to Italy, in search of Suze, only to find that she had already returned to New York.

4. The instrumental piece usually referred to as 'The Cough Song,' recorded in 1963, appears on *The Bootleg Series* under the title 'Suze.'

5. Dylan retrospectively claimed that the song was written for his wife, Sara: 'Stayin' up for days in the Chelsea Hotel, / Writin' "Sad-Eyed Lady of the Lowlands" for you' (L 390). Of course, he also claimed that 'Sara,' the song in which he made this claim, was not written for his wife! Critics who accept this claim point to the line about 'your magazine-husband.' Robert Shelton refers to Sara's previous marriage to 'Victor Lownes, the Chicago and London executive of the *Playboy* magazine empire' (325). (Shelton does not explain how 'Lownes' became 'Lowndes.') Bob Spitz, who spells the name 'Lownds,' identifies Sara's former husband as 'fashion-photographer Hans Lownds' (277). Does a 'fashion-photographer' qualify as a 'magazine-husband'? Those other critics who persist, despite Dylan's denial, in thinking that the 'Sad-Eyed Lady' was Joan Baez have equally strong evidence in the text: 'Spanish manners,' for instance, or even the word 'Lowlands' itself. The traditional British folk song, 'Lowlands,' sometimes known as 'The Lowlands of Holland,' was part of Baez's repertoire in the early 60s; it appears on *The Best of Joan Baez*, Squire SC 33001. On the basis of the song itself, it is impossible to state definitely who Dylan had in mind when he wrote it. However, from 1975 on, the claim made in 'Sara' becomes an inescapable part of the song's intertext.

6. A similar argument can be made for other songs of this period that feature a triangular structure, such as 'She's Your Lover Now' (L 244) or 'Fourth Time Around' (L 237). Even in 'Visions of Johanna' (L 223), the division between the singer and Louise, in what they each desire of the absent Johanna, is not an absolute one.

7. None of this need rule out the alternative interpretation of these lines as drug references, in which the 'warehouse eyes' are dilated pupils, the 'Arabian drums' are amphetamines, and the 'gate' is the entry point of a hypodermic needle.

8. A similar configuaration (woman claimed by the ghost of a dead sailor) occurs in the traditional ballad 'House Carpenter,' which was sung by both Dylan and Baez in the early 1960s. No recording of Dylan's version was available until *The Bootleg Series*. And again the Zimmerman/carpenter translation should be noted.

9. After 'You're the other half of what I am, you're the missing piece,' any Hallmark greeting-card versifier could have produced 'And I love you more than ever with that love that doesn't cease' (L 350). Curiously, *Lyrics* flattens out some of the best lines in this song. On record, Dylan sings 'Love you more than madness, more than dreams upon the sea,' but the printed text gives 'more than *waves* upon the sea.'

10. This is one of the few direct references in Dylan's work to the town in which he was born. Duluth had been recalled in '11 Outlined Epitaphs,' and it also appears in the *Planet Waves* liner notes, which are unaccountably missing from *Lyrics*: 'Duluth—where Baudelaire lived & Goya cashed in his chips, where Joshua brought the house down!'

11. The same is true of the September versions of 'If You See Her, Say Hello' and 'You're a Big Girl Now,' both of which are more sympathetic than the later recordings. The earlier version of 'You're a Big Girl Now' was later released on *Biograph* and the other September takes, including 'Idiot Wind,' on *The Bootleg Series*.

12. The same idea is handled much better in 'Call Letter Blues,' a fascinating song of this period that remained unreleased and even unbootlegged until 1991.

13. Spitz claims that Dylan recorded the song without warning, springing it on Sara in the studio. Spitz quotes one of his many unnamed sources as saying that Dylan 'turned and sang the song directly at Sara, who sat through it all with an impervious look on her face' (466).

CHAPTER SIX NOTES

1. For the purposes of this chapter, I have adopted Bicker's numbering of the scenes in

Renaldo and Clara, and my references to the film will be annotated accordingly. I realize, of course, that his pamphlet has had an even more limited circulation than the film, but there is, for the moment, no other convenient way of identifying particular scenes.

2. The interview was conducted in 1977, but not published until 1989: see under 'Ginsberg' in Works Cited. My general practice has been to rely very little on statements made by Dylan in interviews, partly because Dylan interviews have to be carefully weighed to see whether he is giving straight answers, and partly because I believe that statements an artist makes outside the work carry no special authority. But in this case, it is clear that Dylan is giving very honest, careful answers, and interviews like this one have become almost a part of the text of *Renaldo and Clara*.

3. Ginsberg 27; also in an interview in *Playboy* (March 1978): 'Ramon, the dead lover of Mrs Dylan, appears as a ghost in the bathroom.'

4. In a different interview: this one is in *The Telegraph* 12 (June, 1983).

5. In this way at least, *Renaldo and Clara* resembles Sam Peckinpah's *Pat Garrett and Billy the Kid*. Peckinpah's film, like Dylan's, was commercially released in a badly cut version. Recently, a complete print of *Pat Garrett and Billy the Kid* has been shown, which enables one to see that the whole film is built on a series of doubled characters, incidents, even small gestures.

6. Even an innocuous scene like that of the roadies setting up the equipment for a concert (35) contains the line 'There are two cables, one gold and one violet,' while someone else complains that he has twin amps and the serial numbers don't match.

7. Scene 5 features The Masked Tortilla (Bob Neuwirth) talking about a black poet called Tony Curtis. Although the actor Tony Curtis is never mentioned, his name surely occurs to an audience. Bicker quotes Dylan as once saying that, if a film were to be made of his life, 'he hoped Tony Curtis would play the leading role' (31). There is also a contemporary *British* poet called Tony Curtis, though it is unlikely that The Masked Tortilla would have been aware of him.

8. Another Cohen reference just misses being included. The performance of 'Isis' (9) begins, in the film, at the second verse. The full performance (recorded in Montreal and released on *Biograph)* begins with Dylan's dedication, 'This is for Leonard, if he's still here.'

9. Shepard may be confusing the two concerts, importing the 'Bob Dylan mask' from the 1964 comment and imposing it on the 1975 Richard Nixon mask. Larry Sloman's version: 'And in honor of Halloween Neuwirth and then Jack Elliott come out in masks. After Jack's set, Dylan bounds on, in black leather jacket, long Indian scarf, and a grotesque, transparent plastic-sequined mask.... He's so intense that he forgets one small detail as he starts into the harmonica break: it's hard to blow harp through a mask. A quick swirl, the mask goes, and the audience explodes at the sight of the familiar face' (74). Sloman also writes that he mentioned the 1964 Halloween concert to Dylan, who seemed to agree with the connection (177).

10. Cf. the ending of 'Lily, Rosemary and the Jack of Hearts': 'She was thinkin' 'bout her *father,* who she very rarely saw, / Thinkin' 'bout Rose*mary* and thinkin' about the *law*' (L 366, emphasis added). I will return to this song in Chapter Eight.

11. There may be an additional joke in the pairing of Ronnie and Ronee as the fictional married couple. Ronee Blakley was best known for her performance in Robert Altman's *Nashville* (1975), where she played Barbara Jean, an idolized singer assassinated by a fan. See Sam Shepard's *Rolling Thunder Logbook* (60, 89) for further comments.

12. This theme has been tragically extended by the subsequent deaths of some of the major figures involved in the making of *Renaldo and Clara*, notably Howard Alk and David Blue.

13. One line in this Blake song—'the hills are all covered with sheep'—is later echoed by Dylan in 'Ring Them Bells': 'the mountains are filled with lost sheep' (OM).

14. This theme is extensively treated by Jacques Derrida. See *The Ear of the Other:* 'Inasmuch as *I am and follow after* [je suis] my father, I am the dead man and I am death. Inasmuch as *I am and follow after* my mother, I am life that perseveres, I am the living and the living feminine' (16); also *Glas:* 'the mother ... follows absolutely, she always survives ... what she will have engendered, attending, impassive, fascinating and provoking; she survives the interring of the one whose death she has foreseen' (116bi-117bi).

15. Similarly, the driver of the carriage wears Renaldo's distinctive jacket (the one Dylan

wears in the cover photo on *Desire).* In the first few shots we do not see his face, and it is only toward the end of the sequence that we can be sure it is not Renaldo driving.

CHAPTER SEVEN NOTES

1. This movement from an outward-looking social critique to an inward-looking individualism is repeated over and over. Not only is it the movement from folk-protest to folk-rock, it is repeated *within* each phase: it is the shift from *The Times They Are A-Changin'* to *Another Side of Bob Dylan,* and also from *Highway 61 Revisited* to *Blonde on Blonde.* So, years later, it is also the movement from *Slow Train Coming* to *Saved.*

2. Two possible exceptions are 'Neighbourhood Bully' and 'Union Sundown,' from *Infidels.* 'Neighbourhood Bully' is a simplistic defense of Israel, which reduces the complexities of the Middle East to black-and-white clichés. 'Union Sundown' could be an attack on trade unions, but the word 'Union' can also refer to the USA as a whole.

3. 'Strengthen the things that remain' is an apocalyptic phrase, from Revelations 3:2.

4. Again, this aspect can also be found in early works. The 'Masters of War' are told that 'Even Jesus would never / Forgive what you do' (L 56)—theologically, a dubious proposition.

5. The Crucifixion may also be alluded to in a phrase from 'Idiot Wind': 'I been double crossed now for the very last time and now I'm finally free' (L 368). In Wim Wenders' film *Im Lauf der Zeit (Kings of the Road)* (1975), one of the characters stands in front of a roadside crucifix, spreads out his own arms to double the cross, and quotes Dylan's line in English.

6. See the entry on 'Judas' in the *Supplement* to the *Oxford English Dictionary,* which gives 1914 as its earliest citation for this phrase.

7. Strictly speaking, 'Caribbean Wind' was not recorded as part of *Shot of Love.* Clinton Heylin specifies that it was recorded in early April, 1981, several weeks before the main *Shot of Love* sessions. This recording was subsequently issued on *Biograph,* and its text is included in *Lyrics.* Among several variants, the most important is a version performed in San Francisco on November 12, 1980, whose text was printed in *The Telegraph.* 'The Groom's Still Waiting at the Altar' was released as the B-side of the single 'Heart of Mine' and was later included on reissues of *Shot of Love* and on *Biograph.* A text is included in *Lyrics,* but it is widely divergent from the released version. 'Angelina' was not released until 1991 and is not included in *Lyrics.*

8. In the earlier concert version of 'Caribbean Wind,' the central female character is described as coming 'from Haiti.'

9. The 'pale white horse' conflates two different, indeed opposing, references in Revelations. At 6:8, 'behold a pale horse: and his name that sat on him was Death'; but at 19:11, 'behold a white horse; and he that sat upon him was called Faithful and True.' The latter reference immediately follows the description of the marriage of the Lamb.

10. Could the link be taken even further back, to 'Farewell Angelina' (L 184)?

11. For the best discussion of 'Jokerman,' see Day 131-143.

12. Bert Cartwright suggests that the woman who 'owned the world' is the Queen of Sheba, and he cites 1 Kings 11:1, 'king Solomon loved many *strange women*' (emphasis added). See Cartwright 56.

CHAPTER EIGHT NOTES

1. The historical John Wesley Hardin, minus the g, has very little relevance to the song. He was not a romantic character but a squalid and unsuccessful outlaw. There are two minor footnotes to his story: one of the lawmen who eventually captured Hardin was also involved in the manhunt for Billy the Kid; and some writers claim that Hardin was a distant relative of the folk singer Tim Hardin, author of 'If I Were A Carpenter' (Zimmerman again!).

2. Michael Gray offers a political reading but oddly inverts the positions of the protagonists. He argues that 'the voice here is post-Vietnam America, confusedly asking the Third World to reveal the way things really are' (208).

3. There is one earlier appearance of Billy in Dylan's work. 'She's Your Lover Now' refers to 'her picture books of the pyramid / And her postcards of Billy the Kid' (L 244). In one recorded version, 'postcards' becomes, perhaps more ominously, 'snapshots.'

4. In performance, Dylan emphasizes the D and slurs the R so that one almost hears 'the Dylan in the wall.'

5. The combination of 'diamond mine' and 'silver cane' may also recall William Zanzinger, 'With a cane that he twirled around his diamond ring finger' (L 102).

6. Later, she does say 'I've missed you so,' but this comment occurs in the 'missing' stanza 12.

7. The structure of the final lines—thinking about a, b, and c, but especially about d—is repeated in the final lines of 'Tweeter and the Monkeyman': 'Sometimes I think of Tweeter, sometimes I think of Jan / I don't think about nothing but the Monkeyman.'

8. It was to be extended further, by Lawrence Ferlinghetti, in a poem entitled 'The Jack of Hearts (for Dylan),' published in 1976: 'the Jack of Hearts / the black-eyed one who sees all ways / the one with the eye of a horse / the one with the light in his eye / the one with his eye on the star named Nova ... when all is said and all is done / in the wild eye the wide eye / of the Jack of Hearts.'

C H A P T E R   N I N E   N O T E S

1. All quotations from 'Brownsville Girl' are transcribed from *Knocked Out Loaded* and will be annotated (BG). All quotations from 'Danville Girl' are transcribed from the earlier recording and will be annotated (DG).

2. See *Rolling Thunder Logbook:* 'Shifty Jacques Levy, who blitzed off-off-Broadway some years back with his head-on Brechtian style, is responsible for at least one theatrical bravado act' (117). Shepard goes on to describe the second-act apparition of Dylan and Baez.

3. Dylan also may have picked up the recurring phrase 'Got my mind made up,' which occurs four times in the film, and used it as the title of the song, coauthored with Tom Petty, that immediately follows 'Brownsville Girl' on *Knocked Out Loaded.*

4. *Paris, Texas* is, as it happens, distributed by 20th Century Fox, but it was produced by Road Movies Produktion, Berlin, and Argos Films, Paris (France).

5. Harry Dean Stanton also appears in *Pat Garrett and Billy the Kid.* Unconfirmed and probably apocryphal rumors contend that he once recorded a tape of country and western songs with Bob Dylan.

6. For a full account of this theory of the cinema spectator, see Christian Metz, *The Imaginary Signifier* (Bloomington: Indiana UP, 1981).

7. Note also that in the Song of Solomon, the Bridegroom addresses the Bride as his sister: 'I am come into my garden, my sister, my spouse' (5:1).

8. See John Bauldie's study of *Desire*, especially pp. 26-35, in which he writes of the Soror Mystica, the mystical sister in the tradition of Alchemy.

9. He also dedicated the song: 'This is for Leonard, if he's still here.' Cf. various references in Cohen: the song 'Where Is My Gypsy Wife Tonight?'; the appearance of Isis in *Beautiful Losers;* the version of 'God said to Abraham, "Kill me a son"' in 'Story of Isaac'; etc.

10. Robert Shelton suggests that Graves is a source for much of the imagery on *Desire*, but he does not specifically say that Dylan had been reading *The White Goddess.* See Shelton 463-465.

11. Sam Shepard's *La Turista* features an American couple in a motel in Mexico; the man falls sick, and the woman sends out for a doctor. The parallel is suggestive but far from exact.

12. Brownsville, Texas, was the site of the last battle of the Civil War, fought by irregular Confederate troops a month *after* the surrender at Appomattox. In 1906, it was the site of a race riot, the aftermath of which developed into a major scandal for the Roosevelt administration.

P O S T S C R I P T   N O T E S

1. Earlier versions of this postscript were delivered to the Victoria Dylan Group and to the Under the Red Sky convention in Las Vegas, October 1990. In a slightly different form, it has also

been published as a pamphlet by Rolling Tomes, P.O. Box 1943, Grand Junction, Colorado 81502.

    2. For a full list of these quotations, see the pamphlet referred to in the previous note.

    3. Compare my discussion of such songs as 'You Angel You' in Chapter Five.

WORKS CITED

All Across the Telegraph: A Bob Dylan Handbook. Edited by Michael Gray and John Bauldie. Introduction by Bob Willis. London: Sidgwick & Jackson, 1987.

Barthes, Roland. *Image-Music-Text.* Essays Selected and Translated by Stephen Heath. Glasgow: Fontana/Collins, 1977.

——. *The Pleasure of the Text.* Translated by Richard Miller. London: Jonathan Cape, 1976.

Bauldie, John. *Bob Dylan & Desire.* Wanted Man Study Series #2. Bury: Wanted Man, 1984.

Bauldie, John and Chris Whitehouse. 'On the Heels of Rimbaud.' *The Telegraph* 24 (Summer 1986): 47-64.

Bicker, Stewart P. *The Red Rose and the Briar: A Commentary on Bob Dylan's Film 'Renaldo and Clara'.* Privately printed, 1984.

Bowden, Betsy. *Performed Literature: Words and Music by Bob Dylan.* Bloomington: Indiana UP, 1982.

Cartwright, Bert. *The Bible in the Lyrics of Bob Dylan.* Wanted Man Study Series #4. Bury: Wanted Man, 1985.

——. 'Like a Dead Man's Last Pistol Shot?' *The Telegraph* 29 (Spring 1988): 109-114.

Cavendish, Richard. *The Tarot.* London: Michael Joseph, 1975.

Clément, Catherine. *Opera, or the Undoing of Women.* Translated by Betsy Wing. Foreword by Susan McClary. Minneapolis: U of Minnesota P, 1988.

Cohen, Leonard. *The Energy of Slaves.* Toronto: McClelland and Stewart, 1978.

——. *The Favourite Game.* Toronto: McClelland and Stewart, 1970.

Cohen, Scott. 'Don't Ask Me Nothin' About Nothin' I Might Just Tell You The Truth: Bob Dylan Revisited.' Interview by Scott Cohen. *Spin* I, 8 (December 1985): 36-40, 80-81.

Corcoran, Neil. 'Going Barefoot: Thinking About Bob Dylan's Lyrics.' *The Telegraph* 27 (Summer 1987): 93-98.

Davidson, Robert. *Genesis 12-50.* Cambridge: Cambridge UP, 1979.

Day, Aidan. *Jokerman: Reading the Lyrics of Bob Dylan.* Oxford: Basil Blackwell, 1988.

De Lauretis, Teresa. *Alice Doesn't: Feminism, Semiotics, Cinema.* Bloomington: Indiana UP, 1984.

Derrida, Jacques. *The Ear of the Other: Otobiography, Transference, Translation.* Texts and Discussions with Jacques Derrida. English edition edited by Christie V. McDonald. Translated by Peggy Kamuf and Avital Ronell. New York: Schocken, 1985. Cited in the text as EO.

——. *Glas.* Translated by John P. Leavey, Jr., and Richard Rand. Lincoln and London: U of Nebraska P, 1986. Cited in the text as G.

——. *Limited Inc.* Translated by Samuel Weber and Jeffrey Mehlman. Evanston: Northwestern UP, 1988.

——. *Margins of Philosophy.* Translated, with Additional Notes, by Alan Bass. Chicago: U of Chicago P, 1982. Cited in the text as M.

——. *Of Grammatology.* Translated by Gayatri Chakravorty Spivak. Baltimore and London: The Johns Hopkins UP, 1976. Cited in the text as OG.

Ferlinghetti, Lawrence. *The Jack of Hearts (for Dylan).* Pamphlet. San Francisco: City Lights Books, 1976.

Gans, Terry Alexander. *What's Real and What Is Not.* Munich: Hobo Press, 1983.

Ginsberg, Allen. '"It's Not Rational But It's Logical": Allen Ginsberg interviews Bob Dylan.' *The Telegraph* 33 (Summer 1989): 6-33.

Graves, Robert. *The White Goddess: A historical grammar of poetic myth.* Amended and enlarged edition. London: Faber and Faber, 1961.

Gray, Michael. *Song and Dance Man: The Art of Bob Dylan.* London: Hart-Davis, MacGibbon, 1972. Revised Edition, New York: St. Martin's Press, 1981. Unless otherwise indicated, citations are to the Revised Edition.

Herdman, John. *Voice Without Restraint: Bob Dylan's Lyrics and Their Background.* New York: Delilah Books, 1982.

Heylin, Clinton. *Stolen Moments: The Ultimate Reference Book.* Romford: Wanted Man, 1988.

Hinchey, John. *Bob Dylan's Slow Train.* Wanted Man Study Series #1. Bury: Wanted Man, 1983.

Ions, Veronica. *Egyptian Mythology.* Feltham: Paul Hamlyn, 1965.

Kamuf, Peggy. *Signature Pieces: On the Institution of Authorship.* Ithaca and London: Cornell UP, 1988.

Kearney, Richard. *The Wake of the Imagination: Toward a postmodern culture.* Minneapolis: U of Minneapolis P, 1988.

Marcus, Greil. Liner notes to *The Basement Tapes.* CBS Records, 1975.

McGregor, Craig, ed. *Bob Dylan: A Retrospective.* New York: William Morrow, 1972; revised edition, Da

Capo, 1990. Page references are to the original edition.

Mellers, Wilfrid. *A Darker Shade of Pale: A Backdrop to Bob Dylan.* London: Faber and Faber, 1984.

Metz, Christian. *The Imaginary Signifier.* Translated by Alfred Guzzetti et al. Bloomington: Indiana UP, 1981.

Miles, Barry, ed. *Bob Dylan In His Own Words.* New York: Quick Fox, 1978.

Nicholas, Tracy. *Rastafari: A Way of Life.* New York: Anchor Press Doubleday, 1979.

Pelikan, Jaroslav. *Jesus Through the Centuries: His Place in the History of Culture.* New York: Harper & Row, 1987.

Pichaske, David. 'The Prophet and the Prisoner: Bob Dylan and the American Dream.' *The Telegraph* 26 (Spring 1987): 36-98.

Pound, Ezra. 'Vorticism' (1914). In *Ezra Pound: A Critical Anthology.* Edited by J.P. Sullivan. Harmondsworth: Penguin, 1970.

Scaduto, Anthony. *Bob Dylan: An Intimate Biography.* New York: Grosset & Dunlap, 1971.

Shelton, Robert. *No Direction Home: The Life and Music of Bob Dylan.* New York: William Morrow, 1986.

Shepard, Sam. *Fool for Love.* San Francisco: City Lights Books, 1983.

——. 'Interview.' *Rolling Stone* 489/490 (December 18, 1986-January 1, 1987).

——. *Motel Chronicles.* San Francisco: City Lights Books, 1982.

——. *Rolling Thunder Logbook.* New York: Viking, 1977.

——. *Seven Plays.* New York: Bantam, 1981.

——. 'True Dylan.' *Esquire* Vol. 108, 1 (July 1987): 59-68.

Sloman, Larry. *On the Road with Bob Dylan: Rolling with the Thunder.* New York: Bantam, 1978.

Snow, Craig. *Folksinger and Beat Poet: The Prophetic Vision of Bob Dylan.* Ph.D. Dissertation, Purdue U, 1987.

Spitz, Bob. *Dylan: a biography.* New York: McGraw-Hill, 1989.

Stokes, Geoffrey. *Rock of Ages: The 'Rolling Stone' History of Rock & Roll.* New York: Summit Books, 1986.

Tatum, Steven. *Inventing Billy the Kid: Visions of the Outlaw in America, 1881-1981.* Albuquerque: U of New Mexico P, 1982.

Walker, Barbara G. *The Woman's Encyclopaedia of Myths and Secrets.* San Francisco: Harper & Row, 1983.

Webster, Patrick J. 'Everybody's Going Up The Castle Stairs.' *The Telegraph* 16 (Summer 1984): 14-30.

Williams, Paul. *Performing Artist: The Music of Bob Dylan. Volume One, 1960-1973.* Novato, California, and Lancaster, Pennsylvania: Underwood-Miller, 1990.

Witt, R.E. *Isis in the Graeco-Roman World.* London: Thames and Hudson, 1971.